SPCM 200

PUBLIC SPEAKING NOW

Textbook and Coursebook for **SPCM 200: Public Speaking**

1st Edition

Thomas R. Dunn

Colorado State University

Printed in the United States of America

10 9 8 7 6 5 4 3 2 1

ISBN 978-0-7380-8316-2

Macmillan Learning Curriculum Solutions
14903 Pilot Drive
Plymouth, MI 48170
www.macmillanlearning.com

Dunn 8316-2 F19

Sustainability

Hayden-McNeil/Macmillan Learning Curriculum Solutions is proud to be a part of the larger sustainability initiative of Macmillan, our parent company. Macmillan has a goal to reduce its carbon emissions by 65% by 2020 from our 2010 baseline. Additionally, paper purchased must adhere to the Macmillan USA Paper Sourcing and Use Policy.

Hayden-McNeil partners with printers that use paper that is consistent with the environmental goals and values of Macmillan USA. This includes using paper certified by the Forest Stewardship Council (FSC), Sustainable Forestry Initiative (SFI), and/or the Programme for the Endorsement of Forest Certification (PEFC). We also offer paper with varying percentages of post-consumer waste as well as a 100% recycled stock. Additionally, Hayden-McNeil Custom Digital provides authors with the opportunity to convert print products to a digital format to use no paper at all. Visit http://sustainability.macmillan.com to learn more.

TABLE OF CONTENTS

Acknowledgements

Written on behalf of the Department of Communication Studies at Colorado State University by Thomas R. Dunn. This project was made possible with the support of the Department of Communication Studies at Colorado State University. Special thanks to Kristina Lee, who served as a research assistant in Summer 2018 and assisted with recommendations and revisions of the first edition. I would also like to extend my thanks to Dr. Ellie Light, who provided some images for the text and offered comments on earlier drafts. Many thanks as well to Heather Landers, who piloted the first draft of this text in several classes on campus and provided valuable feedback on the final product. In addition, the author would like to thank the Department of Communication Studies' Basic Course Committee for their guidance in designing the framework of this book. The committee consisted of Dr. Allison Prasch, Dr. Carl Burgchardt, Dr. Evan Elkins, Heather Landers, and Kristina Lee.

Unit 1

THE VALUE(S) OF PUBLIC SPEAKING

Chapter 1

SIX FACTS TO KNOW ABOUT PUBLIC SPEAKING

As a student, you might find yourself enrolled in classes that you don't know anything about. Public speaking is almost certainly *not* one of those classes.

That is not to say that public speaking is something you know how to do or even know a lot about.

But the fact that you know what public speaking is—at least at some level and without Googling it—tells us something meaningful: namely, that *public speaking is a common, widespread act that holds an important place in our societies.* Think about it. Public speaking is something that you've seen people do before, probably many times. It is something that you have likely done as well, regardless of whether it comes naturally to you or if it is something you just stumbled your way through. You almost certainly know that public speaking is something that many people dread but that some people seem to really enjoy. And you know that, regardless of our own feelings about public speaking, our families and friends, professors, employers, customers, clients, and fellow community members will all expect us to be able to speak in public effectively and confidently over the course of our lives and careers. This text focuses on helping you do just that: become a more effective and confident public speaker.

Over the next several chapters, we will work toward these goals in three ways. In Unit 2 of this book, we investigate and practice key concepts and skills that every public speaker should have in order to be successful in public speaking situations. In Unit 3, we will focus on particularly common types of speeches most people will be asked to complete during their lifetimes. By the end of that unit, you should have a better idea of the expectations and pitfalls of each of these speech types and how to deliver them effectively for personal, professional, and public success. However, we begin this book in our current section, Unit 1. In the remainder of this chapter and the next, we will set the stage for these later conversations by providing you a clearer sense of what public speaking is, what we need to know about public speaking, and how speaking fits into our broader need for communication in an increasingly pluralistic society and world.

For the Record: What Is Public Speaking?

While we might all have some idea of what public speaking is, it is best to make sure we are all on the same page before we go any further. So, what is public speaking? A good working definition of **public speaking** *is* speech *in*, *by*, and *for* the public.

This working definition has two primary parts we need to understand. First, public speaking is about **speech**. In the most explicit sense, "speech" simply means talking to someone. But, of course, the word "speech" implies more than just talk. For example, giving a speech is *more formal* than having a casual conversation. Unlike a conversation, a speech is often prepared with great care and forethought in advance. Likewise, a speech is *goal-oriented*. Speakers are not just talking for the sake of talking; rather, they have something they want to achieve by giving a speech. In addition, "speech" implicitly *prioritizes face-to-face talk*. To speak to or with someone nearly always assumes sharing a space with that someone. This presumption has changed as technology has created new ways to approximate the immediacy of being in the same room with someone even if you are thousands of miles apart; however, the preference and authenticity of speaking with someone in physical proximity is still present in the term "speech." We also can't ignore the fact that "speech" implies *communicating orally*. While there are certainly some exceptions to this assumption—particularly for people whose different communication abilities do not permit them to do so via verbal language—most public speakers will be expected to communicate with their own words and in their own voice out loud for others to hear. All of these assumptions about speech are built into our working definition of public speaking.

Second, public speaking is as much about the "public" as it is about "speech." **Public** is a term used to describe *the presence of something before or in the hands of the community, what we might think of as the people*. Like speech, the word "public" has lots of meanings and is used to modify our understanding of other words in important ways. In the context of public speaking, "public" means at least three things. For one, the "public" in public speaking means to give a speech *before others in the public*—what we will come to think of as an audience. As we will see shortly, to speak in public means more than to speak in front of one or two other people; rather, a good standard is that for a speech to be "public" it must be given before at least ten people. In addition, the "public" in public speaking implies that the topic of the speech will be of *public concern*. That is to say, what you speak about in public speaking should matter to your audience and our shared lives as a community. Finally, the "public" in public speaking is about what is in the best interest of the people, what we commonly think of as the *public good*.

When we put these two terms together, we should have a stronger sense of what we mean by public speaking. As public speakers, our task is to share with an audience—orally, authentically, and in person—our ideas, thoughts, and feelings about how we can live our lives better together as individuals and as a community. When we speak in this way, we are participating in **public discourse**—*the ongoing, simultaneous conversations community members have with each other about how to maintain and remake the world*. As we will see, in a democracy, a vibrant and healthy public discourse is essential; therefore, by becoming a better public speaker, you are not only improving your own skills, but also participating in a process to make our collective world a better place.

While we now have a better grasp of what we mean by public speaking, there are still several points we need to know before we can start to put public speaking into practice. These points are:

- Public speaking is a form of communication.
- Public speaking is always goal-oriented.

- Public speaking has personal, professional, and public dimensions.
- Public speaking is cultural.
- Public speaking is a form of free expression.
- Public speaking is an ethical undertaking.

In the remainder of this chapter, we'll examine each of these six points to learn about public speaking in greater depth.

Public Speaking Is a Form of Communication

The first thing we need to know about public speaking is that it is a form of **communication**—*the exchange of symbols between people in an effort to understand or influence each other's perception of the world.* The study of communication in its various forms is one of the oldest of human interests, dating back to ancient times and a diverse set of oral traditions and cultures that span the globe. Over time, scholars and practitioners formalized and refined the study of communication, resulting in several comprehensive models of how most communication interactions work.

Claude Elwood Shannon and Warren Weaver developed the most influential of these contemporary models in 1949 when they codified and standardized existing understandings of communication as part of their work for a telephone company that would later become AT&T.[1] In 1960, Dr. David Berlo, a Professor of Communication at Michigan State University, synthesized Shannon and Weaver's thoughts on communication into a working model for identifying and analyzing the communication process.[2] Over the years, others added to this framework, leading to what we think of today as the **Standard Model of Communication**, *a holistic attempt to account for the major attributes that are at work in most communication interactions.* This model provides a common basis from which people across fields of study and cultural experiences can talk about what it means to communicate effectively (or ineffectively); therefore, we can use this model to begin to understand public speaking as a communication process.

The Standard Model of Communication, which you can see outlined in Figure 1-1, includes several parts. The **sender** in the model represents *the person or institution that initiates a communication interaction.* The sender does this by creating a **message**—*a form of symbolic representation (a statement, a question, an exclamation, etc.) that contains information or an inquiry from the sender to another party.* Messages can take many forms in a communication interaction—including the spoken word, a hand gesture, a conversation on a cell phone, a text message, a film, or an advertisement, just to name a few—all of which can dramatically affect how a message is interpreted. *These diverse forms and media in which messages travel* are called **channels**. When a sender relays a message through a channel, another party is meant to receive that message. That other party—the other part of the communication interaction—is called the receiver. The **receiver** is *the person, persons, or institution for which the sender prepares a message and from whom the sender expects a response.* These four aspects—sender, channel, message, receiver (SCMR)—of communication represent the pillars of the communicative process established by Berlo.

Of course, anyone who has ever had a conversation in the real world knows that communication is much more complicated than simply saying something to another person. Real-world communication is filled with confusion, misinterpretation, cultural and generational references, contextual cues, and environmental challenges, among many other factors. As such, scholars have added a number of features to both Shannon and Weaver's and Berlo's original models to reflect these realities.

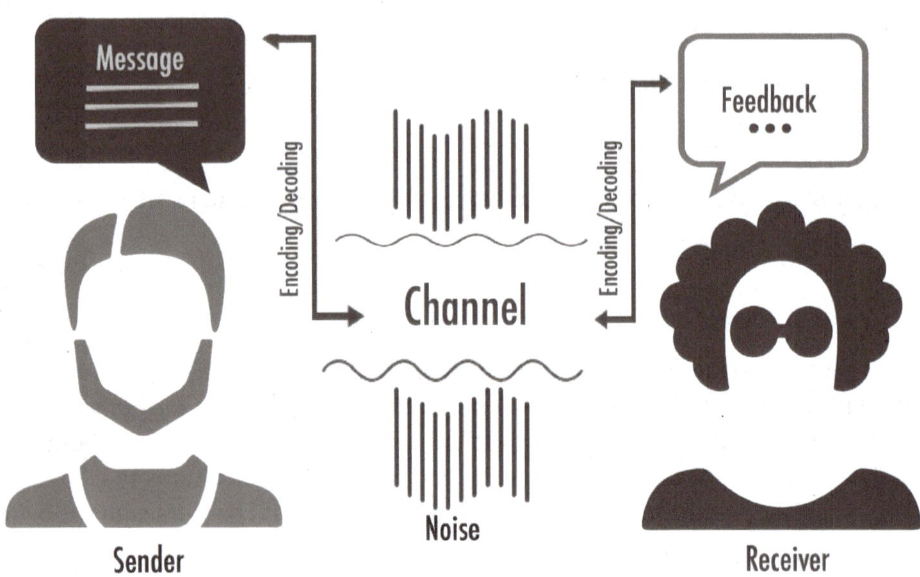

Figure 1-1. Standard Model of Communication

Two of the most important of these additions are the notions of encoding and decoding. **Encoding** describes *the work that a sender does to a message to put it into a format appropriate for communication in a particular situation.* Examples of the type of work a speaker does to encode a message include selecting the appropriate words, using proper syntax, and even putting ideas into a particular language. **Decoding**, by contrast, is the work done on the other end of the communicative interaction, namely *the work the receiver or receivers do to translate the speaker's encoding into a format they can interpret and understand.* In some cases, encoding and decoding occur with minimal transmission error; in other cases, our inability to encode and decode messages is a major factor in communication failures. Feedback is also an important addition to the SCMR model that was incorporated into the Standard Model of Communication. **Feedback** refers to *the verbal and non-verbal signals a receiver provides a sender in the course of communicating.* Typically, feedback includes elements such as applause, smiles, frowns, tears, boos, even something as simple as attention. Each of these elements of feedback can add to, emphasize, or call into question the message. Finally, **noise** describes *anything that interferes with the successful transmission of a message.* The most obvious examples of noise are sounds that disturb the proper hearing or seeing of a message: people talking, a passing vehicle, a loud air conditioner or heater, or someone doing construction out the window—all literal noises. However, noise can also include harder to recognize forms of interference, including stereotypes, prejudgments, distractions, and even physiological concerns like having a headache.

While the Standard Model of Communication is an excellent foundation for understanding how public speaking functions, this model is continually in need of updating and reassessment. Notably, scholars have argued that the Standard Model privileges certain cultural understandings of communication that are Western, patriarchal, and human-centric. For instance, the Standard Model privileges a single speaker as opposed to a set of speakers; it also implies turn-taking, which does not reflect all real-world communication interactions (for better or worse). These privileges embedded in the Standard Model can make it difficult to explain types of communication that occur in non-Western contexts, across gender identities, and between human and non-human subjects. However, for the purposes of this book, the Standard Model will provide us a shared language from which to think about the act of communication—even as we recognize it is imperfect.

While it is important that we understand how communication works in general, it is also important to recognize that public speaking is only one form of a series of different types of communication that operate according to Standard Model of Communication. Communication scholars who study how communication works at all levels of the practice typically conceive of six basic forms of communication:

- **Intrapersonal communication**: *communication that takes place within a person's own mind, primarily through thinking and internal dialogue.*
- **Interpersonal communication**: *communication that takes places between two to three people and typically concerns the creation, maintenance, or disillusion of personal relationships.*
- **Group communication**: *communication that takes place among a small group of people—particularly teams—and is often focused on the completion of a task.*
- **Organizational communication**: *communication that takes place within and between large institutions and their members.*
- **Mass communication**: *communication that takes place through media of many kinds, including television, film, and social or print media, and is transmitted to large audiences.*
- **Public communication**: *communication that takes place between a speaker (or speakers) and an audience with the aim of engaging that audience on a topic of shared concern about the public interest. Public communication is always done within a public setting.*

The act of public speaking can conceivably appear in several of these communicative forms. For instance, many public speeches are delivered over mediated platforms, making it a form of mass communication. In addition, public speaking can be a strategy for changing the culture of a corporation or workplace, making it a dimension of organizational communication. However, because all public speaking is delivered before an audience of at least ten people and concerns the interests and affairs of that audience, it is always best to think of public speaking as primarily being a form of public communication.

Public Speaking Is Always Goal-Oriented

A second thing we need to know about public speaking is that all public speeches are goal-oriented. In other words, all speakers deliver public speeches with the intention of achieving a specific task, usually with the assistance of the audience. This explicit focus on achieving some goal in a speech is something that separates public speaking from other forms of communication—although most forms of communication are always trying to do something implicitly.

As you step into the world of public speaking, you will quickly realize that the act of giving a public speech effectively contains many minor goals. By **minor goals** we mean *small, targeted tasks that the speaker hopes to achieve over the course of a speech in order to improve its effectiveness.* These minor goals connect to the numerous particular parts of public speaking that you will be working to improve on or to execute flawlessly. For instance, a novice speaker might have the minor goal of reducing the number of "ums" and "ahs" they say during the course of a speech. Meanwhile, a more experienced speaker might aim to deliver their conclusion fully memorized with passion and great eye-contact—a significant but still relatively minor goal. The feedback you receive from your instructor will help you identify the minor goals you should focus on as you proceed from one speech to the next in the class.

While speakers should always be mindful of their minor goals, they do not constitute the full extent of effective speechmaking. Instead, all speeches also have primary goals that are central to determining whether a public speech is successful or not. We define **primary goals** as *the single, focused, overarching achievement the speaker hopes to attain with her audience by the end of the speech in order to be successful.* Traditionally, public speaking textbooks identify three kinds of primary goals novice speaker should master: informing, persuading, and praising. To be sure, you will learn to meet all of these goals in your speeches in this class as well.

However, in this textbook, we take a slightly different approach to thinking about primary goals. More specifically, we believe that students should recognize from the start that all speeches have the primary goal to **persuade**—*to encourage the audience to think about an issue or see the world in a way advocated by the speaker.* Within persuasive speaking, however, students in this class will focus their energies toward meeting several specific primary goals, all of which have persuasive intent. They include:

- To persuade the audience *to learn* important information about a new topic
- To persuade the audience *to consider* perspectives other than their own
- To persuade the audience *to adopt* a solution to a public problem advocated for by the speaker
- To persuade the audience *to value* the life and experiences of another person

As you become a more advanced public speaker, you will start to see other primary goals that you might want to achieve by delivering a speech; however, as a novice speaker, these primary goals—in addition to the minor goals you will work on with your instructor—will be the focus of our time in class.

In order to achieve our primary goals, all public speakers must have a clear and understandable thesis statement in their speech. A **thesis statement** is *a single, declarative sentence in which the speaker makes the central, overarching argument of their entire speech.* A speech without a thesis statement is a speech without a point. Quite literally, a speech without a thesis statement is what we colloquially refer to as "bullshit": the unending, pointless blather of someone who only wants to hear himself speak. Luckily, few public speakers are interested in being bullshit artists. Nevertheless, many public speakers who enter a speech with every intention of having something meaningful to say find themselves in the midst of a speech without a thesis statement. They make supporting arguments and have evidence, but that evidence and argument do not lead anywhere in particular. A list of facts, quotes, and statistics is not a speech or an argument, but a list. However, when we add a thesis statement to a speech, it provides a direction for those facts, quotes, and statistics. It gives them a destination—the primary goal of the speech—and the speaker's job is to arrange the entirety of the rest of the speech so that each part gets us closer to arriving at that destination. Therefore, a thesis statement is a vital investment in the time and energy of a speaker. Without it, your speech will be rudderless and adrift in a sea of information.

Given how important thesis statements are to achieve our primary goals as public speakers, we will return to how to create effective thesis statements several times in this book. However, for now, it is important to know that the thesis statement is central to public speaking as a goal-oriented undertaking.

Public Speaking Has Personal, Professional, and Public Dimensions

A third thing we need to know about public speaking in this book is that it has a valuable role to play in three aspects of our lives: the personal, the professional, and the public. As we have already seen, given the public nature of public speaking, we know that giving a speech has a powerful role to play in *public* discourse generally. As speakers, we give voice to community concerns, identify community problems, and offer solutions for the consideration of the community. All of these acts connect us to the local, regional, national, and international communities in which we live.

In addition to these public dimensions, public speaking also has *professional* dimensions. If you are reading this book as a part of a class, it is highly likely you are taking public speaking as an assigned course in your major or program of study. Indeed, at Colorado State University, public speaking is a required course for more than 30 different majors across multiple colleges. This requirement is based on the view shared by many professions that everyone should enter the job market with previous public speaking experience. Depending on your major or career goals, the need for this class might be apparent. If your future career will require you to give presentations, lead meetings, train others, recruit job candidates, engage public officials, request support from the community, or work with customers or clients (among others), the professional skills you will acquire in public speaking will likely help you as you find a job and rise through the ranks in a way that peers without this class will not.

For others of you, the need for public speaking skills might not be as apparent at first glance. It is quite possible that people in your profession recognize ways in which you will need these skills that you cannot at this stage of your education and career. It is also possible that, while you may not need public speaking skills in your first position, you will need public speaking skills to be promoted or to succeed in a more senior-level position—and who wants to learn those skills for the first time then? Regardless, data from universities, corporations, and other employers for decades have made the same point repeatedly: written and oral communication skills are among the most highly sought skills in all corners of the job market. Indeed, data shows that—particularly in science, technology, engineering, and mathematic (STEM) fields—finding applicants with those solid communication skills is an ongoing challenge for employers of all kinds.[3] Therefore, learning how to become a more effective and confident public speaker is vital to your professional outlook.

Not to be overlooked: public speaking also has important *personal* dimensions you should consider. Regardless of our professional or public lives, nearly all of us will find ourselves called upon to give a speech on behalf of a friend or family member at some point in our lives. Indeed, for many people, giving speeches at family events or personal occasions will be the most prominent way in which they use their public speaking skills. Just think about all the kinds of speeches that take place in our personal lives surrounded by friends and family: marriage proposals, wedding vows, wedding toasts, anniversary cheers, after-dinner toasts, retirement speeches, prayers, eulogies, holiday toasts…the list goes on and on. The point is clear: unless you intend to go through life without friends or family—however you define them—you will almost certainly need to give a few speeches among the people who matter to you most, typically around life-changing events. These are times and people for which we want to show up and show up well, making public speaking not just a public or professional good, but a personal good too.

Public Speaking Is Cultural

Let's be clear from the start: there are many ways to be an effective and powerful public speaker. We know this to be true because of how public speaking has spanned cultures from around the world through time.

For millennia, people from all corners of the world used speeches delivered before others to build, refine, and shape the earliest human communities. These *earliest practices of speechmaking and storytelling by which societies shared and passed on histories, common sense, and culture* are what we refer to as **oral traditions**. Oral traditions are rich and varied practices traced to all corners of the world. Indeed, long before the ancient Greeks began training people in speechmaking, civilizations in what we think of today as Central and South America, China, and Sub-Saharan Africa participated in public discourses through oral traditions. It is because of the rich and diverse history of speech in all human societies that we can say so clearly that there are and always have been many ways to be an effective and powerful public speaker.

However, for centuries, public speaking handbooks, instructors, and classes like this one worked very hard to hide the rich and diverse traditions of making speeches that existed across the globe through history. Indeed, by the age of European colonialism, many diverse kinds of people worldwide were taught there was only one model of public speaking that worked—what we might call the dominant paradigm of public speaking. By **dominant paradigm of public speaking** we mean *the belief that effective public speaking should* ***only*** *be formal, be rational, emphasize Western values, and be practiced almost exclusively by white men.*

The dominant paradigm of public speaking became dominant for several reasons. For one, it was written down and formalized in way that many oral traditions were not. The dominant paradigm also benefitted significantly from it valuing of reason, a key cultural term since the Enlightenment and Scientific Revolution. In addition, the dominant paradigm of public speaking thrived because it was connected to certain centers of power throughout the history of world—the West, patriarchy, colonialism, and white supremacy—that gave it great durability. Indeed, we should never forget, for example, that formal and informal rules, practices, and laws in the U.S. explicitly prevented people of color from learning to speak and write and stopped women from speaking in any public setting that included men. Of course, while acknowledging the significant problems with the dominant paradigm of public speaking, we also need to remember that there are significant and important strategies and theories about public speaking that emerge in this model—ideas that we do not necessarily want to throw out. Indeed, history is replete with powerful public speakers like the escaped-slave and anti-slavery leader Frederick Douglass who did not fit this dominant paradigm but used the lessons of the dominant paradigm to undermine institutions like slavery. Nonetheless, the view that there is only one way to be a great speaker forwarded by the dominant paradigm is an illusion—an illusion we need to discard early and directly in this text.

Instead of strictly adhering to the dominant paradigm of public speaking, this course will argue for a multicultural paradigm of public speaking. The **multicultural paradigm of public speaking** *acknowledges that there are many speaking traditions and ways in which those traditions can be integrated or used independently in order to do effective and confident public speaking.* Key to understanding this approach is recognizing that all people share numerous different **cultures**—*socially created practices and values for understanding the world*—including different cultures around speech. These cultures can be national or transnational, regional or local, gendered or gender-nonconforming, raced, faith-based, embodied, alternative, subcultural...all of these and more are ways in which we learn to understand the world and how to communicate in it that can be used to give a speech effectively. Some examples of the ways in which cultures might shape our public speaking include:

- **How we use our hands**: some cultures use grand hand gestures where others use few or understated hand gestures.
- **Eye contact**: some cultures encourage deep and engaging eye contact whereas others promote careful, limited eye contact.
- **Structure**: some cultures rely on highly linear structures to explain ideas whereas others use circular, narrative, or even rhythmical forms of talk and explanation.

These examples are just some of the many ways in which our different cultures can be a resource for us to become successful public speakers. We will talk more about issue surrounding public speaking and the differences inherent in human communication in Chapter 2.

Public Speaking Is a Form of Free Expression

A fifth and key thing to understand about public speaking is that it is a form of **free expression**. This statement means that speechmaking is *an exercise of the human right to share ideas and opinions with others without interference from governments or other forms of authority*. Note the phrasing of this last sentence: to share one's ideas and beliefs freely is a human right. It is something inherent to all people, regardless of their age, race, class, gender, religious affiliation, nationality, ability, and so on. Indeed, the right to speak our minds is something that makes us human beings; without it, we become less than a full person. As such, it is important that we do not infringe on another person's right to free expression.

In the United States, the right to free expression and speech is outlined in the U.S. Constitution and the Bill of Rights—the primary governing documents of the nation. However, the right to free expression is not a uniquely U.S. value; rather the protection of free speech is a value shared by many nations across the globe. Indeed, Article 19 of the *Universal Declaration of Human Rights*, which most nations signed in 1948, declares that:

> "Everyone has the right to freedom of opinion and expression; this right includes freedom to hold opinions without interference and to seek, receive and impart information and ideas through any media and regardless of frontiers."

Unfortunately, while much of the world has long celebrated the right to free expression and speech, in practice, securing the right of every person to speak their mind freely can be much harder than it seems. In some nations, governing documents, laws, or custom do not guarantee the right to free expression, making speech vulnerable to censure and silencing. Elsewhere, those who speak their minds freely are subjected to active hostility, leading to the violent suppression of speech and sometimes, the intimidation and murder of people who speak out against those in authority. As such, when we rise to speak our minds, we should never forget that our right to speak is not shared by many millions of people worldwide—and that it is always in need of reaffirmation here as well.

However, while the United States often prides itself on it robust respect for the freedom of speech and expression, we have also agreed as a society to limit free expression in select cases. Indeed, the freedom of expression we uphold in the U.S. is not absolute for good reason: while it may sound upright to protect all speech at all times, in reality no society can function effectively without some reasonable limitations on free expression. In the U.S., the legal system has been our primary means for determining which limitations are reasonable and which are not, with the U.S. Supreme Court often serving as the final decision maker on these difficult issues. More than two centuries of legal debate have led to the establishment of *a few circumstances in which the U.S. does not protect the right to free expression*—what we refer to as **free speech exceptions**—four of the most common of which are vital for novice public speakers to know. They are:

- **Incitement**. One of these free speech exceptions is incitement. **Incitement** is *speech that advocates the use of force in a lawless and immediate way.*[4] An example of incitement is a speaker who advocates for the immediate lynching of the suspect of a crime by a mob. In this example, because the speech calls for illegal violence and for it to be done immediately, this speaker would be considered guilty of incitement and their speech would not be protected.

- **Defamation**. Another free speech exception is called **defamation**—*a knowingly false statement made in public that harms the reputation of another person or entity.* An example of defamation is when a person goes on television and falsely and knowingly calls another person an adulterer or cheater. Because the person making the charge knows the statement is untrue, says it anyway, and says it in a public setting that harms the reputation of the accused, the speaker's speech would not be protected and they could be found guilty of defamation.

  Defamation is a broad category of free speech exceptions that typically takes two forms:

  - **Slander**, which is *defamation that occurs in speech.*

  - **Libel**, which is *defamation that occurs in print or visual media.*

  Statistically, most cases of libel and slander are made against the press or media figures when they are covering or analyzing people in the news; however, many of these cases fail for a simple reason: if the derogatory statement made in the press or media is true, there is no case. In other words, because the statement was not false, no defamation occurred. It is also important to know that it is extremely difficult to find someone guilty of libel or slander when the criticism is of a public figure, like a politician or civic leader. That is because U.S. courts have found that it is vital for individual citizens and the press in a democracy to be able to criticize their leaders in public discourse without threats of libel or slander.

As a public speaker, it is important for you to recognize that there are limitations to the right of free expression that you will be held responsible for, not only in the classroom but in your personal, professional, and public lives.

While many people are surprised that the freedom of speech and expression is limited by exceptions like incitement and defamation in the U.S., many other people are surprised to learn that some forms of objectionable speech are, in fact, protected, even though we might think they should not be. This is particularly true on the question of hate speech. **Hate speech** is defined by the American Bar Association as *"speech that offends, threatens, or insults groups, based on race, color, religion, national origin, sexual orientation, disability, or other traits."*[5] Most reasonable people can agree that hate speech is unethical, immoral, objectionable, and has no place in public speaking or public discourse. However, hate speech is protected as a form of free expression under current Constitutional interpretations, unless it leads to incitement.

Many people often feel uncomfortable when they learn that hate speech is permissible speech in the U.S.—and rightfully so. Who wants to live in a society that protects intentionally offensive and threatening speech, particularly when it is most often directed at minorities or marginalized communities? But, in a free society, hate speech is protected speech for several reasons:

- **The principle matters.** The principle of free speech and expression matters, and we show our commitment to that principle even when we have to defend the right of someone to say something we find horrific.

- **Who decides what is hateful and what is not?** While we might think we can easily detect hate speech when we hear it, in reality, it is not always so clear. Language grows and evolves through time, some words lose their meanings, other gain new meanings, and all the while how do we keep up? Who, then, gets to decide what is hateful and what is not?

- **When speech is restricted, minorities suffer the most.** Research shows that when free speech and expression are restricted—even when it is intended to protect minorities and marginalized communities—those same communities often end up being harmed most by those policies. Indeed, the greatest beneficiaries of restrictions on speech—even hate speech—are those people and groups who are already secure and well represented in government and the halls of power.

Given these reasons, in the U.S. generally and in SPCM 200 in particular, we defend the right to free expression, even when we find it objectionable. In this class, we show our commitment to the freedom of speech by encouraging all students to select topics and make arguments that truly represent their point of view as long as they fall within the parameters of a given assignment.

But what do you do as an audience member who is confronted with a hateful form of speech? As audience members in SPCM 200, listening to speeches we disagree with or even find offensive is expected even when it is difficult. However, that does not mean that students in class do not have opportunities to make their disagreement with their classmates known. Indeed, Colorado State University's *Principles of Community* strongly assert that all people are welcome here and imply that all members of the community should feel empowered to confront hatred when they see or hear it on campus. What does that confrontation look like? Strong, safe, and legal responses to a controversial student speech include:

- expressing disagreement with the student *after* their speech in class discussion.
- asking the student a question in their Q&A session.
- offering a different perspective or rebuttal in a post-speech discussion or dialogue.
- identifying and explaining a logical fallacy in the student's speech.
- challenging the source or credibility of the student's evidence.
- offering a different source or evidence with stronger credibility.
- expressing your disagreement with the student in a private conversation.
- expressing your disagreement with the student in a letter to the editor of the student newspaper.
- preparing a speech to counter the student's claim for your own speech assignment.

You should also feel encouraged to speak with your instructor or the SPCM 200 Course Director directly if you have concerns about the kind of speech that is made in your SPCM 200 classroom.

It may feel strange to speak out against a fellow student in the classroom even if you vehemently disagree with their position or assumptions. However, thanks to the First Amendment and the assurances it provides, the only one who can silence you is yourself. For the same reason, when people of ethics and characters remain silent in the face of hate, we risk becoming complicit in the very hatred we would usually stand against.

For more information on the Freedom of Speech on the CSU campus, please see the First Amendment website at https://firstamendment.colostate.edu/.

Public Speaking Is a Moral and Ethical Undertaking

Not only do we have legal responsibilities as they relate to respecting other people regarding public speaking, but we also have moral and ethical responsibilities, as well. That is because public speaking is always a moral and ethical undertaking. Another way to think about this point is to recognize that while speakers are granted extensive freedom to say whatever they please as human beings in the world, we are also bound by personal and community standards to ask ourselves whether we *should* say anything we want without regards to the impact of our words.

But what do we mean by morals and ethics—two terms that often are used interchangeably but have important variations? Let's begin with what each term has in common. Both morals and ethics are guidelines for determining acceptable and unacceptable conduct in life—what is "good" and "bad." **Morals**, however, are *the personal and consistent principles that individuals use to determine what is good and bad*; meanwhile, **ethics** are *the socially-defined expectation of good and bad behavior, which are almost always variable by context.* As we navigate our lives as individuals and parts of a community, we rely on both our personal morals and our social ethics to guide our choices about the proper way to act. In many cases, morals and ethics align closely, placing a significant imperative on us to act in a particular way. In other cases, morals and ethics can come into conflict. When morals and ethics do conflict, however, we cannot be paralyzed by inaction; instead, we are obligated to make choices between what values matter most to us and the community in that moment.

Morality and ethics appear in prominent ways in the public speaking situation. For instance, morals and ethics both shape what we select to speak about in our speeches: what moves us, what we believe, what we care about, and what we do not care about. Morals and ethics also influence how we treat our audience and how we as audience members treat speakers—both those we agree with and those we disagree with. In addition, morals and ethics both appear in *how* we speak about our ideas, beliefs, and values. How we research and use evidence in our speeches also has strong ethical and moral components. These are only some of the ways that moral and ethics appear in the public speaking process, suggesting that the public speaker must make moral and ethical decisions numerous times in their own public address.

While morals can vary from person to person and ethics tells us that there is never one and only one correct way to act ethically in a given situation, most public speakers—both as individuals and members of a community—prioritize particular kinds of values in their speaking, including:

- **Accuracy**: *the expectation that public speakers will share information with an audience about the world that is verifiable, specific, and true.*
- **Honesty**: *the expectation that public speakers will share their viewpoints without deceit or malice.*

- **Transparency**: *the expectation that public speakers will be upfront and clear with the audience about their own investment in an issue, why they believe what they do, and where their information or evidence comes from.*
- **Empathy**: *the expectation that public speakers will put themselves in the place of their audience and use that perspective to shape what and how they speak.*
- **Vulnerability**: *the expectation that public speakers will risk exposing intimate parts of their lives to others in a genuine effort to communicate and connect.*
- **Accountability**: *the expectation that public speakers will be held liable for what they say and will acknowledge both their successes and their failures.*
- **Authenticity**: *the expectation that public speakers will speak to their audience in a real way with the best interests of audience in mind.*
- **Consistency**: *the expectation that public speakers will hold the same beliefs, values, and positions when speaking to different audiences, even as they might change how they speak about those beliefs, values, and position for rhetorical effect.*

In addition to championing certain values, moral and ethical public speaking also obligates a public speaker to actively avoid other kinds of speech—speech that is protected by the First Amendment but that can constitute significant moral and ethical failings on the part of a public speaker or an audience. In particular, most speech communities agree that moral and ethical public speakers should:

- **Reject hate speech**. As we have discussed, hate speech is *not* prohibited by the U.S. Constitution and has been upheld numerous times under judicial review. However, as moral individuals and ethical community members, it is important to recognize that using public speaking to intentionally offend, harm, or threaten communities different from our own—particularly when those communities are minorities or have been the subjects of persecution through history—is highly problematic. That is ***not*** to say that we cannot or should not speak about issue of disagreement about how we as a society navigate topics like race, color, religion, sexual orientation, etc. Indeed, a speech in opposition to same-sex marriage, for example, is not necessarily hate speech, but could simply be a disagreement about a contentious issue related to sexual orientation. However, when we do discuss contentious issues around differences in our communities, we should speak about these issues respectfully, genuinely, open-mindedly, and with the best interests of our diverse audience in mind.
- **Reject demagoguery**. Moral and ethical public speakers should also choose to reject demagoguery as a tactic in their public speeches. A **demagogue** is *a speaker who appeals to popular prejudices rather than reason and argument*. The demagogue is a long-standing figure in the history of public speaking. They excel at using public speaking to whip a crowd into a frenzy, fueling people's worst instincts and using their rage, anger, and resentment to achieve their own political or personal ends. Many of history's most notorious warmongers and mass murderers achieved their goals through the use of demagoguery, illustrating how dangerous this unethical and immoral form of communication can be. Indeed, the founders of United States and many other democratic nations designed their governments and laws in explicit ways to minimize the rise of demagogues. However, much like hate speech, demagoguery is not illegal; it can only be defeated through moral and ethical choices not to engage in demagoguery as speakers and to reject demagogic appeals as audience members.

- **Reject baseless claims**. In public discourse, our ethics and morals should also lead us to reject claims and assertions made without evidence or support of any kind. As we will discuss in later chapters, using evidence in our arguments is vital to be an ethical and moral speaker. Indeed, evidence-based argument and research has been a primary source of scientific innovation and cultural progress in nations across the globe for centuries. Unfortunately, this has not stopped some speakers from relying extensively on **baseless claims**—*arguments that cannot be supported with credible evidence*. Indeed, in our hyper-partisan era, far too many speakers and audiences are willing to overlook the lack of evidence surrounding a claim purely to support their preferred candidate, party, or worldview. This has led some critics to suggest we are moving into a **post-truth society**, *a world in which people are willing to believe only their own interpretation of the world, even when there are no facts to support that the world actually exists in that way*. The move toward a post-truth society is dangerous because when we make and believe arguments without evidence, we are creating ethical and moral quandaries in public life that make it impossible to engage in a vital, public discourse about our honest disagreements. The fact is: we may not like a particular course of action or outcome in a public debate, but it is morally and ethically dubious to deny reality purely to make ourselves feel good or comfortable.

The moral and ethical values listed above are not the extent of the values you will face and be responsible for in your role as public speaker; indeed, as you start public speaking, you must recognize that you have a responsibility to consider the moral and ethical implications of each of your speaking choices.

These six facts about public speaking are important for framing the work we will do in this book and in this class; yet, they should also provide you with a set of principles to think about what you are doing when you speak in a public setting. As should be clear from the points in this chapter, public speaking is never simple, minor, or unimportant; rather, public speaking is a deeply important, complex, and culturally significant act—one that needs to be appreciated, studied, and practiced.

Chapter 2

SPEAKING *ACROSS* DIFFERENCE IN A PLURALISTIC SOCIETY

> *"The future of our earth may depend upon the ability of all [people] to identify and develop new definitions of power and new patterns of* ***relating across difference****. The old definitions have not served us, nor the earth that supports us. The old patterns, no matter how cleverly rearranged to imitate progress, still condemn us to cosmetically altered repetitions of the same old exchanges, the same old guilt, hatred, recrimination, lamentation, and suspicion…* ***Change means growth, and growth can be painful.*** *But we sharpen self-definition* ***by exposing the self*** *in work and* ***struggle together with those whom we define as different from ourselves****, although* ***sharing the same goals****. For Black and white, old and young, lesbian and heterosexual [people] alike, this can mean new paths to our survival."*[6]
>
> *—Audre Lorde*

As a person living in the 21st century, you will be giving public speeches in one of the most diverse human societies the world has ever known. Today, in the United States, there is greater racial, ethnic, and religious diversity than at any other time in the nation's history. According to Census data, 98% of all the metropolitan areas in the United States became more diverse since 1980. Meanwhile, 97% of most small cities and 90% of all rural areas in the U.S. also saw an increase in diversity from earlier decades.[7] To put it simply: no matter whether you live in the city, suburbs, or country, your community is quickly becoming more racially, ethnically, and religiously diverse.

We see this change at an accelerated rate in Colorado, one of the fastest diversifying states in the nation. Across the state, the white population has dropped precipitously from 75% to 70% in just ten years while the share of non-white communities has grown robustly. According to the state demographer, while African American and Asian communities in Colorado have all grown in recent years, the Hispanic community has grown at the most vigorous rate, from 17% to 21% of the population between 2000 and 2011.[8] This is not just a trend in urban Colorado; diversity has grown significantly in most rural counties as well. Indeed, in some rural Colorado counties, the Hispanic community represents the single largest population category.[9]

In addition, the world will only become more diverse during your lifetime. By mid-century, white people will no longer constitute the majority of the U.S. population; meanwhile, Hispanics, Asians, and African Americans will continue to grow to represent larger and larger percentages of the population overall. Indeed, in thirty years, there will be no majority racial or ethnic group in the U.S.

By 2050, the number of people globally who identify as Muslim will match the number of people who identify as Christian, while the percentage of people unaffiliated with a religious faith will be the largest faith group in the nation.[10] The United States will also be an older nation by 2055, with just about as many people age 65 and older as there are 25 to 44 or 45 to 65.[11] And while the nation and the world continue to diversify, we will see more and more personal and intimate relationships across these categories, with significant increases in interfaith and interracial marriages, international marriages, and multiracial families and children.

This short summary of the changing demographics of our state, nation, and world illustrates that growing diversification is a reality of the 21st century—a reality we will all be able to enjoy in the years to come. Indeed, research shows that states and nations with dynamic changes in immigration, intercultural experience, and background not only enrich their neighborhoods but also supercharge their economies, providing even greater opportunities for future generations.[12] Still, change can be difficult and noticeable changes in the makeup of our communities can make some people uncomfortable and confused.

This is just one reason why it is crucial that all future public speakers learn the importance of speaking across difference effectively. Public speakers who include and affirm difference are not just well-prepared for success in the business and politics of our changing communities; they can also play an important role in development of our increasingly **pluralistic society**—*a society constituted by many different kinds of people who believe many different kinds of things yet work in common cause and tolerance for the betterment of the community as a whole.*

Getting Perspective on Difference

As the definition above suggests, key to understanding how we speak in a pluralistic society is coming to understand difference better. What is difference? In this book, we use the word **difference** to refer to *the various ways in which people's experiences in and understanding of the world are expressed in their sense of self and others.* In other classes or conversations, you may have come across other words that have a meaning similar to difference: tolerance, diversity, multiculturalism, inclusivity, and so on. While these words all have value, in this class, we use difference for some very specific reasons:

- **Difference can take many forms**. Other terms highlight particular forms of difference—race, class, gender, sexual orientation, faith, military service—each of which is an important aspect of the differences that distinguish people and communities. However, by using the word "difference," we do not get locked into any single set of particular differences; rather, "difference" allows us to more easily anticipate and include the many ways in which people relate to each other.

- **Difference is a relational term**. The term "difference" does not privilege one identity over another or imply that one community is "mainstream" or "traditional" while the others are not. Rather, "difference" recognizes that what distinguishes us can only take on meaning in context. In other words, the nature of our differences only becomes meaningful when one person experiences the world in manner that is not the same as another person.

- **People can have and experience multiple forms of difference**. Other terms often highlight particular dimensions of a person's experience (their skin color, their abilities, their nation of origin, etc.) as if that was the only thing that matters about them. But "difference" recognizes that all people are complex with many layers of identities and knowledge simultaneously shaping our experience in the world.

- **Difference is situational.** The term "difference" also foregrounds the fact that difference is always attuned to particular times, places, and events. What might be "familiar" or "typical" in one place might be "different" in another place. "Difference," then, is not a static term; instead, it foregrounds the dynamic and evolving ways in which we might be different.

- **Difference draws attention to experiences we might like to ignore.** "Difference" is directly opposed to the blasé idea that human beings are inherently "all the same." While there are many things people have in common, much of our social lives are lived in and across differences. Using the term "difference" makes it harder to ignore this fact and demands that we pay attention to the ways difference enriches and harms the lives of ourselves and others.

This book and this class take the viewpoint that differences within human communities, for their challenges, are a wonderful gift. Just like biodiversity enriches our ecosystems and competition enriches our economy, human differences enrich our speaking environments, giving us more interesting things to talk about, new experiences to try, and disagreements that illuminate the human condition.

Yet, difference is also at the root of many of the most stubborn issues facing human society. Our differences of experience, opinion, belief, worldview, resources, opportunities, and so on are often what drive so much of the disagreement and partisanship on which our public discourse seems to turn. We might be under the illusion that, if we could just keep our societies homogenous—if we could all just be the same—we could cure all the disagreements that plague us and finally get something done. But the horrors of genocide, "ethnic cleansing," and mass murder throughout human history should always remind us that such ideas are morally repugnant and simply wrong. Therefore, discovering ways to speak *across* difference becomes a vital tool for our future success.

Speaking across difference, however, can be challenging, particularly because research tells us there is no way to avoid difference when we use language. The 20th century rhetorical scholar Kenneth Burke, for instance, showed convincingly that difference is inherent in all forms of language use, because it is simply impossible to see and describe the world to another person exactly as we see it. If we did not need to use language, Burke argues, it might be possible to avoid the disagreements and arguments that derive from our different understandings of the world. However, because we largely communicate with each other through language—an inherently imperfect medium—our communication will *always* reflect differences of perception, accuracy, or perspective.[13] To put it another way: there will never be the perfect word, description, or expression of an idea that every person in the world agrees to, because language simply is not perfect enough. It is always flawed from the beginning. As such, until we invent telepathy, all humans speaking to other humans will have to tackle difference as a part of the communication process.

So, if our language is always going to reflect (and sometimes, inflame) our differences, what can we do about it? Thinking about ways to anticipate, minimize, and circumvent issues between speech and difference is much of what we will do in this chapter. To begin, let's spend some time thinking about the ways in which we get defensive about difference.

Getting Defensive about Difference

Because speaking across difference is hard work and often makes people uncomfortable, some people have fallen into defensive positions about speaking across difference. These defensive positions often come in one of two forms: either people assume that any and all words and actions by someone different from them is meant to harm them or people assume that all concern about difference is pointless, whiny, or unsubstantiated. Neither of these approaches to difference is helpful, but at some level, they might be understandable. That is because doing the work of social change is hard and can be exhausting and scary. As such, it might make sense to some people to always be looking for the worst in others or to just try to ignore a potentially uncomfortable set of realities. However, if most or even a substantial minority of people in a democracy falls into defensive positions about an issue as important as speaking to people who are different from us, we're creating a recipe for disaster. Therefore, it is vital that we as public speakers learn to recognize two very common knee-jerk reactions that we need to avoid: rejecting political correctness and demanding safe spaces.

"I HATE POLITICAL CORRECTNESS"

Over the last two decades, one term has become particularly contentious in how we learn to speak to each other in a pluralistic society: political correctness. Traditionally, **political correctness** refers to *the belief that language and behaviors that offend marginalized communities in a given society should be curtailed and replaced with statements and acts that affirm these communities' place in that society.* Among the most common features of political correctness are the disavowal of racially inappropriate terms and the use of more contemporary and sensitive terms to discuss others, typically ethnic and racial minorities and women.

Expectations that speakers will be politically correct in their language emerged prominently in the 1980s and 90s when marginalized communities began to demand that they be addressed by others in ways that rejected old biases and affirmed the values and contributions of their communities to society. For example, women in the workforce began to challenge men who referred to them as "girls" because it was patronizing and belittled the valuable work that women did as professionals. Likewise, "African-American" or "Asian-American" became socially preferable terms for talking about different communities in the United States because the language recognized those communities as full-fledged Americans even though the term "American" has been historically connected with the idea of a person who is white. In addition, many communities adopted the term "Native American" as opposed to "Indian" because it finally broke free from a false description of the native peoples of North America made by Europeans centuries earlier. In each case and many others, the recognition of the power of using different words and terms to address minority and marginalized communities in affirming ways was an important step in correcting historical mistreatment and building a more fair and equitable future.

However, more recently, some people have characterized political correctness as nothing more than an attempt to stifle conversations about the world. The complaint goes that being politically correct somehow suffocates a speaker's ability to "tell it like it is," to engage in genuinely felt criticism of others, or to make others uncomfortable even when the topic of debate is justified. Yet, in many cases, these anxieties about the consequences of political correctness are often misplaced. In a robust democracy, no subject of political debate is off limits and most people's speech is protected under law, even if those people refuse to abide by recent conventions about what is moral and ethical speech (something we discussed in Chapter 1).

Meanwhile, in some cases, calls to end political correctness represent veiled admissions that some people of historically dominant categories in the United States do not want to do the work needed to alter their language to reflect changing times. No doubt: learning the new and socially responsible words that are different from the terms we grew up with can be tricky and sometimes requires real struggle. It can also lead us to make mistakes that can be embarrassing and uncomfortable. Some people even fear trying to update their language because they fear the social consequences of getting it wrong. Still, it is important to note that while some of these anxieties and concerns are understandable, the same sympathy and respect is almost never extended to historically marginalized communities in the U.S. In fact, U.S. society has a long and horrific history of controlling, manipulating, and punishing the speech and language of people of color, Native Americans, immigrants, sexual minorities, religious minorities, and women through convention, law, and violence. This inequity raises the question: why should some people be excused from working to use language that creates a more respectful society when marginalized others have been compelled to do so for centuries?

Learn More: Examples of How the Speech of Marginalized Communities Has Been Controlled and Punished

As noted above, while some people may contemporarily bemoan having to do work to learn the socially acceptable way to speak about communities different from their own, U.S. history is full of vivid examples of the speech and language of marginalized communities being prevented, controlled, policed, and punished. For example:

- Laws throughout the U.S. made it illegal to teach slaves how to read, write, or speak in public for centuries.
- By law and custom, women in the U.S. were expected to avoid speaking to audiences of men and women, what was described as a "promiscuous" audience; rather they could only safely speak in public to women-only audiences.
- Black people in the Jim Crow South—particularly young black men—were beaten, murdered, and lynched for speaking back to white men or speaking to (and sometimes even looking at) white women at all.
- Men who were presumed to have a "gay lisp" have been subjected to prejudice, discrimination, and violence for much of the 20th century.
- For centuries, non-English speakers have been locked out of employment, housing, education, and more even though there is no official language in the United States.

Regardless of your feelings on politically correct language, to successfully speak across difference, there is no set of required words to say or not to say; rather, speaking across difference requires speakers to make smart calculations in particular moments about what the best, most appropriate, and most meaningful word is and choosing to use it. There might be times when a particular speaker may say an otherwise inappropriate word because it furthers their argument against that word (for instance); for other speakers in other situations, those words might be simply unacceptable if the speaker is trying to win over their audience. What is without dispute is that all public speakers must make smart choices in the use of their language in order to be effective advocates across communities of difference.

FROM "SAFE SPACES" TO "BRAVE SPACES"

While it is important for public speakers to avoid the laziness that comes from making a blanket rejection of learning about difference, it is also vital that public speakers and their audiences come prepared to do the work necessary to hear things they dislike.

Part of this work is recognizing that public speaking situations are not safe spaces. **Safe spaces** are *locations, places, and sites in the world in which individuals and communities can take refuge from opinions, expectations, and assumptions other people make about them.* ***All of us*** have safe spaces that we go to in order to relax, recharge, rest, or rant. It could be at home with your family or a weekly meet up with a group of friends. Your safe space might be a cultural center in the Student Center or a quiet place in the library. Your safe space might be a particular club where you feel like you can be yourself or a campus facility where you feel valued, respected, and encouraged. Each of us needs these spaces to let loose, to be affirmed, and to simply stop, if even for a second, having to put up with all the things in the world that people different from us don't get or understand. Without these spaces, we can burn out, become alienated, feel isolated or threatened, or worse. So, it is vital that all kinds of people have spaces in which they can exist in a comfortable and reassuring way.

However, while everyone deserves a safe space, some people have access to safe spaces more often and in greater quantity than others. If you come from a historically-dominant culture or identity in Fort Collins, you may never have thought about your safe spaces because almost every place in the city, state, or nation is relatively comfortable, familiar, welcoming, and reassuring to people like you. This is not the case for people who come from historically-marginalized communities and identities. For instance, people who identify as LGBT or queer tend to have very few safe spaces in which they can be themselves openly, without judgment or harassment, or simply with people like themselves. Is that true everywhere in the world? No—each part of the world has its own mix of safe and unsafe spaces for different communities. The Castro District in San Francisco or the Chelsea neighborhood in New York City, for example, are places in which LGBT and queer people tend to feel quite safe. For residents of those cities, their need for a safe space might not be as great.

Meanwhile, in a community like Fort Collins, there are relatively few safe spaces for LGBT and queer people, particularly off-campus. So, the need for safe spaces for that community is greater. Think, then, about yourself and all the ways in which you are similar to or different from the other people in your class, the campus community, or the Fort Collins community generally. How often do you feel unsafe in the spaces in which you circulate on a daily basis? What do you need or do in order to feel safe to be yourself? How many places can you go where you won't feel judged or misunderstood by people different from you? Based on your answers to these question, should people different from you have more access to safe spaces in your community? Or, should a person like yourself be more open to others having these kinds of spaces in your community? Thinking about these kinds of questions is important when we hear people complain about safe spaces; often, the loudest complainers are those with the most security in their own community.

While safe spaces are vital for all people to be happy and healthy members of a pluralistic society, it is also important to remember that not all spaces ***can*** or ***should*** be safe spaces. *This is not a question of physical security*: everyone has the right to feel free from the use or threat of physical violence, harassment, and intimidation, both on-campus and off. But should we expect that all our ideas, values, and beliefs also be free from questioning, disagreement, or judgement? To put a finer point on it, *are public speaking situations safe spaces*?

In both a democracy and an institution of higher education, the answer is a firm "No." In fact, democracies are founded on the belief that all ideas, beliefs, values, policies, plans, and viewpoints benefit from explicit, vigorous, and thoughtful questioning and challenging. Further, we believe that an idea or belief that is scrutinized in public and maintained becomes a stronger and more credible idea. As a public university, Colorado State University is committed to the vigorous debate of ideas on campus; however, that also means that, as public speakers, when we express our ideas or value or beliefs in our classrooms or in a paper or outside the Student Center, we cannot nor should not expect these words and ideas to always be encouraged or appreciated or agreed with. In fact, quite the opposite: **when we speak in public, we should always expect our ideas, beliefs, and values to be put under a microscope, challenged, and scrutinized**.

Unfortunately, when we put our ideas and beliefs out into the world, not everyone challenges or questions those ideas politely. In an ideal world, people who disagree with a speaker would respond by listening carefully, thinking critically, and offering constructive criticism. However, in the world as it is, sometimes speakers can be met with heckling, booing, mischaracterization, and general mean spiritedness. This fact does not always make public speaking comfortable or reassuring, but that is the nature of the process. In fact, the rights that protect an audience member's rude and unhelpful challenges are the same rights that protect your choice to speak more powerfully, passionately, and persuasively against them. It is not a perfect system, but it has created the conditions under which we are more able to discuss difficult topics than other communities around the world.

How, then, do we steel ourselves as public speakers and audience members in spaces which are not safe spaces? The answer is to create brave spaces. **Braves spaces** are defined as *sites in which "we emphasize the need for courage rather than the illusion of safety" in public discourse.* In brave spaces, we recognize that people will disagree, that they will make mistakes, that conflicting viewpoints will be held, and that people will not always be comfortable. But brave spaces are needed because we recognize that being unable to speak to each other across difference or have difficult conversations does not make our public life better; in fact, it makes things much worse. As such, SPCM 200 leans into the idea of the public speaking classroom as a brave space, one that can be challenging but serves a vital public good.

Creating a space that is brave is not easy. It will take effort on the part of your instructor who has been trained in the parameters and goals of a brave space. It will also take the whole class to be willing to set and abide by ground rules for how we will speak to each other and respond as audience members about topics on which we agree and disagree. In addition, it will take you as an individual to be willing to speak, listen, and engage in uncomfortable terrain. As a class, you will devote some time to defining what the exact "brave space" of your classroom looks like; however, you might think about the following ground rules suggested by Brian Arao and Kristi Clemens in their article, "From Safe Spaces to Brave Spaces: A New Way to Frame Dialogue Around Diversity and Social Justice"[14]:

1. Controversy with Civility.
2. Own Your Intentions and Impact.
3. Challenge by Choice.
4. Respect.
5. No Ad Hominem Attacks.

As part of your work in this unit, read more about each of these terms in Arao and Clemens' full essay on Canvas; then, be prepared to discuss how you and your class can build a brave space in your particular section of SPCM 200.

Mistakes in Speaking Across Difference

One of the hardest parts about learning to speak effectively across difference is that all of us are prone to make mistakes. For example, sometimes in our attempts to be assertive, we shut down different points of view. Or, we might say something with the best intentions only to find out later we did so in a way that was inaccurate, impolite, or even offensive. Inevitably, each of us—even those of us with a great deal of training and experience in our diverse world—will make mistakes speaking across difference. With practice, however, we can keep these mistakes to a minimum. Part of this practice involves knowing and anticipating some of the most common mistakes people make when speaking across difference. These include:

- **Generalizing Our Experience**. One of the most common mistakes that we make as public speakers is that we assume our own experience in the world has been the same as everyone else's experience. This mistake is understandable considering how important speaking from experience is in public speaking today. As we will discuss, public speakers who are willing to pick topics that they have had personal experience with and to share those personal experiences in an authentic way in their speeches can be extremely powerful and quite successful. In a homogenous society, where most everyone experiences the world the same, talks the same, and grew up in the same way, speaking from our experience in such sweeping terms might work. But, we do not live in that world. Instead, most groups of people today—at school, in work, on the street—have very different experiences from our own, even if those experiences might not be evident to us. As a result, when we make assumptions about our audience or use phrases like, "We have all seen..." or "everyone knows..." we are generalizing our experience to others. In doing so, we are also extinguishing someone else's experience and disinviting them from our speech.

- **Bias**. The word **bias** refers to *the interpretation of the world in a way that only reflects our own limited experiences*. Bias is a natural part of being a human being. When we come into the world and take it all in, we all do so from our very specific point of view. As we age and grow, this point of view becomes more complex and develops aspects that we share with some people and do not share with others. Nonetheless, even as we find others like us who share similar biases of how the world does or should work, none of us shares exactly the same biases. In other words, everyone interprets the world differently, even from those people we think of as exactly like us.

  A simple way of understanding bias is by laying on the ground with a group of people on a beautiful day and watching the clouds pass by. If you ask everyone to tell you what they see in the clouds, people's biases will start to be revealed. Where someone sees a dog, another person sees a cat; my train is your snake. None of these answers are right or wrong, but each one represents a different interpretation of the world through our bias. And those biases are shaped by each of our individual experiences in the world to that point.

  These differences in interpreting the world are pretty harmless when all we are doing is watching clouds float by; but when our biases are used to interpret other people and their actions in the world, biases can cause problems. The same biases that lead us to distinguish a train from a snake in the clouds, might lead us to interpret a colleague's handshake as friendly or intimidating, a co-worker's joking as lighthearted or discriminatory, or a public speaker's argument as common sense or offensive. Because these interpretations are based on our biases, we can't avoid them. However, to successfully speak across difference, it is important to admit that we do have biases, to ask ourselves where those biases come from, and to reconsider our biases if we learn that they are wrong, unhelpful, or inaccurate.

- **Stereotyping**. Like biases, stereotyping has to do with the way we make sense of the world; however, unlike biases, **stereotyping** is *the projection of a bias onto a category or group of people so that we assume all people in a group act, think, or believe in the same way*. Like biases, stereotypes are difficult to avoid in the social world. They often come from having to make quick decisions about how to interact with another person based on our previous experience with a person who is similarly different from ourselves. Yet, many times, our stereotypes are not based on personal experience; rather, most stereotypes are created and maintained by what we see or hear in the media, in stories, on the news, or even in conversations with our family and friends. That makes stereotypes quite dangerous: they encourage us to make judgements about a person, not on their unique behavior or our personal experience with them, but by our own categorization of that person. Ironically, this can mistakenly lead us to believe something about a person that is the exact opposite of what they believe themselves. For example, racial and ethnic stereotypes about what certain communities of people enjoy eating might actually be the least favorite food of a particular person who comes from one of those racial or ethnic groups. The danger of stereotypes even applies to so-called "positive" stereotypes. Indeed, assuming that a person from a certain community is talented at something because that community is stereotyped as such might actually harm the individual who is not talented in that area and may need assistance. As public speakers, stereotypes are problematic. Unlike biases, which are largely internalized, stereotypes are spread implicitly or explicitly by public speakers (and others) who don't look for the differences that separate us as individuals. As such, public speakers need to be sure to avoid stereotypes and to seek more information about individuals and communities rather than make snap judgements about them.

- **Ethnocentrism**. Public speakers sometimes also mistakenly present their own experience as if it is superior to others. More to the point, public speakers can practice **ethnocentrism**—*the belief that one's own culture is superior to others*. When a speaker uses their time before an audience to denigrate another culture or people and praise their own, they are practicing ethnocentrism. For example, if a speaker praises their own culture's native music while calling all other culture's music "trash," they are making ethnocentric statements. Ethnocentrism is destructive to speaking across difference. It begins with the assumption that cultures are "right" or "wrong" rather than people's actions or ideas. From there, ethnocentric speakers go on to attack an entire community of people without regard for differences within a community, the views and agency of individuals, and the limitations of the speaker's own culture. A common question regarding ethnocentrism is how it differs from pride in one's upbringing, background, community, or culture. The key distinction is not the pride someone has for their own culture or community, but the implicit or explicit denigration of another person's culture or community. To put it frankly: ethnocentrism is the active belief that there is only one right way to live in the world and an active intolerance of others' differing worldviews and experiences.
- **Speaking for Others**. When we speak on behalf of other people, we almost always believe we are doing something helpful. In our minds, we are actively thinking about others and trying to include them into our present discussion—a discussion which they might not be a part of or have access to. However, when we choose to speak for others, we commit a serious offense, namely: we take away another person's ability to speak for themselves. In doing so, we treat people like **objects**—*things that exist in the world and belong to other people*—rather than **subjects**—*mindful, thoughtful people in the world who can act, think, and speak on their own*. It should come as no surprise that women, people of color, people from other nations, and children are the most likely people to be spoken for in contemporary U.S. society.
- **Only Seeing One Side of a Person**. For centuries, people in the Western tradition have been taught to think in either/or terms. Something is either "right or wrong," "good or bad," "thumbs up or thumbs down," "black or white," or "masculine or feminine." However, in a pluralistic society, our tendency to speak in either/or terms can cause significant problems. In particular, when we place people in one of two categories, we risk only seeing a small fraction of the many complex parts of a person's life. Indeed, as our discussion of difference suggests, all of us have many types and degrees of difference when we are in changing sites, spaces, and communities. Think about it: if all people saw when they looked at you was your gender, for instance, and they ignored every other aspect of your life; how little would they know you? And how unwilling would you be to give their speech a fair hearing when addressed through that lens?

- **Defensive Speaking and Listening**. At times, both speakers and listeners assume their viewpoints, opinions, or arguments will be met with hostility. Yet, when a speaker or audience member assumes that they will be met with hostility and proactively become defensive, it prevents us from speaking across difference. Defensive speakers, for instance, might take an angry tone, make assumptions about their audience's beliefs, or convince themselves they will not be heard let alone considered fairly. Defensive audiences ignore a speaker, plan their responses during the speech, and make assumptions about the speaker without cause.

- **Disengagement**. It is not uncommon that speaking in situations with people different from ourselves can produce fear. Indeed, it is a natural human response to be nervous or anxious when we engage with a person, place, or experience that is new to us. However, when some people are confronted with voices, faces, and experiences different from their own, they react by disengaging from the situation. What this disengagement looks like can take many forms: they avert eye contact, stop listening, look at their phones, walk away, or simply freeze. But all forms of disengagement are counterproductive in speaking across difference. Indeed, disengagement is an attempt to flee difference; to keep ourselves from having to acknowledge or consider other people in the world and how those people's needs and desires might impact us. Turning to disengagement is therefore very problematic: it short-circuits any genuine communication between people and leaves the other person isolated, unheard, and disrespected. Importantly, while some people from privileged communities use disengagement all the time, disengagement is not an equal opportunity tactic. Many minority and marginalized communities do not have the choice to disengage a threatening or confrontational situation without risking their own safety and livelihoods.

By knowing and recognizing these challenges in speaking across difference, we can better prepare ourselves to address audiences more fully and openly.

Strategies for Speaking Across Difference

While learning to anticipate and avoid mistakes in speaking across difference, public speakers and audiences can also take proactive steps to encourage genuine and meaningful communication across difference. These include:

- **Listen to criticism, admit mistakes, and grow**. One of the most important things we can do as speakers and audience members is to listen to criticism about speaking across difference, admit when we made a mistake, and grow from that experience. As a public speaker, we might find ourselves in a situation in which we are "called out" by a colleague or audience member for a mistake we made in speaking across difference. These call-out moments can be awkward and embarrassing, and our natural instinct may be to run, hide, or even deny our intention or our statement. But these are all counterproductive responses—they keep us from learning as speakers and tell those different from us that we do not value or care about their views or feedback. Instead, speaking across difference requires public speakers to listen to criticism intently, think about it meaningfully, and admit mistakes when we make them. In an ideal situation, we might also lay out how we will do better next time to prevent those mistakes from happening again.

- **Use inclusive language**. When public speakers *use terms and phrases that include, invite, and represent the widest number of people possible, they are using* **inclusive language**. As we know, language is a reflection of the time and place in which it was first used; as such, language can also become outdated and damaging when it reflects social and cultural conditions that have actively been altered or changed in our society. By discarding outdated and exclusive terms and using inclusive language, not only do we make more people feel included in our speech situation, but we can also help move outdated and offensive words out of public discourse. There are various types of inclusive ways of speaking that we should learn, many of which are highlighted for you in the chart in Chapter 9; however, a good practice is to describe people and communities different from yourself by using preferred language identified by that individual or community.

- **Speak for yourself and invite others to speak.** To counteract our tendency to treat others as objects and speak on their behalf, speakers can choose to speak for themselves and only themselves. However, our efforts cannot stop there. Speaking across difference also relies on the willingness of speakers to invite others to speak. Indeed, as speakers with access to a podium or platform to be heard, it is vital that we recognize when our voice is meaningful and when we should defer our own voices so that other voices can be empowered. In fact, in some situations, choosing not to speak on a particular subject or on a particular occasion and to support the speech of another person might be the best way to speak across difference.

- **Take up less time and space.** An often-unconscious way in which public speakers prevent speaking across difference is by taking up excessive amounts of time and space. Indeed, the position of the public speaker often comes with a lot of privileges as it relates to time and space: from the podium you can make some assertive decisions about how long you wish to speak or how much space on the program you want to fill with yourself and your ideas—even when limits are placed on you! In taking up more than one's fair share of time or space, however, speakers actively limit the amount of time and space available for other people, particularly people with marginalized identities or viewpoints. Therefore, we can support speaking across difference by actively limiting our use of time and space in public speaking. By selecting to speak only as much as we need to in order to be heard and then stepping back, we ensure there are opportunities for voices different from our own with which to engage.

- **Be open-minded.** As we have seen, listening or speaking defensively sets up strong barriers to speaking across difference. Instead, practice open-mindedness in your public speaking situation. **Open-mindedness** refers to *the willingness of a speaker or listener to hear views, perspectives, and beliefs that are different from their own and fully consider them before accepting or dismissing them.* Open-mindedness is essential for all forms of public speaking; however, it is especially essential when we speak across difference.

- **Be self-reflective.** Many of the mistakes we make when speaking across difference are a direct result of our sometimes-unconscious attempts to shield ourselves from discomfort, new ideas, or change. Being self-reflective can be a powerful tool to limit these mistakes. **Self-reflectiveness** refers to *the ability of a speaker or listener to recognize when they are acting uncritically in a communication situation and to investigate why that is.* Self-reflexivity involves two related tasks: making conscious behaviors that we do unconsciously and making a commitment to consider the roots of those behaviors. Self-reflexivity is a skill that takes time and effort, but it can pay innumerable dividends in speaking across difference as well as other parts of our lives.

- **Ask questions but do *your* work first.** Finally, speaking across difference by definition involves speaking with and about people who are different from us. Inevitably, this means we will have gaps in our knowledge about the right word to use, how to address someone, or any number of other issues that may come up. In these cases, some public speakers barrel ahead mindlessly; they try to hide the gaps in their knowledge by just saying things assertively or quickly or ignoring key areas of discussion. This almost never goes well and can lead to greater barriers to speaking across difference. Instead, speakers should ask questions when they do not have the information or knowledge they need to speak across difference. When a speaker raises these questions proactively prior to a speech, a speaker can avoid many problems and help create a more engaging conversation for all people in the audience. However, it is important to recognize that while having and asking questions is valuable, **it is not the responsibility of those different from you to educate you**. Instead, it is up to you to do the work necessary to find out what you don't know, seek out those answers on your own from reliable sources, and only then to ask questions once you've done your fair share of the work needed to speak across difference.

Speaking across difference is not easy; it can be challenging and intimidating and often requires us to be open minded and open to criticism and mistakes. However, when we choose to speak across difference, we not only choose to become more effective speakers; we also choose to take a first step toward creating a more just and fair society.

Unit 2

STRATEGIES FOR EFFECTIVE SPEAKING

Chapter 3

ANXIETY: STRATEGIES THAT WORK AND DON'T WORK

There is an old statistic that has been repeated for years: that people, on average, fear public speaking more than they fear death. That means, in the words of comedian Jerry Seinfeld, that, "if [people] have to go to a funeral, they'd be better off in the casket than giving the eulogy."[15] While much has been made of this statistic in the news and popular culture, people who read their research carefully can tell you this statistic is quite misleading.[16] In reality, while the number of people who report a fear of public speaking is higher than those who report a fear of death, people in those surveys also always rate death as a more important fear than public speaking. But that does not change the fact that public speaking is a major source of nervousness, angst, and anxiety for many people around the world.

In fact, fear of public speaking continues to affect large portions of the U.S. public. According to the 2016 Chapman University Survey of American Fears, **25.9% of the respondents reported a fear of public speaking.**[17] That's one out of every four people! That means that fear of public speaking is quite real. And it doesn't matter who you are: any of us could be susceptible to a fear of public speaking—even if you consider yourself a pretty confident public speaker. It occurs in people of all races, classes, genders, faiths, nationalities, sexualities, and abilities. It does not matter how old you are or what you look like. People who are introverted and extroverted can each experience anxiety when they speak in public. It does not matter if you are a first-time speaker or someone who has been doing this for years. Experiencing a fear of public speaking is simply quite common. So, if you have a fear of public speaking, now or in the future, don't worry: you're in good company.

But if so many people are so afraid of speaking in public, *why can't we just agree not to do it anymore*? While that might sound appealing, the reality is that we need competent and confident public speakers to make our societies work. People have real problems and exciting solutions for fixing them that we need to talk about at the level of the community. Making the world a better place, whether that means fixing a pothole or rethinking health care, requires buy-in from everybody. Unless we can come together to talk about what matters to us and how we address those problems as a community, we are never going to fix them. Posting on social media, talking to our friends, or answering a poll does not explore options, build consensus, or commit each other to action, **but public speaking can**. Our communities need everybody to be able to stand up and speak their mind effectively. We cannot let nerves get in the way.

Myths about Public Speaking

If we want to overcome our fear and anxieties related to public speaking, the first things we need to do is to dispel a lot of bad information and advice that is out there on how to make public speaking "easy." Public speaking, like dance or art or poetry, is an *art form*—and there is no such thing as a "quick fix" for doing something that takes real effort. So, let's take a moment to explode some of the most common pieces of bad advice we hear about public speaking.

- **Everybody is naturally a good communicator.** This myth goes back centuries and appears in ancient Greece and Rome, early Christendom, and even in the Scientific Revolution. The gist of the myth is probably something you've heard before: most human beings pick up language as babies and learn to speak all on their own; therefore, most of us are born knowing how to communicate effectively and anyone who wants to give a great speech can do so with no effort. However, any of us who have been in a boring lecture or listened to a painful speech by a politician know that is simply not the case. In fact, the people who abide by this myth are often the very speakers who perform badly once they make it to the podium. The reality is that language acquisition is not easy, even as a child. We learn to speak from years of listening, imitation, trial and error, parental and family training and correction, and formal education. Learning to be a great public speaker also requires a great deal of effort, failed attempts, practice, and education. Luckily, thanks to all the hard work you've done to this point in your life to acquire language skills, you have a good base of knowledge and experience, which means you can become a good public speaker in a relatively short amount of time.

Example in Action: In February 2018, the nation was mesmerized by the students of Marjory Stoneman Douglas High School. After a horrific school shooting resulted in the death of 17 students and school employees and hundreds of injuries, the students banded together to protest, petition, and speak out for changes in gun control policies at the state and federal level. Dozens of students took the microphone at rallies, spoke at marches, appeared on television shows, and debated in a nationally-televised town hall about their shared tragedy and what they wanted to see change. To many observers, the eloquence and skills of these students must have been a combination of luck and raw talent. But it simply didn't make sense as an explanation for such a concentrated, large group of great speakers. A week after the attack, a better explanation was discovered: the school district's superintendent explained that the student's success was based in large part on the "district's system-wide debate program that teaches extemporaneous speaking from an early age." In other words, unlike many other school districts, the students of Marjory Stoneman Douglas had spent years practicing speech, debate, and argument in the public. So, what appeared to some to be a lucky pocket of speaking skill was actually evidence that people well-prepared in speech can always have those skills at their disposal when the need arises. For more on the students and their speech training, see:

Kyra Gurney, "Last fall, they debated gun control in class. Now, they debate lawmakers on TV," *Miami Herald*, February 23, 2018, http://www.miamiherald.com/news/local/education/article201678544.html

- **Either you have it or you don't.** This is another myth that has spanned ages and cultures that needs to be debunked. Put simply, this myth suggests that the world is broken down into those who are naturally talented speakers and those who are not, and those in the latter category will never acquire the skills to be good speakers. Unlike the first myth, there is some truth to this idea. Scholars and thinkers, including the likes of Cicero—the great Roman orator and political leader—have often acknowledged that there are people who through nature, genes, divine intervention, or luck are born talented speakers. It makes sense to them instinctually with little or no training. Some speakers might even be so excellent that we could consider them a genius or prodigy in the art of speaking. Others of us, frankly, know that for a variety of reasons, we are not these people. But while the first half of this idea has some truth to it, the second half is where the myth takes over. It is not true that those of us who are not naturally talented speakers can never be good speakers. Instead, centuries of evidence suggest that people without natural skill can become immensely successful speakers with the right training and effort, so much so that they can match the speaking abilities of the naturally good speaker. What's more: naturally good speakers can excel even more in speaking with proper training and practice. In short, while we may not all begin our lives as good speakers, we can all become better speakers.

- **Public speaking is just reading aloud**. Regardless of what you may have heard there is a significant difference between giving a speech and reading from a paper or PowerPoint. This difference is summed up in the distinction between what we call the oral style and the written style. The **oral style** is *the preparation of words and ideas for speech* while the **written style** is *the preparation of words and ideas for reading*. To be successful in the 21st century, we need to be proficient in both the oral and written style. However, while both formats can use words, argument, and evidence, how they will ultimately be delivered matters a great deal in their preparations. Think about it. In the written style, where a document is prepared to be read, proper grammar is vital, evidence can be cited textually, and a document must follow proper conventions in order to be considered "good." Meanwhile, a document that is prepared to be spoken is very different. A speaker needs to be relatable and more casual or conversational. A speaker needs to know not just how to spell a word but how to say it properly. Evidence that is not said aloud will never be appreciated by the audience because the audience will likely never see the written document's Work Cited. And a speaker who is too busy reading in front of her audience is unlikely to make good eye contact, use gestures, move around the room, or notice that the audience has fallen asleep from boredom. So, do not be fooled: no matter what you might think, a document that is *read* to an audience will never feel or work like a speech *spoken* to an audience.
- **Substance without style or style over substance**. Have you ever listened to one of these two types of speakers? The first speaker has lots of evidence, research, and ideas but sounds like a robot spitting out computations. The second speaker is a flashy, gregarious talker who loves the sound of their own voice but never really says anything that matters. If you've ever suffered through listening to either of these kinds of speakers, you know that neither of them is actually successful at speaking. The former, while full of information, doesn't seem like a human being with feelings or emotions or anything that we can relate to. The latter is a bullshit artist, whose words might be pretty but who offers the audience nothing of value or interest. Neither one of these speakers is sufficient on their own; but together they might make a fully interesting speaker. In this example, we learn another lesson about public speaking: there is no speech situation in which style beats substance or substance beats style. A good and effective public speaker always has to do both. If you have nothing of value to say, then don't say anything; likewise, if you can't convey passion for your important ideas, ask yourself why that is. A public speaker is a well-rounded speaker and you have to be good at several parts of the job to do it well.
- **Speed solves everything**. Just before a nervous speaker begins to talk in front of their audience, a little voice sometimes pops up with a foolish idea: "You know, the faster you talk, the faster this whole thing will be over with. And the sooner it is over with, the better we'll feel." There is something appealing in that logic; indeed, it is only human to want to minimize our discomfort. Therefore, why not take the quickest path to doing so? In reality, speed is not your friend in public speaking. Sure, you might ease your discomfort more quickly and you still might get credit

for your number of points and evidence. However, as a practical matter, speed is a speech-killer. An audience can only process information so quickly, especially when the information is new, different, or challenging. A speedy speech forces arguments and evidence down an audience's throat. It makes them confused, angry, and likely to lose interest or stop trying. Frankly, it is disrespectful to a group of people who genuinely want to hear what you think about the world for a few minutes to waste their time and abuse their senses with a fast speech. A good and generous speaker is conscious of their time limits and speaks within them at a steady rate that gives the audience time to consume and consider their points. Taking your time might very well make you more uncomfortable. But few people in human history have ever been rewarded for a fast speech.

- **Procrastination**. Do any of us really believe that waiting until the last minute to prepare for anything improves our chances of succeeding at it? Realistically, I don't think so. So, it may be unfair to call procrastination a myth for success. But much like the voice in our head described above, there is something inside us that tells us something positive will come from minimizing discomfort. In this case, we are promised a momentary relief if we put the stress and anxiety of preparing our speech off for another hour, another day, or another week. For many of us, it is certainly true that procrastination does give us that momentary high. The problem, of course, is that it is only momentary. To make matters worse, the cost of that temporary relief is higher stress and less time to prepare for the speech that is still coming, one way or the other. So, while it might not be the case that there is a myth that procrastination will make a better speech, it is certainly the case that avoiding a task is no way to succeed at that task.
- **"Wing it."** More than a few people have tried to make it through a speech by the old strategy of "winging it." In other words, some people's approach to public speaking is to actively do no preparation prior to the speech and hope that everything comes together at the last possible second all on its own. The misguided belief bets that inspiration will strike like lightning, saving the day at the last possible moment. The "winging it" strategy, however, is an urban myth: a belief that someone somewhere once gave an amazing speech by not preparing at all. Most likely, this myth comes from popular culture, which is full of extraordinarily eloquent speeches that come out of thin air and perfectly capture the moment (think *Braveheart* or *Independence Day*). Ask anyone who has tried the "wing it" approach and they are sure to tell you: this strategy is a surefire loser. Sure, you might come up with something interesting and heartfelt to say in a timely moment. But most speeches are not about your most recent thought or spit balling in front of an audience. Rather, most speeches in the real world are about this quarter's profit margin, policy solutions to challenging public issues, or articulating complex feelings in front of others. In other words, the reasons we speak in public usually require more thought than what a person can achieve in the moment. If a moment's notice is really all that is required to conceive and say something sufficient about a topic in question, it is likely that topic does not merit a speech in the first place.

Examples in Action: Popular culture is full of examples of amazing and inspiring speeches given by speakers who just "wing it." And why not? Hollywood loves to create tension, surprise its audience, and tell stories about an underdog succeeding when the odds are against them. But just because something makes a great Hollywood ending does not mean it makes sense as a way to prepare for your next big speech. To see an example of how Hollywood creates the false belief that good speeches come from "winging it," check out Will Ferrell's character delivering a surprisingly effective debate rebuttal during a "black out" from the film *Old School* (2003).

- **Picturing the audience naked**. This is one of the most famous pieces of advice about public speaking in the world. We have no idea where it came from. Frankly, I have never heard anyone try it successfully. On the rare occasion a student has told me they tried to picture the audience naked, they reported it made them feel uncomfortable at best and queasy at worse. I even had a student break into a minute-long laughing fit in the middle of their speech after trying this technique. So, does picturing the audience naked work? Maybe for someone somewhere once upon a time it did. But in the day-to-day lives of public speakers, this strategy is a bigger myth than Big Foot, the Loch Ness Monster, or a pot of gold at the end of a rainbow.

Whether we're talking about 300 B.C.E. or today, public speaking continues to give people anxiety. And that anxiety continues to produce a futile search for an "easy" way to handle, avoid, or overcome that anxiety. Now that we know some of the most common myths about public speaking that should be avoided, we can begin to seriously consider tools and strategies that can and will help us become effective speakers. The first part of that process is learning to better understand our main obstacle: public speaking anxiety.

Public Speaking Anxiety: Speaking, Nerves, and Apprehension

If we're going to better understand that awful feeling you have before you give a speech, we need to start by getting the name right. While many people refer to this feeling as a "fear of public speaking," that name is misleading. Most people are not *fearful* of speaking as they are fearful of spiders or ghosts. Unlike the latter two examples, most people do not scream and run away in terror at the mention of the word "speech" or the sight of a podium. What is common, however, is that people who need to give speeches feel nerves, angst, or anxiety about doing so. That is why the better name for what we are talking about is public speaking anxiety. **Public speaking anxiety** (also known as **glossophobia**) is *a common form of nervousness people feel before, during, and/or after speaking before groups of people in a public setting.* If you have ever given a speech before, you probably know this feeling. If you have never given a speech before, the experience of having public speaking anxiety is not unlike the nerves you get before a job interview or asking someone out on a date. Researchers in Communication Studies who study public speaking anxiety survey large groups of people on what they experience during public speaking and the results are what most of us would expect. The most common experiences reported by respondents are increased heart rate, sweating palms, a nervous stomach, a sense of disorientation, and numb feelings, usually in the arms or legs.[18] These feelings are not particularly comfortable. Actually, they are pretty frustrating and inconvenient. But when compared to most people's worst fears about public speaking, these feelings are pretty rational and manageable.

We should also note that public speaking anxiety is part of a larger category of anxieties that we call communication apprehension. **Communication apprehension** is *a broad term for the many types of anxieties people have about communication generally.* Examples of communication apprehensions include anxiety when speaking on the phone, anxieties in intimate conversations, and anxieties about communicating in written form. While public speaking anxiety is the most common form of communication apprehension, it is useful to know that communication can generate nerves in many kinds of people in many different ways.

CAUSES OF PUBLIC SPEAKING ANXIETY

But what causes public speaking anxiety? Most research suggests that public speaking anxiety comes from one of two sources. The first is what we call a trait anxiety. **Trait anxieties** *produce anxiousness around general categories of human experience because of our distinct personalities or experiences.* If your personality gets anxious around dogs or strangers or heights, it is a reflection of you and your unique likes and dislikes. It is not that any *one* dog or any *one* stranger makes you anxious in particular; it's that the *entire experience* makes you somewhat uncomfortable. The same is true of public speaking. For people with trait anxiety, public speaking anxiety may be driven largely by your unique personality and experiences about all public speaking scenarios.

However, while some people may be anxious in almost any kind of communication situation because of their unique traits, it is much more common that particular kinds of communication interactions generate apprehension while other communication interactions do not. This fact leads us to the second source of public speaking anxiety, *anxiety about communication that is linked to a particular situation, circumstance, or moment that we call* **state anxiety**. If, for example, the thought of speaking in front of others gives you anxiety but talking to your friends in a small group does not, you can see how state anxiety works. In state anxiety, our apprehension is specific and limited, in a way that trait anxiety is not. Public speaking anxiety is a great example of a state anxiety: people have apprehension about communication *only* when it is in public and before others. But, as we saw in our earlier discussion of communication apprehension, other kinds of state anxiety exist as well. For instance, some people get anxious when speaking with others on the phone. Others might be anxious when they do not know the person they are communicating with well. Still others might be the opposite: they feel confident talking to strangers but get anxious when speaking with people they know intimately.

Knowing how public speaking anxiety fits into communication apprehension and how communication apprehension does or does not appear in your life can better prepare you to tackle whatever anxieties might come up in your social interactions.

WHY MINIMIZE PUBLIC SPEAKING ANXIETY?

While public speaking anxiety and other kinds of communication apprehension are very real, there is no magic pill that can make them disappear. Pharmaceutical companies would like us to believe otherwise. They would like us to believe that public speaking anxiety is a disease—like cancer or a heart condition—that can be "cured" with the right combination of very expensive drugs. But a fear of public speaking is not a disease. Certainly, there are severe and specific anxiety conditions that affect a small part of the population for whom medication is an invaluable benefit. But the vast majority of people who get nervous while giving a speech (or going on a job interview or a first date) are just responding in a very natural, human way to a challenging situation. Meanwhile, if we're realistic about it, we can make public speaking anxiety a minor roadblock on the road to successful speaking.

While it might not be possible to eliminate public speaking anxiety, it is possible to manage it. In fact, the world is full of examples of successful people who have managed their public speaking anxiety. We don't usually think of great leaders and speechmakers like Abraham Lincoln, Winston Churchill, Thomas Jefferson, or Mahatma Gandhi as having a fear of public speaking. And leaders of million-dollar corporations like Warren Buffet and Richard Branson who give speeches to stockholders and testify before Congress couldn't do their jobs with a fear of public speaking, right? Certainly, someone like evangelical preacher Joel Osteen must have no concerns when he delivers a sermon before a church of thousands. And celebrities like Oprah Winfrey, Conan O'Brien, and

Leonardo DiCaprio must be adept public speakers since they spend their careers on stage and on camera? But each of these people has said repeatedly in the press that they have struggled with public speaking throughout their lives and careers.

What's more, managing public speaking anxiety is important for several reasons. First, **public speaking remains a highly sought-after skill in today's workforce**. Annual, large-scale studies by organizations like the National Association of Colleges and Employers, Bloomberg, and Forbes regularly show employers desperately seek candidates well-equipped to give speeches and presentations, even in this increasingly digital age. In fact, Bloomberg reported in 2016 that "communication skills" like public speaking were identified in a survey of more than 500 major companies as one of the "most common but hardest to find" job skills. In that same survey, industries as diverse as Technology, Health Care, Finance, Chemicals, Manufacturing, Pharmaceuticals, and Transportation all rated communication skills as their "most important" skill for future job candidates.[19] In other words, people who can manage their public speaking anxiety are in high demand in the 21st century workforce.

Second, research suggests **you can actually scare yourself into doing worse in a speech if you let your anxieties get out of control**. For instance, scholarship has shown that public speaking anxiety can lead to "poor decision making" in the days leading up to a speech, leading a speaker to choose meager topics, cite poor sources, and manage their time ineffectively. Another research study on public speaking anxiety demonstrated that fear of public speaking actually contributed to "poor speech preparation." That means that people who experienced anxiety avoided preparing for their speech that, in turn, lead them to do worse on their speech than they would have if they prepared. In other words, public speaking anxiety can be a self-fulfilling prophecy if it gets out of control, so it is important to face it head on with a plan to limit its effects.[20]

Finally, communication research has shown that **if people don't take steps to manage their public speaking anxiety, they can start to actively avoid public speaking situations in the future**. While never speaking in public again might seem like a good idea to some people, it can have big consequences in people's everyday lives. Imagine losing a new job opportunity or a promotion just because it might require you to give a speech once a year? That could have significant consequences in terms of job satisfaction and financial worth. Or imagine how it would feel to refuse to be in your best friend's wedding party because you would have to give a brief speech congratulating them? What impacts could that have on your personal relationship? Avoidance is simply not a good option.

Luckily, there are many proven ways to help people manage their speech anxieties.

Effective Strategies for Managing Public Speaking Anxiety

We have already examined a lot of bad advice for thinking about public speaking and the nerves it can produce in a speaker. Now let us review some time-tested and proven strategies that can actually work to make the nervous speechmaker more effective.

Before we review the following strategies, there are two important points to keep in mind about these strategies. First, this list is by no means the entirety of all the solutions to public speaking anxiety. Without a doubt, you might hear from others or discover your own strategies for managing public speaking anxiety that are not on this list and that are quite effective. If that is the case—great! Do not be afraid to try something new to ease your anxiety and improve your speaking. Second, not all of these strategies will work for every person; meanwhile, some people may find multiple strategies successful. People become nervous before, during, and after public speaking for a variety reasons. For some of us, this anxiety is based in our personalities or experiences generally. For others, these anxieties come from more specific or targeted factors. You might get anxiety from one factor or a combination of factors might affect you. And the intensity of this anxiety may vary significantly depending on the person in question. Given the diversity of ways in which we experience public speaking anxiety, it is best to take a trial and error approach to strategies for combating it. Think about your own sources of public speaking anxiety and then, work your way through the list, making note of what helps and what does not. None of these solutions is one size fits all, but most people will respond positively to several of these strategies.

That said, let's review some of the most common strategies for managing public speaking anxiety.

Be Confident in What You're Going to Say. The opposite of anxiety is confidence; therefore, to beat public speaking anxiety, we want to do everything possible to make ourselves a confident speaker. In some ways, confidence is about our personalities and partially outside of our control. But confidence is also about a set of choices. In other words, we become confident—in life as well as in speaking—because we feel good about the choices we have and continue to make. Therefore, to increase our confidence as a public speaker, we should make choices that we will feel confident about so that that confidence shines through on speech day. Some choices we can make that will make us feel confident as public speakers include:

- **Pick a topic you know and care about**. One of the most important places you can intervene in the public speaking process to minimize anxiety is in the topic selection phase. In most public speaking situations, the speaker has significant freedom in what they choose to speak about. Certainly, there will be constraints on topics by an assignment, authority, or situation; but even in highly constrained situations, speakers still retain a great deal of freedom. Use that freedom wisely and select a topic for your speech that you know and care about. There is certainly value in using a speech to learn about something new. But from the perspective of being a more confident speaker, choosing to speak on a subject with which you are familiar, have experience, already know about, and enjoy talking about can make a world of difference.

- **Prepare in advance**. You should also make the choice to prepare your speech well in advance of the time to speak. As we have already discussed in this chapter, procrastination often drives public speaking anxiety and puts us in a vicious cycle of failing to prepare and speaking poorly. But research in Communication tells us that the anxiety that leads to procrastination is misplaced. Indeed, research shows that most populations report their greatest moment of anxiety about public speaking is *when they discover they have to give a speech*. That means that, for most of you, **you have already experienced your most anxious moment** about an upcoming speech. That does not mean you will not have moments of nervousness again going forward, but it does mean that the worst of your anxiety is probably already over.[21] So why wait? Choosing not to procrastinate empowers the speaker to know that time will not be against them. If you complete your speech well in advance, you can walk into the speech occasion confident that you did everything you could in order to be successful. It will minimize self-doubt and give you real security in what you say.

- **Practice, practice, practice**. As with all things in life, practice makes perfect, and the same is true of public speaking. There is such a thing as over-practicing but, typically, most novice public speakers fall far short of the level of intensity where it can be counterproductive. Generally, a speaker should have practiced their speech in full and aloud at least five (5) times before giving their speech when it counts. And it should come as no surprise that doing so will convey a great deal of confidence on the speaker. When you have practiced your speech enough that you can anticipate the next sentence, the next argument, and the next piece of evidence, your speech will not feel like a strange land you are visiting for the first time, but like returning to a familiar spot in your hometown. That feeling of comfort and familiarity that comes with practice is the soil in which confidence grows.

- **Give yourself flexibility in your speech**. Finally, make the choice to give yourself flexibility in your speech in order to improve your confidence. A lot of anxiety in public speaking comes from the unknown and the unanticipated: what will I do if I start to run out of time? What if something relevant happens in the news the day of my speech? What if I get lost in my outline? These things happen but they can also be major driver of our anxiety—and a poor speech performance—even if they don't happen in our speech. To feel more confident in the face of these possibilities, think through in advance what you will do if something goes awry in your speech. This might mean thinking about a section of the speech that you could cut in the moment if time gets tight. Or you might build time into your day to check the news so that you are confident you are caught up on current events. You might also plan out what you will do if you get lost in your outline: what will you say, what will you do, and how will you get the speech moving again? For many of us, our anxiety comes in large part from the unanticipated. So, anticipating the unanticipated can make us significantly more confident speakers, even if our worst fears never materialize.

Be as In Control as Possible. A major contributing factor to anxiety in public speaking is that speakers feel out of control. That is totally natural. Indeed, unlike a scientific experiment, human interactions in the real world can never be entirely controlled for. For example, consider that you will never be able to control what your audience thinks about your speech, you will never be able to know 100% that your technology will not fail, and you may not even have complete control over your speech, particularly if it is for a class assignment, given at the direction of your boss, or for a paying audience or organization. Therefore, *accepting that you won't be able to control every factor of your speech situation is a prudent first step*. However, you can follow up this first step with another: while recognizing you can't control everything in a speech situation, *make proactive choices to control what you can*. Another way of saying this is that while you can't control everything in a speech situation, the situation is also not *out of control* either. You can bring some degree of control to the speech by identifying things you can reasonably control and doing your best to make them work to your advantage. As such, consider some of the following points you may be able to control in your speech:

- **Select the date and time of your speech**. If there is flexibility in when you speak, choose a date and time that will work best for you. Think about issues like: what date will give me enough time to prepare and practice my speech? Do I have other commitments on a given date or week? Am I more awake and engaging at certain times of day? In a public speaking class, selecting a time and date for your speech may or may not be in your control; however, be sure to figure out how these issues are determined in your class and to do everything you can to fairly earn the time and date that work best for you.
- **Select the order of your speech**. Similarly, if you will be one of many speakers on a given day, do your best to select where in the speech order you will speak. This issue may be of no concern to some speakers; however, for others, their anxiety increases depending on if they go first or last or if they follow a particular person.

- **Know your speech requirements.** In SPCM 200, students are provided well in advance with both the descriptions of their speech assignments and the critique sheets they will be graded with (attached in the Appendix in this book). Therefore, review your speech against the description and critique sheet in advance. If you are sure you have covered all of the components in each, you will feel more in control entering your speech day.

Get to Know Your Audience and Environment. A third factor in driving public speaking anxiety is unfamiliarity with our audience and where we will give our speech. These are, again, totally understandable human responses to something challenging and different. For many speakers, our anxiety comes overwhelmingly from the strangeness of the strangers we will be talking to. Will they like me? Will they judge me? Do they care about my ideas? All of these are natural feelings. Ironically, some people actually feel more comfortable speaking in front of strangers and the real anxiety comes with being known by your audience too well. Likewise, a new space can contribute to anxiety. Concerns as simple as knowing if there will be a podium, how the lights work, and what your voice sounds like on a microphone can all be preoccupations that drive public speaking anxiety. Luckily, in most cases, we can take proactive steps to manage these aspects of our anxiety.

- **Get to know the audience.** Depending on the situation of our speech, we may or may not have the opportunity to get to know our audience. But in some cases, we absolutely do. In particular, if you are in a Public Speaking class, you have ample opportunity before your first speech to introduce yourself to and have a conversation with your future audience. Doing so will answer many of the questions you might have about the audience before you speak and reduce anxiety. Outside of a classroom, you may not know anyone who will be at your speech prior to a few minutes before the speech begins. In that case, you might introduce yourself to a few people in the first few rows. You'll be surprised how sharing some simple pleasantries with an unknown audience all of a sudden brings a sense of reassurance to you as the speech begins.

- **Visit your speech site in advance.** Again, if you are in a public speaking classroom, you will almost certainly get to know your speaking space well before you give your speech. But in other cases, you may know nothing more about your speech site than its name. To reduce anxiety, plan to take a trip to visit your speech site a few days before your speech. Most public venues are open to the public and can give you ample access. Private venues might be happy to assist you with a "walkthrough" of the space if you ask politely. They may even walk you through the room's technology and speaker system. Knowing that the space is safe, accessible, and familiar in advance through these steps can make a big difference in reducing your pre-speech anxieties.

Anticipate and Relieve Stress. Public speaking anxiety can also be alleviated by mitigating the physical and physiological effects of anxiety as best as we can. In other words, know that as someone who is about to do something challenging, you will almost certainly feel the symptoms of stress. Since these symptoms themselves can exacerbate public speaking anxiety, managing these symptoms can contribute to our overall feelings of positivity on the day of the speech. While stress and anxiety reveal themselves quite differently in different people, some of the steps below might be worth consideration.

- **Be well rested.** A good night's sleep the evening before your speech is always a good idea. Regular and substantive sleep balances out of body's rhythms, attunes our memory, keeps us alert and attentive, and settles our mood; therefore, sleep can take the edge off of some of anxiety's worst effects. By contrast, while regular and restful sleep can provide great benefit for a speaker, irregular sleep may actually produce worst results. As such, be mindful of "power naps" that attempt to compensate for a good night's sleep. They might lead to lethargy or confusion instead.

- **Eat healthy, consistently, and strategically**. Athletes carefully plan their meals before major sporting events to maximize their performance. Public speakers with public speaking anxiety might likewise think about their food intake during the 48 hours before a big speech as a helpful strategy. Consider avoiding heavy, unsettling, or unhealthy food within 24 hours of your speech. An upset stomach may lead to or exacerbate speech anxiety. Don't over caffeinate as it can lead to jitters and unexpended energy.
- **Provide an outlet for existing stress.** One way to manage public speaking anxiety physiologically is to actually provide an outlet to burn through your excess nerves or energy just prior to your speech. Exercise is a great way to do so, particularly the morning before a big speech. In fact, consistent exercise during the entire speech preparation process can pay positive dividends throughout and may minimize procrastination. Talking through your anxieties with a trusted friend might also help you keep those anxieties under control. One very small study several decades ago even showed that speakers who engaged in safe and consensual sexual activity the evening before a speech reported much lower levels of anxiety in their speeches![22] While finding a relaxing outlet can be a great resource to manage public speaking anxiety, choose to actively avoid alcohol and drugs for at least a few hours before a speech since neither has a correlation with successful speech performance.

Introduce Comfort Items. A little discussed strategy to minimize public speaking anxiety is the use of what we call comfort items. **Comfort items** are *small, unnoticeable objects that a speaker can bring with them to a speaking situation that give them a sense of calm, confidence, and support.* Comfort items can take on any number of forms. A student of mine once brought a lucky rabbit's foot with her on a speech day. Several students have told me they wore a crucifix on the day of their speech to give them confidence. A college football player confided in me once that he kept a picture of his mom in his polo shirt pocket when he had to talk to the press. And I once helped a speaker who was highly anxious about losing his speech by encouraging him to keep a second copy of his speech in his jacket pocket. Did he ever need to go to his second copy of his speech? No. But having it with him alleviated significant anxiety and helped him excel in his speech. While comfort items can be any number of things, they do share two qualities. One is that they work through the same principles. In several studies, researchers have found that people who are given a task with an object deemed lucky or special performed significantly better at that task than those who did not. In these studies, what the object was had little impact on the result; what mattered was the participants' belief that the object would help them. So, it doesn't matter what comfort item you might bring with you to your speech; what matters is that you believe it could help.[23] The second quality shared by all good comfort items is that they should not be evident to the audience. If the item becomes visible to the audience, it risks becoming a distraction and could affect the speaker's credibility. So, while comfort items can be a good idea, keep them out of sight of the audience while speaking.

Be Realistic. Our final piece of advice for minimizing public speaking anxiety is to set realistic expectations about the speech and its outcome. Communication researchers have shown over and over again in scientific studies that many anxious public speakers wildly exaggerate what they think could go wrong in a speech. Speakers share false beliefs like the audience is out to get them or wants them to fail, that they are unique in their challenges and anxieties, and that other speakers are significantly better and less likely to be anxious than them. But this research also shows speakers' fears are just an unrealistic as they sound. Most people in most audiences want the speaker to succeed and most speakers have more in common about anxiety than not. As such, it is important to set realistic expectations for your speech in order to put aside these anxiety-inducing misperceptions. A helpful exercise to do so is visualization. **Visualization** is *an exercise in which the speaker imagines himself or herself succeeding in the act of giving a speech.* Visualization is the opposite of the faux-failure images we cook up in our nervous state. Rather, it involves positively picturing success in hopes of reaching those goals. To be sure, positive visualizations can go awry if we are not careful. Simply *imagining* a great speech is no replacement for the work necessary to *do* a great speech. However, putting aside outlandish negative expectations and embracing affirming visualizations can make a significant dent in our feelings of anxiety and inadequacy.

Public speaking anxiety is a common concern for many public speakers; however, as we have discussed in this chapter, it need not be a concern that limits anyone's success. With the right mindset, practice, and preparation, public speaking anxiety can be successfully managed, leading to more effective public speaking.

Chapter 4

SPEAKING AS A SITUATED ART

Back in the 2nd century B.C.E., a well-regarded student of Plato named Aristotle became one of the era's greatest thinkers of rhetoric and public speaking. While Aristotle was not himself a great speaker—history tells us he was quite an anxious speaker—he nonetheless wrote the book on the subject that lays out many of the sentiments we still teach today about how to speak well. Aristotle offers a number of strategies for success, but his most important insight may be that public speaking always takes places in "a given situation." The situated-ness of public speaking is the focus of this chapter.

What does Aristotle mean when he says that effective speaking requires attention to a "given situation"? Simply said, Aristotle is arguing that public speaking is a situated art. That means that, unlike numerous other areas of knowledge, public speaking can never really be considered something that is *universally* true, effective, or consistent. Mathematics, for example, is a form of universal knowledge because 2 + 2 = 4 everywhere in the world throughout time. Physics pursues universal knowledge about the cosmos from the perspective that the rules of the universe do not change or alter; rather they are universally consistent. Even some of our more humanistic forms of knowledge like philosophy and religion have universal features in the forms of beliefs, values, and virtues that are believed to apply to everyone reliably no matter the circumstance. These and many other forms of knowledge and practice do not vary from situation to situation. Instead, they seek to explain the things that are universal and unchanging in the universe.

Public speaking, by contrast, is never universal; rather it is a kind of knowledge and performance that depends almost entirely on the *particulars* of what is happening in a given moment of time. For instance, the joke you tell in the middle of your speech will only work if it resonates with the specific audience present the day of your speech. Your evidence, also, is highly situated: it is only good if it is recent and regularly updated to the standards of the topic. Speech topics are also quite particular, for example, because what matters to your audience in January may not matter to them at all in August. As these examples show, an effective speech will never be universal because effective speechmaking is always based in the moment—and when that moment passes, a speech needs to be redesigned in order to be effective in a new moment, with a new audience, and a new world of concerns and cares.

In this chapter, we will focus on understanding the situated elements of a public speech so that we can assess what situation we are stepping into in our own speeches and how we can design those speeches to rise to that situated moment effectively.

Dimensions of a Speaking Situation

As we already discovered with the Standard of Communication, there are key dynamics to all communication situations as well as specific dynamics that separate types of communication from each other. To understand the public speaking situation better, we will need to dig into the more specific aspects of what is at play in these kinds of situations. For the purposes of this chapter, we want to highlight six dimensions of the situation: the speaker, the audience, the occasion, the time, the place, and the immediacy.

The Speaker. Perhaps one of the two most obvious dimensions of the public speaking situation is the speaker. Without a speaker, there can be no public speech. But the speaker matters to the public speaking situations in ways beyond being the sender of the message or the source of a public speech. For instance, much of what can or will be said in a speech is determined by who the speaker is. Indeed, as we will discuss shortly, the speaker's life experience, personal struggles, education, culture, and interests often form the foundation of many public speeches. On the flip side, however, the speaker also dictates what is not said in a speech situation. As a general rule, a speaker who does not have experience or expertise in a particular subject should avoid speaking on that topic. In addition, the speaker's strengths and weaknesses as a public speaker dramatically affect the public speaking situation. A dynamic and engaging speaker, for example, might have a radically different impact on the public speaking situation as opposed to a speaker who is more reserved. It should then be clear that no public speaking situation can be understood without making time to think about the identity, experience, and skills the speaker brings to the situation.

The Audience. Besides the speaker, the other most obvious dimension of a public speaking situation is the audience. An **audience** is *a gathering of individuals addressed by a speaker whom are asked to change their opinions or actions based on the speaker's address.* Just as we can say confidently that a public speaking situation cannot exist without a speaker, it can also not exist without an audience. Certainly, a person can choose at any point to stand and start speaking; however, if that speech is not listened to by anyone—if there is no audience addressed in the speech—a public speaking situation is not present. Because audiences are central to the speaking situation, they can play a dramatic role in shaping a speech. As such, a speaker must always seek to identify an existing audience or call one into existence, speak directly to their audience through compelling words, ideas, and delivery, and ultimately earn and maintain the audience's attention. To put it another way: Consider that audiences need to, first, be *addressed* by the speaker. Audiences must also feel that the speech is relevant to them and their interests. Audiences also need to be *engaged* in the speech: if the audience cannot follow the speaker's points or arguments, the entire situation can go off track. Audiences then have significant role in the public speaking situation.

To account for the ways in which an audience can impact a public speaking situation, speakers often conduct an audience analysis to learn more about their audience. An **audience analysis** is *an assessment of members of the audience's identities, interests, and beliefs that can help the speaker shape their message.* Audience analyses work from one simple principle: the more a speaker knows about their audience, they better they can find a message that will keep the audience attentive, interested, and engaged in the speech. Depending on the speaking situations, speakers can conduct audience analysis in many ways. For instance, a speaker might conduct a **demographic survey** of her audience prior to preparing her speech to learn more about the audience members' individual identities. A demographic survey is *a written document that asks the audience to provide the speaker with information about the audience's race, class, gender identity, sexual orientation, or other similar information.* A speaker might also do an **informant survey** by *reaching out to the speech organizer and asking that person for their assessment of the likely audience makeup.* If the speaker does not know in advance of the speech who is in the audience, he might also do a **visual survey** of his audience, *quickly judging for him or herself purely on what they can see, what kinds of people are in attendance at his speech.* Finally, a speaker with little information about her audience or who is seeking information about her audience that cannot be discovered through a visual survey might use a **hand survey** *where the speaker asks the audience to raise their hand if they fall into a particular category or have had a particular experience.*

Each of these methods of audience analysis have their own benefits and pitfalls. A demographic survey, for example, can provide a speaker with all the information they might want to better understand their audience; however, it is rare outside of a public speaking classroom that a speaker will know in advance who their audience will be. An informant survey can solve this problem by relying on an informed person to relay this information; but, an informant survey is only as good as any particular informant. Visual surveys can be quite helpful and require no advance time. Indeed, most speakers can tell quite quickly from a visual survey if their audience is, for instance, largely young adults, people in middle age, elders, or a mix of the above. However, a visual survey can be dangerous if the speaker makes too many assumptions about an audience based purely on how they look, particularly since many dimensions of difference are not visible (refer back to Chapter 2 for more pitfalls on making assumptions and stereotyping). A hand survey might remedy this situation by empowering the audience to characterize themselves and their beliefs, but a speaker can only use a hand survey one or twice in a speech before it becomes tedious and not every audience member will feel comfortable sharing information about themselves in public. As such, a speaker who wants to try to account for an audience in a public speaking situation is likely best off if she uses a mixture of these surveys and comes prepared to a speech confident and ready to make adjustments to her text in the moment.

The Occasion. Another important aspect of a speech situation is the occasion of the speech. By **occasion**, we mean *the event or moment that a speech is meant to mark.* It is quite rare for a speaker to stand up and give a speech without an occasion. How many times, for example, can you remember someone giving a speech on a bus or in the middle of the airport? Rather, most speeches are linked to particular occasions: weddings, funerals, political rallies, inaugurations, lectures, conferences, business meetings, and so on. Certainly, some speakers may try to make an occasion by giving a speech seemingly out of the blue. But, in most cases, a speech is connected to an occasion—and that occasion needs to be clear when thinking about the situation of the speech. This clarity is necessary because occasion tells us something about the appropriate decorum of a speech. **Decorum** is *the degree of style and formality that a speech should have to be considered appropriate for a certain situation.* Decorum is what distinguishes a speech at a funeral as opposed to a pep rally: in the first, the speech should be respectful and meaningful and often somber while at the second, a speech that is not loud and boisterous and enthusiastic is probably a bad speech. Therefore, situating a speech within its occasion will tell you exactly what kind of tone your speech should feature if it will be successful with your audience.

The Time. Time is an often-ignored dimension of the speaking situation that can dramatically reflect our choices as a speaker and our effect on the audience. For most novice public speakers, time only refers to the length of time that they are required or expected to speak by their teacher or employer. But if we take a broader look at public speaking in a given situation, we see that there are many ways in which time can impact our speech. Consider:

- **The time of day**. Is your speech early in the morning? Right after lunch? During those difficult mid-afternoon hours? Or maybe after dinner? Depending on which of these times you will be speaking, you will need to make adjustments in your speech in order to be successful. For instance, you might need to be extremely energetic to wake up your audience. Or you might avoid a brash and loud style late at night.

- **The time of year**. In cultures where yearly traditions and holidays reoccur, you might find inspiration for a clever rhetorical resource on your calendar. Is there a holiday coming up that ties into your speech topic or that might give insight on a value you're addressing? Is there an anniversary of a great accomplishment or notable tragedy that occasions saying something in particular? Is there something you may want to avoid in your speech given the spirit of the season?

- **The time during the program**. On some occasions, you may be speaking alongside others at the same event. If so, the time you are scheduled to speak on the program should be of paramount concern. Will you be speaking first and setting the tone for the event? Will you be speaking last and have responsibilities to summarize or respond to the other speakers in the moment? Or will you be speaking in the middle where it will be crucial to distinguish yourself and not be forgotten?

- **The time allotted**. Let us not forget to consider how much time you have been allotted to speak. Your speech slot might be short or long or even variable or undefined. As such, you will need to make sure your speech is designed to fit the time allotted. Will your speech be slow and meandering? Or must you be short and to the point? It might be so unclear how much time you have to speak that you will want to prepare a set of points that can be cut in the moment or stretched out if necessary.

The Environment. Where you give your speech often matters as much if not more than when you give your speech. Some of the greatest speeches of history have taken place in breathtaking or horrifying locations and played a significant part in shaping the effectiveness of the address. Consider how a speech on a blood-soaked battlefield or on sacred ground where thousands of heroes fell might shape your words? Or think how a speech about governing from the halls of Congress would differ from a speech about campaign issues at a rally? Environment clearly can have an impact on a speaker's speech plan. Of course, not every speech environment will have an evident or meaningful impact on what or how your speech goes. Some speeches are perfectly fine given in any of a number of kinds of classrooms, event halls, or corporate boardrooms. But even these rather banal and everyday environments for a speech still contain often-unnoticed features—for good or bad—that a speaker will want to consider. For instance:

- Is the speech indoors or outdoors?
- Is the environment of the speech special and unique or everyday?
- Is the environment related to your speech topic or inconsequential to it?
- Does your speech environment offer particular challenges you will want to control for if possible?
- Does your speech environment offer particular opportunities you will want to take advantage of?
- Is there a podium?
- How large is the room and how much space do you have to move around?
- Is there a projector and, if so, where will the projector screen be?

Exercise: Speech Environment Inventory

Using a piece of paper and the questions listed on the previous page, complete a speech environment inventory of your SPCM 200 classroom. Make notes of the important challenges and opportunities present in your classroom. When complete, compare your inventory with others in your class to determine if you missed key environmental factors. Extra Credit: With the same set of questions, take an inventory of a different speaking environment on campus. Then compare and contrast these two environments. What are the strengths and weaknesses of each?

The Immediacy. A final dimension of the speaking situation that speakers increasingly need to be aware of is the degree of immediacy their speech will have with their audience. The term "immediacy" comes to us from a 16th century word meaning "closeness or proximity." In the public speaking situation, we should be concerned with exactly this: how close or proximate are we the speaker to our audience? For most of human history, the question of immediacy in public speaking was straightforward: all speeches were given face-to-face, in the presence of the audience it was intended for. This made historical speeches—except those read in printed form—immediate: the audience heard and responded to the speaker in real time without a filter. Today, however, public speaking increasingly takes place with lower levels of immediacy: many audiences experience speeches as a transcript, through a screen, or recorded and distributed online. These ways of watching and delivering a speech can be quite beneficial in that they offer a wider audience, a larger circulation, and can be shared easily across social networks. However, both giving and hearing a speech in a less immediate way also poses its own problems, including:

- The loss of immediate feedback from the audience
- The loss of control over the circulation of your words
- The inability to adjust words or delivery mid-speech or to improvise in the moment

These are just some of the challenges and opportunities immediacy can pose in a public speaking situation. For this reason, most public speaking situations today will still take the form of the high immediacy approach that speakers have used for centuries. Nonetheless, we need to learn to work with these new dimensions of immediacy in order to become the most versatile public speakers possible. As such, in Chapter 17 of this book, we will have an opportunity to dig more deeply into understanding how to be an effective speaker in a digital environment.

Topics for Discussion: Holograms

As we have seen, immediacy is a significant aspect of a speech situation. However, new technologies are being developed every day that radically alter our understanding of these situations, for better or worse. With a partner or in a group, consider: how might the advent of full body holograms alter the way we think of immediacy in public speaking? Are they an opportunity for speakers? Are they an obstacle? How so?

Matching Your Speech to the Situation

Once we have a better understanding of our speaking situation, we can then consider ways in which we might adjust our speech to fit the kind of speaking situation we find ourselves in.

For some novice speakers the thought of matching or tailoring your speech to fit various dimensions of a speaking situation might seem uncomfortable. You might be thinking: am I being asked to compromise my ideas, experience, or words to make my audience happy? Or: am I being asked to change my way of speaking so as to not ruffle any feathers? The answer here is a firm "no." While it is important for a public speaker to be mindful of the speaking situation, there is a limit to how far you should adjust your appearance, ideas, delivery, and so on in order to increase your chances of success. In fact, as we discussed in Chapter 1, doing so is unethical and immoral—the stuff of demagoguery that we want to avoid. Rather, public speaking should always be about speaking your truth, being your authentic self, and sharing yourself and your ideas with your audience in a genuine and passionate way.

Nonetheless, avoiding demagoguery is not an excuse for failing to be *strategic* in your public speaking situation. You want to be yourself *and* put your best foot forward in the particular public speaking context you find yourself. So, how should you go about matching the dimensions of your speech situation to crafting the best speech for that situation? We recommend a five-step process:

1. Generate a long list of possible topics, arguments, and evidence for your speech making sure each topic is something that fits you as the speaker.
2. Run each of these topics against the five other dimensions of the speaking situation described previously. Note how each topic gives you particular opportunities or poses particular challenges for you as a speaker.
3. Evaluate all your topics against each other. Which topics provide you the fewest obstacles? Which topics provide you the greatest challenges? This should help you narrow down topics that are too easy or too challenging and reveal the topics that are likely to work well in your particular public speaking situation.
4. Select your favorite topic among those most likely to succeed in your situation. Begin developing your speech with initial research and a first draft of an outline.
5. Finally, as you develop your speech, continue to evaluate your topic, evidence, and arguments with the dimensions of the speech situation discussed previously. If you encounter evidence or arguments that pose a challenge you did not anticipate earlier, consider whether a) you can find other information or arguments that are less problematic instead or b) you will need to address this challenge explicitly in your speech. Similarly, if you encounter evidence or arguments that provide opportunities you did not anticipate earlier, look for ways to maximize those opportunities in your speech.

Think of matching your speech to the situation just as you would match your outfit to a situation. You would and should never wear something that looks horrible on you just to make someone else happy. At the same time, you know that you might have several outfits that are "you" in your closet, while also knowing only some of them will make you shine at certain events. Public speaking works the same way: do not speak on or about a topic to make someone else happy; instead, consider all the various ideas, experience, and styles you have in your public speaking closet and pick the one that you think will work best in the given situation.

Chapter 5

SPEAKING WITH ARGUMENT AND EVIDENCE

What do you think of when you hear the word "argument"? For most people, chances are good that they picture two or more people screaming at each other about different points of views, wagging their fingers and waving their hands, not even hearing each other. No matter whether we think of partisan politicians slugging it out on cable news or couples going after each other over an awkward dinner out, argument simply does not conjure up feelings that are good, helpful, or productive.

But, that's a shame because argument is actually poorly understood through these examples. Indeed, the way we use argument in public speaking comes from a long tradition of high-minded ideals and liberal democratic values. So, how did we get from this noble idea of argument to children fighting over who gets to sit on the swing first on the playground? While there is no easy answer, it seems likely that the idea of argument has devolved because of an assortment of incentives in our society that encourage us to argue in the worst possible ways. From hyper-partisan information sources, to self-sorting ourselves into communities of people just like us, to valuing being "tough" and being "right" over "civil" and "open-minded," our colloquial understandings of argument are just not healthy, let alone productive.

The good news is that we can change this lackluster argument culture by relearning argument and doing it better. Indeed, public speaking is one of the best formats for learning how to do argument with thought, reason, and direction.

So Then, What *Is* an Argument?

If an argument is not a screaming match, a fight, or a set of insults, what is an argument *really*? In reality, an **argument** is a *well-supported and well-reasoned assertion about the world as it is or should be.* It is less a thing or event that happens than a way of making a point. An argument then is only partially about *what* you are arguing for or against; it is also about *how* and *why* you argue for that position.

To better understand arguments, let's break them down into their component parts. Throughout time, there have been a number of different models and views of what constitutes an argument. In this book, we do not have sufficient time to trace each of those models; that is something better done in our Communication Studies class specifically on argument: SPCM 207: Public Argumentation. Instead, for our purposes, we are going to focus on the basic components of argument that all these models and viewpoints share, namely, three elements: claims, evidence, and warrants.

CLAIMS

Of all the parts of an argument, claims are the easiest to understand because they are often what we think of when we imagine argument: a statement about the world. To put a finer point on it, a **claim** is *a statement that conveys a person's sense of how the world is or how it should be.* Everyday each of us hears thousands of claims about all kinds of issues, big or small. When the woman on line at the post office says, "All the bums in Congress should be thrown out of office" or the person talking on their cell phone at the bus stop says, "It just seems like the summers get hotter and drier ever year," they are making claims, whether they know it or not. Importantly, while these claims can be part of an argument, claims do not constitute argument in themselves. This is a point lost on many people in our contemporary argument culture. Just making competing claims *at* one another does not mean you are having an argument. However, it is impossible to have an argument without at least one claim. This is certainly true in public speaking because public speaking is always goal-oriented. When we rise to speak, we are always doing so with the aim of trying to get others to see the world in a way we think makes sense. Since claims are statements about how the world is or should be, it is not possible to speak in public successfully without making claims.

While every public speaker makes numerous claims over the course of a speech, not all of the claims in a speech are of equal importance. To put it another way: every speech has a central and overarching claim that is the reason for giving the speech in the first place. This *single, declarative sentence in which the speaker makes the central, overarching argument of their entire speech* is a claim that we refer to as a **thesis statement**. As you will recall from Chapter 1, a thesis statement is an essential part of a public speech. They are how we express to an audience what our goal in a speech is and what we want them to do by the end of the speech.

However, in most cases, speakers and arguers actually make numerous claims over the course of an argument. Unless you are having a very short and simple argument or giving a very short and minor speech, you will almost certainly need to go beyond a single claim to be a successful speaker. Think about it: the world is a complex and dazzling place. If you want to make a major assertion about the world—as it is or as it should be—you almost certainly will need to detail, describe, or relate other information that support your sense of the world before you can do so. We call *the claims that undergird and support our thesis statement* our **main points**. How many main points are needed to support our thesis statement is up to the individual speaker and their topic; however, most speeches have at least three (3) main points that serve as the foundational claims for a thesis in public speaking. So, if we went back to our previous example of the woman at the post office, we might find her thesis statement that "All the bums in Congress should be thrown out of office" is supported by three main points, namely that the current Congress has been: 1. Ineffective, 2. Out of touch, and 3. Can't work across party lines. Each of these main points supports the thesis statement, but each is also a claim itself; in other words, while each contributes to the overarching claim, the main points are also statements about the world as it is in the mind of the speaker.

If, then, our main points are also claims it should not be surprising that most speeches also have additional, smaller claims that support the main points, in the same way that main points support a thesis. *The smaller assertions we make about the world in support of our main point* are called **sub-points**. Structurally, sub-points act exactly the same way as main points do: they make assertions that undergird the claim above them. In our ongoing example, a sub-point for the main point that "The current Congress has been ineffective" might be that "This Congress has passed fewer new laws than any Congress in forty years."

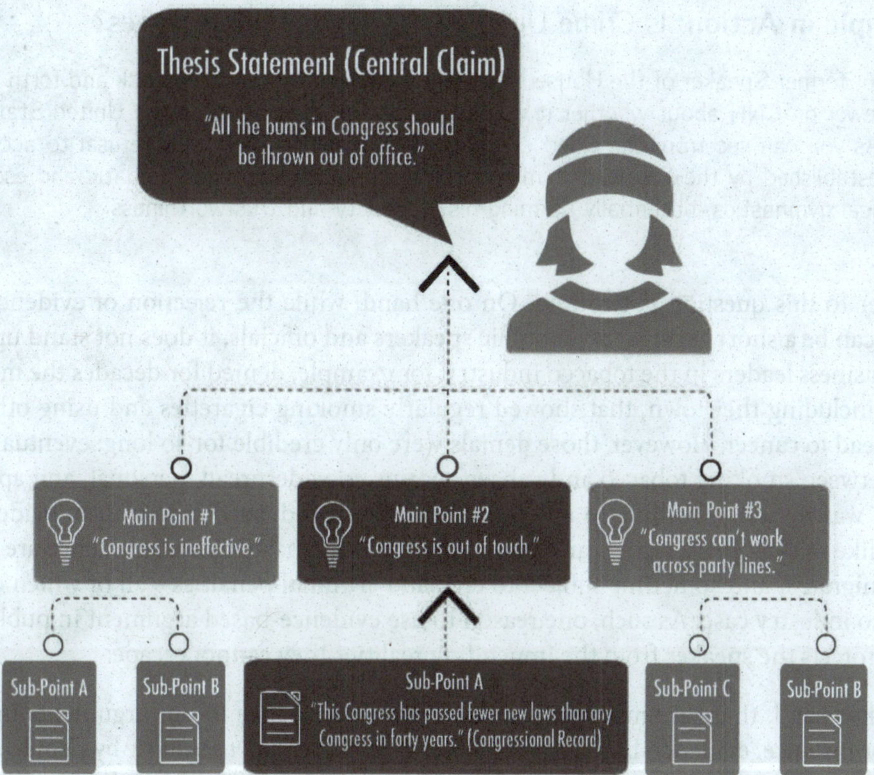

Figure 5-1. A Flowchart of Claims

Now, I know what you're thinking: are there sub-sub-points? And the answer is, frankly, if a speech needed sub-sub-points in order to make a good argument, it should have them. Luckily, however, most speeches (and other forms of argument, too) are not endless exercises in claim-making. Rather, they have a limited scope and a limited time. As such, most speakers will never need to develop points at a level deeper than sub-points.

EVIDENCE

Another essential part of an argument is evidence, or what is sometimes called data. **Evidence** refers to *credible information about the world that can be used to support a claim.* To put it another way, if a claim is an assertion about the world as it is or should be, evidence is the information we use to back up that assertion. Within an argument, evidence is mostly placed within a main point or sub-point to do this work in support of the speaker's thesis.

If you watch our public discourse lately, you may be asking yourself "Why should I speak with evidence?" Indeed, in our contemporary culture, the role of evidence in making good arguments and good decisions has come under assault. Some politicians, business interests, and cultural figures have turned to replacing evidence-based argument with nothing more than strong assertions of personal belief, even when it flies in the face of fact-checking. Similarly, when confronted with evidence, some public figures have rejected evidence out of hand as meaningless and without merit simply because it contradicts their opinion or viewpoint. This vivid dismissal of evidence in our society is worrisome. As such, the question "why use evidence?" is an important one.

Example in Action: Is Crime Up or Down in the United States?

In 2016, former Speaker of the House Newt Gingrich got into a heated back and forth with an interviewer on CNN about whether it was a fact that crime was up in the United States that year. As you can see from the video clip posted on Canvas, Gingrich's refusal to accept the facts established by the FBI leads him to perform a set of highly problematic and escalating rhetorical gymnastics, potentially harming his credibility and trustworthiness.

The answer to this question is two-fold. On one hand, while the rejection of evidence in public discourse can be a short-term tactic of public speakers and officials, it does not stand up to the test of time. Business leaders in the tobacco industry, for example, denied for decades the mountains of evidence, including their own, that showed regularly smoking cigarettes and using other tobacco products lead to cancer. However, those denials were only credible for so long; eventually the connection between smoking tobacco and cancer became so widespread, personal, and apparent that the public was no longer willing to entertain the tobacco industry's rejection of evidence. When moments like this happens, leaders and public speakers who have rejected evidence are often repudiated, denigrated, and sometime subject to civil and criminal penalties—all of which occurred in the tobacco industry case. As such, one reason to use evidence-based argument in public speaking is that it protects the speaker from the impending realities they cannot escape.

On the other hand, there are many good reasons to use evidence in our arguments in the public square. For instance, evidence-based speakers are likely to be *taken seriously* by people and institutions with authority and power. While we might be fooled by politicians or business leaders for a time, people in the areas of law, medicine, banking, science, engineering, the military, and more will tell you with certainty that making arguments without evidentiary support is unlikely to help you make your case (or career!) in these professions. Likewise, people who use evidence-based arguments are likely to *make better claims*—that should hopefully lead to better outcomes for the public. In addition, using evidence-based argument is likely to place speakers on the *winning side* of public debates over time. For all these reasons and more, you will be expected to use evidence and use it well in your public speaking in this course. For more on these issues, refer to Chapter 6.

As a public speaker, there are many kinds of evidence that we can turn to in order to support our claims. In fact, according to Aristotle, there is an entire *taxonomy of evidence*—what he called **forms of proof**—that speakers can rely on in argument. For Aristotle, these many forms of evidence can be broken down into two significant categories: inartistic and artistic forms of proof.

Inartistic Forms of Proof. By **inartistic forms of proof**, we mean *types of evidence that exist in the world that the speaker can point to in their speech as support for their claims.* Said differently, inartistic proof exists outside the speaker and what they can say or do in a speech; it is outside information produced by another person, institution, or group that corroborates what the speaker says themselves.

There are many different kinds of inartistic proof that a speaker might turn to in order to support their argument, many of which you have probably heard of before. In this book, we will focus on six forms of inartistic proof, some of which derive from Aristotle and some of which are more contemporary in nature. They include:

- **Definition.** One of the most important but overlooked forms of inartistic proof is definition. **Definition** refers to *the established meaning and interpretation of a term.* In many cases, definitions may not seem at issue in an argument. However, many of our most contentious debates in public discourse come down to a disagreement about how we define key terms or assign them to entities in the world. For example, much of our decades-long debate about same-sex marriage and abortion are, at their core, about definition, namely: does the term "marriage" apply to all kinds of committed relationships and when should we define a set of cells as being "life"? In these types of cases, setting or refining definitions can be a powerful argumentative tool. By far, the most common way speakers introduce definition into an argument is via the dictionary or some other authoritative source for defining terms. However, definitions can be overused by novice speakers as evidence. A good criterion is to only use definitions as evidence sparingly in a public speech.

- **Testimony**. *Public statements made by a witness that describe an event, idea, or situation* is referred to as **testimony**. Testimony is valuable for a public speaker as evidence because it allows them to demonstrate that their own interpretation of the facts of a case or event in the world is not unique; rather, another person (or perhaps many people) interpreted an event in a similar way. All testimony is not of equal value, so a speaker should consider a few points before choosing to use testimony in their arguments. For example, generally, **quoted testimony**—*the precise words of a witness's statement*—is preferable as evidence to the speaker's paraphrasing of what the witness said. Likewise, **expert testimony**, *testimony from a person trained in and/or credible to speak on the subject or situation at hand*, is considered more valuable as evidence than the testimony of a general member of the public. Finally, **sworn testimony**—*statements given by a witness in the court of law under oath*—is considered more valuable than unsworn testimony because there are legal prohibitions against lying in these statements.

- **Statistics**. When a public speaker uses **statistics** in a speech, they are using *scientifically significant sets of data on a subject of public concern* to advance their argument. Statistics are common types of evidence used by speakers for good reason; typically, statistics condense large, complex data sets into smaller, easier to understand facts. They also tend to be produced by experts in the subject matter, which gives them credence and authority. In addition, statistics benefit from being a quantitative form of evidence, which is often perceived as more reliable and objective in public discourse—even when it may not be in reality. While statistics can be a strong form of evidence, they can also be confusing to audiences that are unfamiliar with certain quantitative measures and terminology. Therefore, public speakers should be sure to use statistics that are reliable, have been confirmed by multiple researchers, and come from credible and expert sources.

- **Laws, Contracts, and Oaths**. *Binding agreements and documents affirmed through the law or the word of another person* are also valuable forms of evidence for the public speaker. **Laws, contracts, and oaths** all fall under this definition. What makes them so valuable is that laws, contracts, and oaths are all social obligations; they are duties that people make a commitment to as members of a society or social arrangement. In addition, they almost all occur at the beginning of a social interaction. As such, when someone violates a law, contract, or oath, these agreements can be brought up by the speaker as evidence of another person's failure to live up to their agreed to expectations. An added benefit of these forms of evidence: they are almost always made in public, either in writing or before witnesses, making them easy to verify. While it is difficult to argue against a law, contract, or oath as evidence, public speakers should make sure that the party in question agreed to the affirmation willingly (as opposed to under duress) and that the document applies to the party in question if they want to ensure their strongest case.

- **Precedent**. *The use of a previous successful finding or occurrence to justify how we should think of a similar contemporary event* is called **precedent**. The logic of a precedent is simple: the situation at hand has already been argued or attempted by others in a favorable way; as such, current similar situations should be treated that way as well. Traditionally, precedent appears most commonly in legal discourse. When a high court rules on a particular issue in a certain way, others moving through the justice system will often look for precedent to confirm their case should be treated the same. However, precedent can also be valuable in proposing policy solutions, particularly when one community or municipality points to another community's policy as justification for trying that same policy in their community. For example, Colorado's successful legalization of recreational marijuana has now become a precedent used by other states and municipalities to argue they should legalize recreational marijuana as well. Precedent can also go the other direction: a poor outcome in one city might lead other cities to not advocate for that policy themselves. In using precedents as evidence, it is vital that the public speaker be sure the findings or policies in question are similar enough to draw comparisons across them; otherwise, they risk making a false analogy (see the discussion of logical fallacies on page 60).

- **Narratives**. Public speakers who relate *a story that sheds light on an issue or exemplifies a point* are using **narratives**. Storytelling is a valuable form of evidence because human beings are natural storytellers. We respond favorably to the format of stories and tend to put lessons and histories into narrative fashion no matter what culture(s) we come from. Indeed, because we hear stories early and often throughout our lives, audiences tend to find narratives a compelling way from which to learn about the world. Like other forms of evidence, not all narratives are equally valuable in public speaking. Indeed, the Communication Studies scholar Walter Fisher identified two important aspects to narratives that make them particularly effective as evidence. One aspect of a good narrative is called **narrative coherence**, *which refers to how well the story hangs together at the structural level.* A good story should have a beginning, middle, and end, sufficient detail, and characters that act in relatively predictable way. Narratives with holes, gaps, or characters that act in odd ways are not viewed as credible by audiences because they are not coherent. The other aspect of a good narrative is **narrative fidelity**—*the degree to which the story fits into how the audience currently understands the world.* If a narrative is true to the audience's understanding of the world, they are likely to accept the story as true; if the story is at odds with the audience's view of the world, they will view it skeptically.[24] However, even a story that is at odds with an audience's view of the world can be valuable for showing privileges, areas for growth, and for gaining the attention of the audience.

Artistic Forms of Proof. Aristotle discusses a second category of evidence called artistic proof. By **artistic proof**, we mean *evidence that the speaker can create in the course of giving a speech to support their own claims.* To put it another way, these are things that a speaker can do to make their arguments more believable. There are three primary forms of artistic proof available to the public speaker:

- **Logos**. When a speaker *presents their information in a clear and logical manner*, they are making an appeal to **logos**. Logic and reasoning appear frequently in public speaking, for example, in the organization of the speech and our use of reasoning. Nevertheless, as a form of proof, logos primarily refers to the rational and often objective delivery of information. This use of logos can make an audience more likely to believe the speaker and her claims. As a general rule, a speaker who incorporates logos into their arguments will ensure that those arguments are clear, well defined, easy to understand, rational and consistent, and free of flowery language.

- **Ethos**. Another way a speaker can use their own speaking as evidence for the audience is ethos. **Ethos** refers to *the credibility of a speaker—particularly their ethics, character, and experiences.* By credibility, we mean how experienced, trustworthy, reliable, honest, and virtuous is the speaker? If an audience finds a speaker to be credible—or to have a strong ethos—in their speech, the audience will have good reason to agree with their argument and support the speaker's claims. If, on the other hand, the audience finds the speaker lacking credibility, they are unlikely to agree with their findings or proposals. Being seen as a credible speaker by an audience is not guaranteed by any single choice a speaker makes; indeed, many audiences across many cultures use different standards for determining ethos. However, most public speakers have success building ethos when they state clearly their qualifications and experience on the topic at hand, cite their sources, address the topic seriously, admit their limitations and what they do not know, and treat the audience with respect.

- **Pathos**. A final artistic proof for the public speaker is **pathos**—*the use of emotional appeals by the speaker*. Emotions are a powerful part of the human experience. We almost always look at the world through an emotional lens—even when we are actively trying to be objective and unemotional. For a long time, public speakers were told to avoid emotion in their speeches for fear that pathos would lead people into a hysteria or incite a mob to violence. Yet while we should be sure as speakers to use appeals to emotion ethically and morally, we should also recognize that a speech without emotion is barely a speech at all. As Communication Studies scholar Richard Weaver proclaimed, "a person is not nor ever can be nor ever should be a depersonalized thinking machine."[25] In fact, many of the most powerful and transformative speeches in human history have relied as much on emotion as they have on logos or ethos. Like ethos, emotionality is not something that all speakers can show or access in the same way in all circumstances. Much of how we think of emotion is cultural and attuned to the uniqueness of a particular moment, event, or location. That said, speakers who use pathos well will be sure do so ethically, honestly, with a genuine concern for the audience, and offer the audience a range of emotional levels beyond just anxiety, fear, or terror.

As public speakers, you will need to become effective at using multiple kinds of evidence in order to complete your speeches well. Indeed, while some topics lend themselves to one or two forms of evidence in particular, most effective public speakers rely on multiple types of evidence to make different kinds of claims in their public speaking.

WARRANT

The final piece of argument that is needed by all public speakers is a warrant. A **warrant** is *a form of reasoning that connects evidence to a claim*. We might describe the notion of a warrant metaphorically as a bridge connecting two cliffs. A speaker and their audience can only cross from one side of the cliff, surrounded by evidence, to the other, where they can arrive at a claim, with a bridge that connects the two. That bridge is the warrant. Indeed, when we think about it, an argument that consists of nothing other than evidence and claims is no argument at all. It is not dynamic; nor would it feature interpretation or synthesis to establish a relationship. For a good argument, we need another component to help us make sense of the evidence and to use it to gain new knowledge. This is how the warrant functions—and why it is an essential part of any good argument.

While you might not be very familiar with warrants in the strictest sense, we use warrants all the time. They are, in fact, probably best thought of as ways of thinking about and processing the world that we often use implicitly. Indeed, this is typically why warrants are the hardest dimension of argument for people to understand: we nearly never think actively and out loud about our reasoning. Instead, it is largely an internal process that we keep to ourselves and only verbalize when someone asks, "how did you arrive at that decision or finding?"

To help us get into the habit of being explicit about our warrants in argument, let's take one of the simplest forms of argument there is: math. If I were to write: 2 + 2 = ? and ask you to tell me the solution, you would instantaneously tell me the solution is "4." And you would be correct. But what is the reasoning you used to arrive at that correct answer or claim of "4"? The warrant that allows you to see two 2s and combine them together as the single digit 4 is what we typically think of as addition. Addition, subtraction, multiplication, division...all of these processes for taking evidence and processing their relationships are forms of reasoning and, therefore, forms of warrants. We don't often talk about them in that way; nor do we often speak about them explicitly once we learn them in school. But every day, we reason out the relationships between numbers in math to arrive at claims that we use to act in the world.

In public discourse, we do the same thing; however, instead of using forms of mathematical reasoning to understand the relationships between numbers, we use argumentative reasoning to understand the relationships between evidence and claims. To be sure, argumentative forms of reasoning are typically much less precise than mathematical reasoning; but that is because human society and human relationships are not standardized or universally the same. Nonetheless, as public speakers, we use argumentative forms of reasoning in much the same way: to process information about the world in order to help us make statements and decisions about the world.

In public speaking, we largely will not be using the reasoning of addition, subtraction, multiplication, or division to warrant our way to a claim. Instead, we'll be using a set of other forms of reasoning that you need to connect evidence and claims in a reasonable way. For the purposes of our speeches as novice public speakers, we are going to focus on a few in particular. They are:

Induction. Induction is *reasoning that uses a number of specific cases to draw a general conclusion or claim*. As a warrant, induction works by connecting a good quantity of similar examples (i.e., evidence) and draws from them a single, overarching take-away (claim).

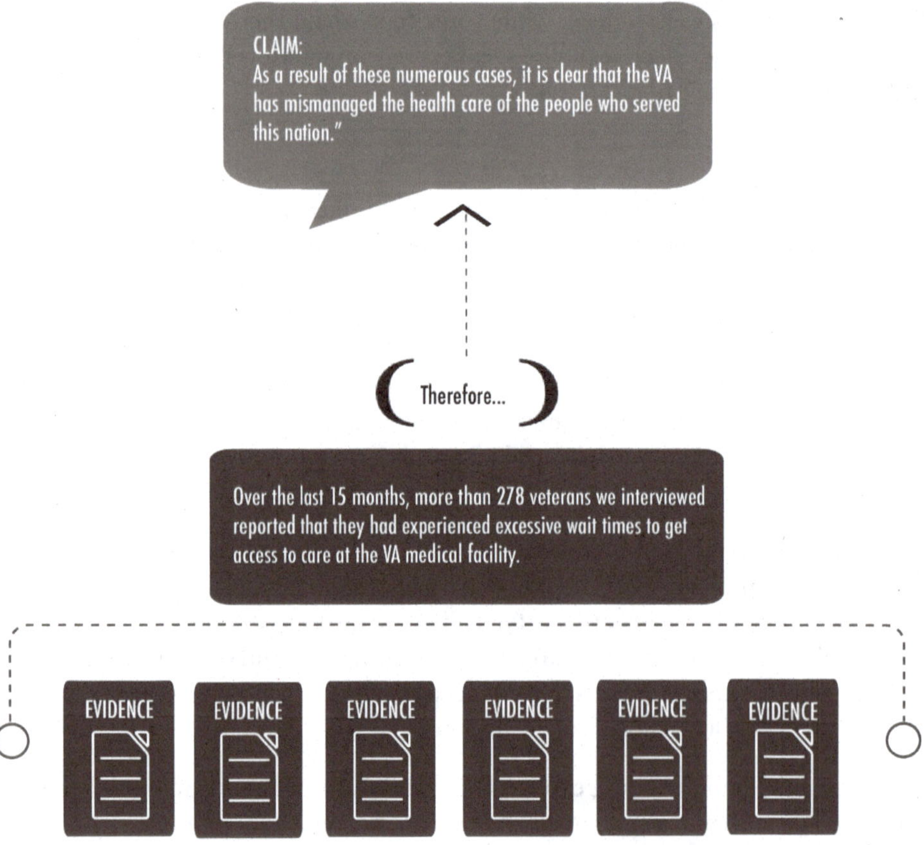

Figure 5-2. Examples of Reasoning by Induction

Deduction. Deduction works like induction but in the opposite direction. Instead of relying on a number of examples to arrive at a claim, **deduction** *uses a general principle to reason what happened in a particular case.*

Figure 5-3. Examples of Reasoning by Deduction

Cause. Reasoning from cause works by *showing that a person, event, or object reasonably produced a change in the world* (i.e., *an effect*). It functions as a warrant by drawing a connection between evidence of certain conditions in the world and what they produced. In public speaking arguments, reasoning from cause is useful for arguing what produced a desirable or undesirable outcome so that the audience can be urged to either foster or eliminate those causal conditions.

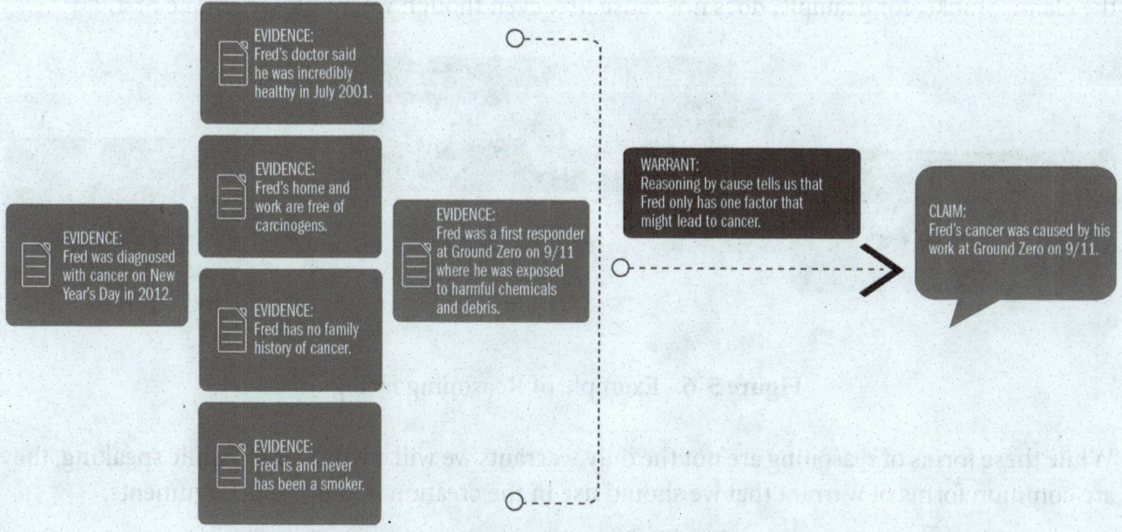

Figure 5-4. Example of Reasoning by Cause

Analogy. Do you remember being asked on college placement exams like the SAT, ACT, or GRE to select the terms with similar relationships? These kinds of test questions are asking you to express your understanding of reasoning by **analogy**—*a form of reasoning that works by identifying the same kind of relationship between multiple kinds of persons, objects, events, or items.* Analogical reasoning is helpful in drawing comparisons between similar situations and suggesting those situations be treated in similar ways. Precedent, which we described previously, is an excellent form of proof that works by the analogical reasoning.

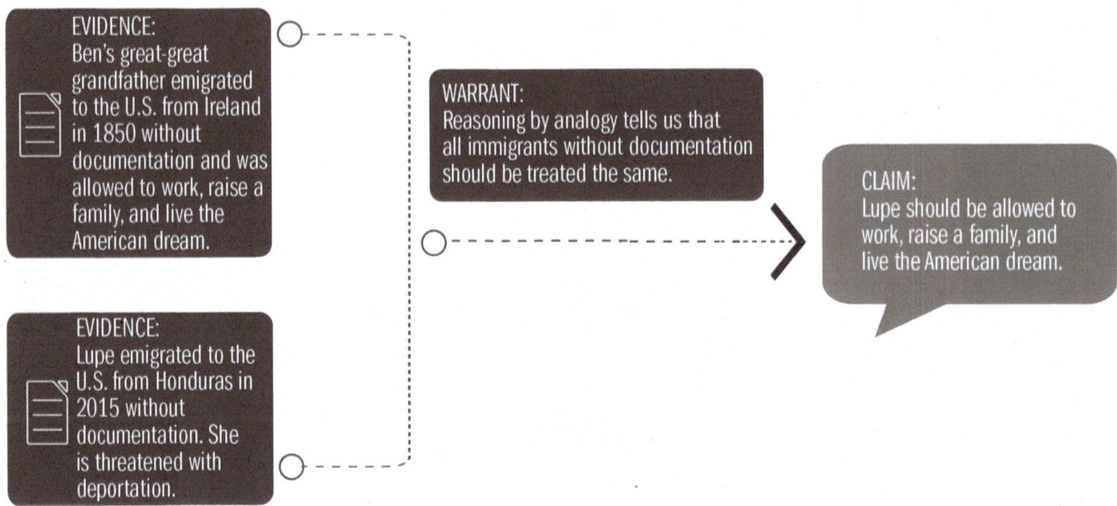

Figure 5-5. Example of Reasoning by Analogy

Sign. Reasoning by sign helps a speaker arrive at a claim *by pointing to something that signifies the presence of something else.* The classic example of reasoning by sign is the phrase "where there's smoke there's fire." In this example, the sight (or sign) of smoke is combined with the speaker's reasoning that smoke is produced by fire; therefore, the speaker can assume there is a fire present in the area when they see smoke, even if they do not see the fire themselves. Importantly, while reasoning by sign uses the presence of a sign to signal the existence of something else, the sign *does not cause* the claim. Smoke, for example, does not cause fire, even though we might see smoke first.

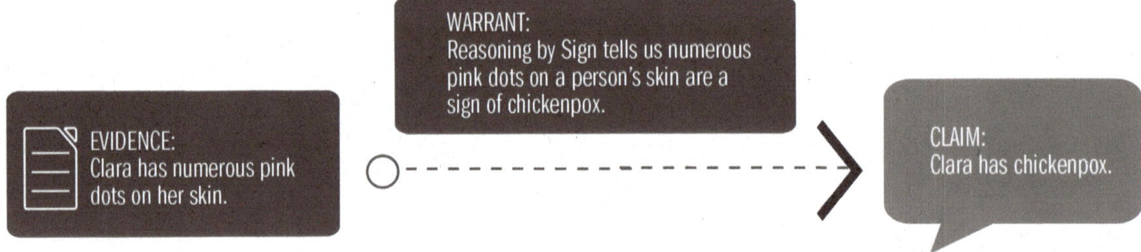

Figure 5-6. Example of Reasoning by Sign

While these forms of reasoning are not the only warrants we will encounter in public speaking, they are common forms of warrant that we should use in the creation of our public arguments.

SECONDARY DIMENSIONS OF ARGUMENT

While claims, evidence, and argument (or something like them) are the primary aspects of most models of argumentation, there are also other dimensions of argument that we should consider in brief. In particular, the Toulmin Model of Argument, which was created in the 1960s to analyze arguments at a deeper level while providing insight on how argument works in everyday talk, suggests an additional three dimensions of argument we should be familiar with:

- **Backing**. Backing is an additional set of data or evidence in an argument; however, in this case, backing is evidence that supports the warrant. In other words, **backing** is *evidence that shows that the speaker's reasoning is credible, authoritative, and makes sense.* If someone questions the warrant of an argument, backing serves as a counterargument against such questions.

- **Qualifier**. While we always want to make the strongest arguments possible, sometimes, in order to be an ethical speaker, we must acknowledge that our argument may not be absolutely certain. A **qualifier** serves this purpose; it is *a statement of the degree to which the speaker is certain that a claim is true or valid.*

- **Rebuttal**. Arguments are situational; that means that a good argument can only remain good for as long as the situation does not change or the facts on the ground are altered. When the situation changes, our evidence may become outdated or wrong or even cease to exist, our warrant can fall apart, and our claim becomes wrong. Recognizing the situational nature of arguments, a good speaker will include a rebuttal in their argument. A **rebuttal** is *a statement that acknowledges the circumstances under which the speaker's argument would no longer be valid.* In this way, it functions as an "escape hatch" for the speaker—a way to maintain their integrity and credibility in a world in which things change. A rebuttal differs from a qualifier because a qualifier hedges on the speaker's certainty about the claim; meanwhile, a rebuttal hedges on the *certainty that the situation* in which the claim is made will stay the same.

Unlike the primary parts of the Toulmin Model of Argument (i.e., claims, evidence, and warrants), the secondary parts are helpful in explaining the "ifs," "ands," or "buts" that often come up in public speaking. To put it another way, the secondary parts of the model help us explain the circumstances under which an argument could go wrong in the real world. As such, they enable the arguer to present their case in a way that acknowledges they may not have all the information, that circumstances can change quickly, and that the speaker made the strongest case they could in that particular moment.

To visualize the difference between the primary and secondary dimensions of argument, let's consider the example of Julio. Julio is a prospective student just admitted to Colorado State University and he wants to know whether he will pay in-state or out-of-state tuition if he chooses to enroll. Using evidence about Julio and a warrant supported by deductive reasoning, Julio's friend Jamal makes the following argument to Julio about his tuition status:

Figure 5-7. Example of Argument with Primary and Secondary Dimensions

In response to this argument, Julio is thrilled. "Great! I'll save so much money then because I am guaranteed to always pay in-state tuition at CSU!"

"Hold on a second," responds Jamal. "That might be true at the moment but, realistically, there are certain caveats and life changes that could affect that argument." Jamal then responds with another argument that acknowledges the ways in which Julio's circumstances could change.

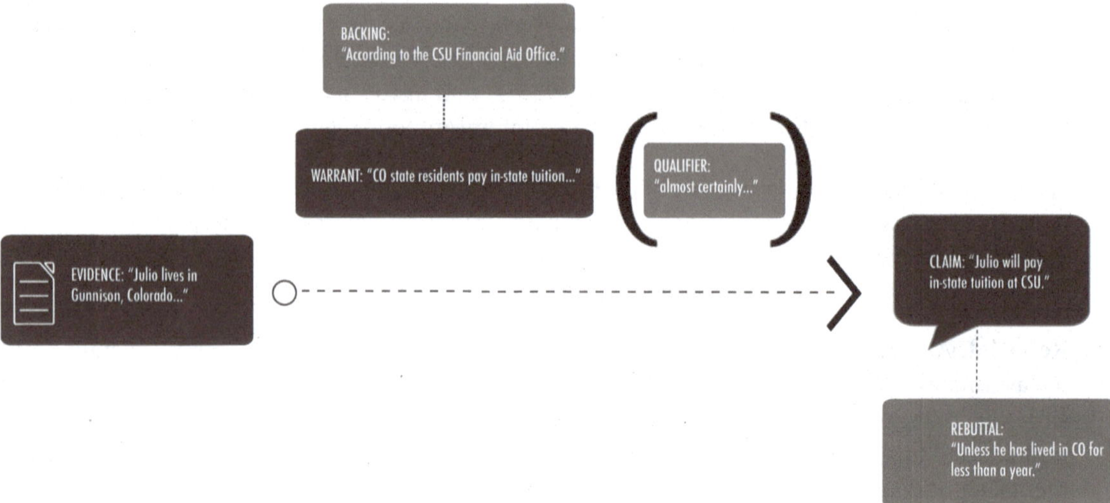

Figure 5-8. Example of Argument with Secondary Dimensions

As we can see by the example above, argumentation is not always as easy as it might seem. As public speakers, we need to make sure that we are doing the primary and secondary dimensions of the Toulmin Model correctly in order to be effective and credible arguers. Meanwhile, as audience members, we must always be vigilant in asking whether the speakers we hear are giving us not just good evidence and warrants, but that those dimensions of argument are well-supported, well arrived at, and mindful of the changing nature of the human world.

Failures of Argument: Logical Fallacies

While public speakers—and the audiences of public speakers—need to learn how to make good arguments supported by sound evidence and warrants, the opposite is also true: it is essential for speakers and audiences to recognize poor arguments so that they can avoid making them or being persuaded by them. There are many different deficiencies that can make an argument poor, weak, or ineffective, including:

- **Unclear arguments**. Arguments that should fail because the speaker does not clearly state their case in a manner the audience can follow.
- **Unsupported arguments**. Arguments that should fail because the speaker has not provided any or enough good-quality support to make their claim successfully.
- **Unethical arguments**. Arguments that should fail because the speaker's argument calls for or is done via unethical or immoral behavior.
- **Arguments made on the wrong terms**. Arguments that should fail because the speaker has made a strong case, but in the wrong context (i.e., a policy argument on a moral question).

These are all poor arguments that we need to know and recognize for our own success as public speakers, but also for our personal, professional, and public good.

While these poor arguments are common enough in public discourse, the most common form of failures in argument that we need to recognize are called logical fallacies. **Logical fallacies** are *unreasonably structured arguments that seek to make poor arguments appear to be good arguments.* Unlike the other examples of poor arguments in this chapter, logical fallacies are particularly dangerous because they seem to be logical and reasonable when, in fact, they are not. Indeed, that is the strength of a logical fallacy: because it seems to make sense, they often work on audiences—even the most thoughtful and educated audiences. And, because people often fall for logical fallacies, unethical speakers often turn to them in their speeches and public discourses, intentionally trying to use bad arguments to make otherwise smart people do illogical, ineffective, counterproductive, and sometimes dangerous things.

Because logical fallacies pose a danger to audiences and public discourse, it is essential that both public speakers and audiences pledge not to use logical fallacies in their speeches and to call out logical fallacies when others make them. As such, we might think of learning fallacies as part of our training in the "defense against the Dark Arts," at least in the realm of public discourse.

Unfortunately, there are dozens of logical fallacies that occur all the time in public discourse; however, for the purposes of this book, we will focus on the nine most common logical fallacies you are likely to encounter in public speaking.

Ad Hominem**.** When translated from its original Latin, *ad hominem* means "to or against a man." As this translation suggests, the *ad hominem* fallacy *attacks a person instead of challenging the person's argument.* In doing so, a speaker tries to use another person's looks, past, or even their identity to discredit their ideas.

- **Example of *Ad Hominem*:**

  "Why would we ever elect someone with a face like that?"

Bandwagon. The bandwagon fallacy *claims that something should be done just because it is popular.* The bandwagon fallacy is particularly powerful in democratic societies because our political systems typically reward candidates that receive the most votes in a given municipality. In other words, when we are not thinking critically, we do not see anything wrong with the majority's opinion winning the day. But in the realm of argument, it is critical to remember that popular opinions are often wrong and even dangerous. Indeed, horrible human atrocities have all been committed in the name of majorities that were later proven to be wrong.

- **Example of Bandwagon:**

  "In the last few years, dozens of nations have taken an increasingly aggressive stance to closing borders and rejecting refugees. Why shouldn't we do the same?"

Slippery Slope. The phrase "slippery slope" conjures a compelling image of a person walking down a hill and then slipping down that hill at an uncontrollable speed. The slippery slope fallacy works in a similar fashion; it is *a claim that a small and reasonable step will inevitably lead to the most severe and outlandish outcome.* As such, slippery slope is similar to exaggeration; however, whereas exaggeration is an over-the-top retelling of what has already happened in the past, slippery slope is an unreasonable claim of what will happen in the future. And that is why slippery slope so often works: it plays on people's fears of change and the future, even when that change is small, well-thought out, and likely to never lead to what the speaker suggests.

- **Example of Slippery Slope:**

  "If we don't win this election, it will be the end of U.S. society as we know it."

What-about-ism. What-about-ism is a contemporary term for a very old logical fallacy called "tu quoque," which means "you too" in Latin. What-about-isms are *a speaker's attempts to avoid criticism by suggesting the critic is actually just as guilty or wrong as the speaker.* This logical fallacy has been around for a long time but has recently become particularly popular again in our partisan political environment. It works in a nefarious way: by making audiences believe that a speaker's opponent, the government, the law, or even the world itself are all evil, unethical, or dangerous (even or especially when they are not). In doing so, what-about-isms excuse the speaker's own evil, unethical, or dangerous actions. While it is not a requirement of the fallacy, the easiest way to recognize what-about-ism at work in public discourse is when a speaker responds to criticism with the phrase "Well, what about..."

- **Example of What-about-ism:**

  Interviewer: "But Congressman, your bank records show you took money from a lobbyist that your committee is supposed to regulate."

  Congressman: "But what about Congressman Stephens? He's been taking dirty money since he was elected ten years ago!"

False Dilemma. Also known as the "either/or" fallacy, false dilemma fallacies *present two options to the audience as their only possible choices when, in reality, there are many actual choices the audience could make.* False dilemma fallacies are popular when speakers want to force the hand of an audience, something they try to do through two steps. First, the speaker ignores the complexity of an issue by presenting *only* two choices to the audience. Second, the speaker makes sure one of the options is their preferred choice and the other is unethical, unappealing, unpopular, or morally bankrupt. Given a choice to either follow the speaker's plan or adopt an objectionable alternative, audiences feel compelled to agree with the speaker. However, in reality, the audience's best choice is to probably reject both of the speaker's options and select among the many other options the speaker chose to leave out of their speech.

- **Example of False Dilemma:**

  "The people of Colorado must make a choice: we either adopt 100% renewable energy in the next decade or submit to another century of nothing but dirty energy."

False Cause. The false cause fallacy works by perverting the reasoning of cause-effect relationships. In particular, a speaker using the false cause fallacy *claims that just because one event happened prior to another event, the first event must have directly caused the second event.* Of course, when we are thinking critically as audiences, all of us can think of examples of something that happened in the past that did not directly cause something in the present. Your decision to get a latte this morning, for example, was not directly caused by the American Revolution in 1776. These events are a long time apart, unconnected to each other, and seem randomly associated, so how could one cause the other? But false cause works by minimizing these obvious misconnections. In other words, false cause fallacies work when the speaker makes the audience *feel* like there might be a connection between two things, even though there is not. The appearance of a cause, rather than an actual cause, is what leads people to fall for this fallacy.

- **Example of False Cause:**

  "Ever since we elected the new mayor four years ago, my job prospects have become worse and worse."

Hasty Generalization. As we have seen, a well-reasoned argument draws from a number of credible examples in order to make a claim about a growing trend or a reality in the world, what we think of as inductive reasoning. Hasty generalizations *pervert the logic of induction to advance an unethical claim.* In particular, hasty generalization fallacies make sweeping claims based on one or too few examples. Because we rely on examples to support arguments all the time in public discourse, people are familiar with the role examples can play in making a claim. However, unethical speakers use this familiarity to their advantage to suggest even a single example of something can justify a claim. If audiences are not mindful—or worse, they are in a hurry to make a decision—they might fall for this fallacy.

- **Example of Hasty Generalization:**

  "The gang member who was apprehended by the U.S. Border Patrol crossing the border illegally just shows that no one who crosses the border can be trusted!"

Red Herring. A classic and popular form of logical fallacy is a red herring. In a red herring fallacy, *the speaker introduces information or ideas into an argument to confuse or distract from the information that actually matters.* In our contemporary world, where we are bombarded by information non-stop, it can be difficult enough to keep people focused on the facts of a case to make a smart and informed decision. Add to that an intentional effort by a speaker to distract an audience or confuse an issue and it becomes all the harder to make a good, reasonable decision. Indeed, the situations in which red herring fallacies are most effective are when the speaker is not actually trying to solve a problem; rather, red herrings work best when the speaker does not want a real or meaningful conversation about an issue to happen in public discourse. In fact, a highly unethical speaker can use a red herring to stop change in its tracks.

- **Example of Red Herring:**

  "You might trust the county's food safety rating, but did they ever stop and think about how the color of the restaurant's walls might impact where people want to eat?"

Strawman. The strawman fallacy occurs when *a speaker intentionally mischaracterizes the position of their opponent and then attacks their opponent for that position.* Just like a scarecrow—from which the fallacy earns it name—is nothing but an imaginary person made of straw, the person attacked with a strawman fallacy is also imaginary; they are a fictitious figure that bears no resemblance to the actual person who stands in opposition to the speaker. When someone is attacked by a strawman fallacy, their first response is often "That's not what I said!" That, of course, is the power of this fallacy; it forces the mischaracterized person to spend their time trying to convince the audience that they are *not* what the speaker describes rather than making an affirmative case for their own positions.

- **Example of Strawman:**

  Politician A: "I believe that abortion should be safe, legal, and rare."

  Politician B: "So you admit that you want unfettered access to abortion to everyone at the drop of a hat with no moral or ethical limitations and no concern for the health and safety of mother or child? Shame on you for your callous disregard for human life and decency!"

As a public speaker, you will find the need to return to the consideration of argument and evidence a common part of the public speaking process. As such, you should think of arguments and evidence not as a roadmap of where to go but as a guidebook that offers you many suggestions for what to do and what not to do on the public speaking journey. As the speaker, your role will involve not just knowing these forms or evidence and argument, but actively making selections of which of these elements make sense for your primary goals in your speech. That, in a nutshell, is part of the creative and exciting possibilities involved with every new public speaking undertaking.

Chapter 6

RESEARCHING TOPICS AND EVIDENCE

What do we mean by research? **Research** is defined as *the act of considering, finding, and collecting ideas and evidence in support of claims about the world.* The definition is a bit vague, but that is because research can take many forms and appear in many ways. Here at CSU, a distinguished research institution, we have faculty that do all kinds of research from translating ancient texts, to explaining legal decisions at the Supreme Court, to growing drought-resistant crops, to finding humane and effective methods for raising livestock. These topics may not seem connected; however, they are all research because each activity demands the researcher consider, find, and collect information about the world as part of their aim to say something meaningful about their given subject. As such, it should come as no surprise that CSU and its faculty care a great deal about their students doing good research in their own academic work.

The importance of research explains why when students turn in "research" that consists of nothing more than the first five items that came up in a Google search, the faculty are more than a little underwhelmed. Entering a word into a search bar and copying down the results is *not* research in the way that real researchers do it. Nor is it sufficient to support current claims about the world or create new knowledge to move our societies forward—what research should ultimately aspire to do. Yet, we know that our students are capable of becoming great researchers. This class will be the chance for you to test your mettle as the researcher we want you to be.

In this chapter, we will begin to build your understanding of research in public speaking by examining three dimensions of the term: researching a topic, researching evidence, and citing your sources at the end of the research process.

Researching Topics: Coming Up with Something to Say

One immediate way in which we use research in public speaking is in the process of **topic selection**—*coming up with something to say.* For some speakers, coming up with something to talk about in a speech is a simple task. For others, identifying and selecting a topic for a single speech, let alone several over the course of a semester, is a challenging undertaking. Regardless of whether you fall into the first or second category, research will be an essential part of the topic selection process, either as a part of brainstorming or selecting and refining your topic.

BRAINSTORMING YOUR TOPIC

Brainstorming is *the process by which a person or group of people generates ideas for further consideration and action.* In public speaking, we use brainstorming to generate a list of topics that might be good for our upcoming speech or speeches. Notice the key words in the previous sentence: "might." Our goal in brainstorming is not to pick *the* speech topic we will do in one pure moment of concentration. Rather, our goal is to generate many possible options that we will come back to for further consideration. Some of these possible options might be great; others might be incomplete or only half ideas, while still others might seem absolutely absurd or random. Then there are those ideas that seem to be going nowhere until something changes and they are revealed as a stroke of genius. In brainstorming speech topics, we want all of these ideas—no idea should be rejected or ignored. Just jot down everything that comes to mind.

While the metaphor of "brainstorming" suggests that the exercise itself is largely a mental one, brainstorming is actually a full-bodied experienced, one that draws inspiration from and relies on some kinds of research to be successful. Indeed, interaction between our brains and some other stimuli is often the key to sparking ideas for speeches. This process of sparking the brain off of contact with something else is one way of thinking about research.

There are many ways to get the sparks flying in your brainstorming process; however, you might start by considering some of the following as catalysts for your brain:

- **Randomization**. If you don't know where to start, begin somewhere random. Go to a dictionary or book on your shelf and turn to a random page and word. What would a speech be on that word? If it's a horrible idea, why is that? What would be better? See? Your brain is already going now.
- **Free association.** Pick a word, idea, or concept. What does it make you think of? Jot it down. What does that word make you think of? Jot it down. See where this chain of associations takes you.
- **Mindlessness**. People tell researchers regularly that they discover their "best ideas" while doing something mindless. Scientists theorize that freeing your mind of thought can actually allow it to bring into focus things we might not see when we're busy. So, consider spending some time doing a mindless activity: sweeping, jogging, brushing your teeth, shredding papers, vacuuming, etc.
- **Be in nature**. Study after study has shown positive correlations between spending time in nature and increased focus and creativity. Go for a walk in nature. What comes to mind?
- **Study abstract art**. Visit the Gregory Allicar Museum of Art and immerse yourself in some abstract art. What do you see in the shapes? In the colors? Where does it take you?
- **Check the news and current events**. Open the newspaper or check out the Coloradoan. What stories are in the news? What does your community care about right now? Do you care enough about it to give a speech on that subject?
- **What's trending?** What's trending on social media? Why? What does that make you think about?
- **Talk with another person**. Have a conversation with a classmate, colleague, or friend. Share some ideas with them. Ask them what they think about your ideas.

SELECTING AND REFINING YOUR TOPIC

Now that you've brainstormed some ideas for your upcoming speech, it is time to select and refine those ideas until you arrive at the one most likely to help you succeed. In other words, this is the process we use to determine which ideas should fall by the wayside and which ones should rise to the top. To make these determinations, you need to ask yourself six questions:

1. **Ask yourself: "What is the primary goal of this speech?"** As we discussed in Chapters 1 and 5, all public speaking is goal-oriented. We never begin to give a speech and do it successfully without having an aim or outcome we are trying to reach. Therefore, if all successful speeches must have a primary goal, you would be smart to start the process of selecting a speech topic by asking yourself: "what is the primary goal of this speech?" From Chapter 1, we also know that all public speaking is largely persuasive, but what persuasive goal do you want to achieve? These goals can take many forms and vary significantly in different aspects of our life. For instance, your primary goal might be to persuade an audience to buy a product or you might seek to persuade the PTA to start a new after-school program. However, in SPCM 200, you will be asked over four speeches to meet each of four pre-established primary goals:

   - To persuade the audience *to learn* important information about a new topic
   - To persuade the audience *to consider* perspectives other than their own
   - To persuade the audience *to adopt* a solution to a public problem advocated for by the speaker
   - To persuade the audience *to value* the life and experiences of another person

   Once you know which of these primary goals you need to reach in this speech round, you will have a good framework for going deeper into the topic selection process. If you are having difficulty identifying or understanding your primary goal for your next speech, speak with your instructor.

2. **Ask yourself: "Who am I and what do I know and care about?"** Once you have a sense of your primary goal for your upcoming speech, you should begin to consider what kinds of topics you are credible to speak about. A public speaker should always choose to deliver a speech on a subject that they know or care about significantly. Why? Because, on one hand, why would an audience listen to or take seriously a speaker who knows or cares little about their subject? On the other hand, selecting a topic you know or care a great deal about will greatly assist in the preparation and delivery of your speech. Your existing knowledge on the subject will serve as a foundation for the new research you will add to the topic as well as likely make you more comfortable in speaking about the subject before an audience. Therefore, within the realm of the primary goal of your next speech, jot down all the topic ideas that you think you know or care a lot about.

3. **Ask yourself: "What does my audience know or care about?"** Working from the list of topic ideas that you know or care a great deal about that falls within the realm of your primary speech goal, begin to consider whether each of these topics is something your particular audience knows and or cares about. This is a vital step in the topic selection process for two reasons. First, if you select a topic your audience already knows everything about, your speech will be considered redundant and useless and, thus, a failure. Second, if you select a topic that your audience does not care about, your speech will face significant inattention from the audience who won't see the relevance of the topic to their own lives. Therefore, you want to ensure that you select a topic that you are both credible to speak about and that the audience will find to be either genuinely new or relevant to their lives. Now, you might be thinking that it is somewhat

unfair for an audience to get a veto on the topic of your speech. But you should never abandon a topic simply because the audience knows it well or does not seem invested in it. Rather, a good public speaker will recognize these challenges presented by an audience and consider if they can find ways to make the audience wants to know more or care about a topic they previously did not. Indeed, some of the best speeches are those that change the audience's thoughts, feelings, or perspective of a topic they thought they knew or that didn't matter to them.

4. **Ask yourself: "Which of these topics will work the best for this speech?"** By now, you should have a few possible topic ideas that meet the primary goal of the speech, reflect something you know and care about, and are or can be made of interest and relevance to the audience. The next question is: *which of these remaining topics will work best?* What counts as "best" of course will depend on you, your speaking situation, and the criteria of the speech; however, typically when you want to identify the best of a set of possible topic ideas, you want to consider issues like:

   - **The currency of the topic**. Is this topic something of current interest or ongoing concern? Or is it outdated, out of fashion, or archaic?
   - **The significance of the topic**. Is this topic something that matters in the world? Or is it something that is of minor concern, passing interest, or just unimportant?
   - **The depth of the topic**. Is this a topic that you can dig into and have enough to say on? Or is the topic so simple and surface-level that it will be hard to expand on in the time frame?
   - **The excitement of the topic**. Is the topic exciting, thought-provoking, unusual, or attention-grabbing? Or is the topic dull, drab, boring, and banal?

   After you have considered your topic list through the perspective of these questions, some should begin to rise to the top of the list and some should fall out of contention. If only one topic rises to the top, you probably have your topic! If multiple topics still seem like good choices, go with the one that excites you the most. If none of your topics check these boxes, go back to the beginning of this process and start again.

5. **Ask yourself: "How do I make this topic the best it can be?"** Now that you have your topic selected, you want to spend a little time refining that topic to make it the best that it can be. Taking time to refine your topic might not seem important; you might think you can just figure it out later. But a lot of time and energy can be saved in researching and preparing your speech by refining your topic from the beginning. Different topics will need to go through different tweaks and changes to make them exceptional, but you might pay special attention to:

   - **Specificity**. Is the topic specific enough? Is it too specific?
   - **Clarity**. Is the topic clearly stated and understood?
   - **Brevity**. Can I condense the topic of my speech into a single sentence?
   - **Terminology**. Am I using the best and most direct language to describe my topic?

6. **Put your topic into the form of a thesis statement**. The final step in selecting a topic for your speech is the ultimate test: assessing whether you can state your topic in the form of a thesis statement. As we discussed earlier, a thesis statement is an essential component of a good speech because it gives both the speaker and the audience a clear sense of the speech and its primary goal. In the next chapter, we will also see that a thesis is an essential part of preparing an effective introduction. Therefore, before making your topic official, you will want to make sure you can express that topic in the form of a thesis statement.

To craft an effective thesis statement, you will want to follow a few rules to make sure the primary goal of your speech is expressed well to the audience. In particular, you will want to make sure your thesis is:

- **Short**. A thesis should be a single sentence. If you cannot make your point in a single sentence, you need to rethink your point.
- **Declarative**. An effective thesis is a claim; therefore, it should take the form of an assertion, a statement that states how the world is, should be, and/or what an audience should do to make it so. In public speaking, avoid framing your thesis in the form of a question since it is less clearly goal-oriented.
- **Interesting**. A thesis should be about something the audience does not already know anything or much about. A speech that only tells the audience what they already know should probably not be a speech. Putting your topic into the form of a thesis can be an excellent exercise to check if you are planning to speak about something genuinely interesting or not.
- **Goal-oriented in language**. A thesis statement should clearly highlight your primary goal, which in most cases will include some dimensions of persuasion. Therefore, most effective thesis statements in public speaking will use the words, "I will persuade you that…" somewhere in the statement. You may also choose to use more specific language about the particular persuasive goal of your speech, such as:
    - "I will persuade you to *learn* more about…"
    - "I will persuade you to *consider* perspectives other than your own about…"
    - "I will persuade you to *adopt* the policy of…"
    - "I will persuade you to *value* the life and experiences of…"
- **Manageable**. A thesis should be able to be expressed realistically in the course of a few-minute speech. "Today, I will persuade you that the meaning of all human life is…," for example, is a thesis statement that fails because few people believe it can be answered successfully in a 7–8 minute speech. By contrast, "Today, I will persuade you to agree with John Lennon, who believed love was the meaning of life" is a more realistic topic to address in a few minutes.

A good thesis includes all of these qualities; if your thesis does not have these qualities, you should seriously consider reviewing and revising it prior to your speech.

Researching Evidence: How Do I Find Support for My Claims?

Now that you've identified and refined your topic for your upcoming speech, you'll want to begin the next phase of the process: looking for supporting evidence for your claims through research. Becoming an effective researcher—for public speaking or any other part of life—takes time and practice, but it is essential to be successful in any number of endeavors. As we saw in the previous chapter, speakers who avoid evidence-based argument set themselves up for short-term and long-term failure. Therefore, you'll want to not only find ample evidence to support all your claims but also select the best evidence from what you find.

To help you think about how to do research more effectively for your upcoming speeches, let's look at some practical tips for doing research and some of the most common sources of research you are likely to use.

TIPS FOR EFFECTIVE RESEARCHING

- **Start early**. One of the best steps you can take to be a successful researcher for your public speech is start early—like now! There is no way around it: effective research is a time-intensive process. It takes hours of work diligently finding, collecting, evaluating, and selecting evidence from different sources in order to meet the high expectations for quality research as a public speaker. Could you find a few sources that touch on your speech topic the night before and work it into a speech? Sure—but the quality of your research is almost guaranteed to be out of sync with what you should be bringing to your speech in order to make it effective. Therefore, in order to guarantee you the most successful speaking experience, you need to start well in advance. Consider: If you have not started researching your speech a week in advance, you're probably in trouble.

- **Think about what you need before you go looking**. When you start your research process early, you can take the time to do something few inexperienced researchers do: take a few moments to think about what you want or need to find to support your argument. Often, novice public speakers find the first few sources that might have something to say about their topic in a search engine and slap those results into their speech. Unfortunately, the first five items in your search may not be your best sources, may not have anything of real value to say on your topic, or, worst of all, may lead you to design your speech to fit the first sources you find rather than the best sources that exist. To avoid all of these problems, think about your claims in your speech. Then ask: what kinds of information would I ideally want to find to support these claims? Keep a list of those ideal pieces of evidence and jot down some initial thoughts about where you might find that kind of evidence. Finally, go looking for that evidence.

- **Use all your available resources**. In many ways, Google has made researchers lazy. It is so easy to find some information online that we ignore the many other areas of research that are not as easy to find online. And this can harm our speech. Indeed, a successful public speech will almost always involve the use of not just many sources, but many kinds of sources, as well. In SPCM 200, we do not have requirements on the types of sources you must use (though other classes do). Nonetheless, you should become accustomed to considering all your available sources as you pursue evidence to support your topic. This is particularly true when your topic is more personal, local, cultural, understudied, or cutting-edge in nature: topics of this sort will likely not have an abundance of resources online for you to use. In the next section, we'll explore some of these other types of sources and evidence.

- **Be open to new or unexpected evidence**. It is important to note that even as you go looking for certain evidence, you must remain open to finding other evidence you did not expect to encounter. If this new information is useful to your speech, include it in your speech. If it is even better evidence than what you were looking for originally, drop the original evidence for newer evidence. If, however, the evidence you find contradicts or problematizes your claims, take it as an opportunity to reconsider and revaluate your topic. Does this new evidence require you to prepare a counterargument? Does this new evidence put your claim in a new light that might require you to reframe your speech? Or, is it the case that this new information leads you to question your own position on your topic altogether? If so, that's a good thing: growth and the willingness to change our minds are essential to a good public discourse. If, however, you do change your mind on your topic, be sure to alter your speech accordingly to reflect your new position and to make sure you remain an ethical speaker.

- **Find a system to track your research**. You've probably been in this situation before: it's the night before a big speech or paper and you've been looking through articles and essays and books for hours. You remember reading something smart that you want to use in your project, but who knows where it was? Which article did it come from? Do you still have that tab open on your browser? Or was it in one of the books spread on your floor? Do you spend an hour looking for that great quote or just give up on it and hope something just as good is out there on the next search result from Google? This situation is frustrating, inefficient, and a nightmare to experience. Unfortunately, it happens all the time to students doing research without a system. The fact is: you live in a world where you are surrounded by too much information. To survive in a sea of facts and figures, you need a way to keep track of what you want, what you need, what you don't, and what you're not sure about. Luckily, there are lots of ways to do this—you just need to find one that works for you. Consider some of these options:

- **Bookmark by idea**. As you are scrolling through websites and articles, create a series of bookmark folders in your browser on your personal computer or tablet. When you find something you even think might be useful, immediately bookmark the page in the appropriate file. That way you'll always have it and it will be initially sorted. This will make finding that quote or idea much easier—particularly with the "Search" or "Find" function on your browser.
- **Use an organizing and archiving app**. Apps like Evernote and Zotero can be a great solution for decluttering your research process. Create an account and then use the program to save documents, links, notes, photos, and screengrabs from the web all in one place.
- **Download everything**. The bookmark system works just as well if you download everything into a set of folders. Make sure you keep your folders neat and connected so that you don't have to find them on your hard drive later. Also, make sure you save your pages and documents in a way that makes them easily searchable, like a PDF.
- **Use your phone**. Cellphones can be a great way to grab a quote or idea right off the page of a printed text. Simply point and snap and then be sure to save to your phone, organization app, or other folders. However, don't forget to take a picture of the citation data you'll need for that source later!
- **Keep a running spreadsheet**. Using Excel or GoogleSheets, create an entry for all the valuable information you come across in the research process. Be sure to include columns for your source's author, title, publication details, a URL (if possible), and the quote or idea you want to include in your speech (along with its page number and proper quotations).

Constantly re-evaluate how your research is going. As you gather more and more evidence to support the claims in your speech, be sure to constantly re-evaluate if and how your research should change your speech and your ongoing research. If you find some types of evidence quickly, consider devoting time to searching for other types of evidence that might come less easily. If you see that you are heavy in evidence from the news media but lacking academic sources, consider spending more time researching in academic databases to fill the gap. In addition, if you have spent two hours in one database, it might be time move to another one. Or, if you have made a good effort and found nothing, maybe you should consider a different topic or refining your topic.

Pick your best sources. One of the biggest mistakes a speaker can make at the end of the research process is trying to put all the evidence they found into their speech. When speakers do this, their speeches can end up convincing, but also bloated, hard to understand, boring, and often over time. In other words, sometimes *too much research* is a real problem. Instead, when you are ready to move from research to preparing your speech, take some time to assess and evaluate all the sources you've collected. Then, select only the best and most effective evidence to include your speech. The evidence you leave out was not a waste of time. In reality, it helped you get to the best evidence and it will be useful to you in addressing counterarguments and questions from the audience. If you pick your best sources and include them in your speech, you've made a smart choice toward delivering a speech that is both well-researched and enjoyable to listen to.

Collectively, these tips will help you make the most of your research experience.

SITES FOR EFFECTIVE RESEARCHING

As a public speaker, you have a world of good-quality evidence of all types at your fingertips. That's why audiences have no time for public speakers who cannot make well-supported arguments for their speeches—you literally have more access to more information than any other generation in the history of the world! With this expectation on our shoulders, let's spend some time assessing the widest categories for good research you're likely to use in public speaking.

Before we begin, we need to make an important distinction in the types of research you'll come across as you look for evidence to support your speech. In particular, you'll want to make sure you know the difference between academic and non-academic sources. **Academic sources** feature *research that is produced by professional scholars and published in peer-reviewed academic outlets.* Meanwhile, **non-academic sources** feature *ideas, reporting, and opinions from writers, critics, leaders, and community members that express their viewpoint or experience.*

In general, neither academic nor non-academic sources are necessarily better than the other; each kind of source has its own strengths and weaknesses. Academic sources, for instance, are excellent because they are the product of extensive focus and years of study on a single subject that is then tested and checked by others in the field. This makes academic sources especially credible and reliable. However, academic sources can also be difficult to read, full of jargon, and too specialized for those who are not in the field. Alternately, non-academic sources are excellent as evidence because they are written for a general audience, deal with the topics of the day, often show clear viewpoints and opinions, and are quickly written and disseminated. However, non-academic sources do not have many checks or reviews of the claims made therein by experts or peers; sometimes, they are just someone's opinion or have an implicit agenda that can skew their claims. Since both academic and non-academic sources have strengths and weaknesses, a thoughtful researcher will likely use both in the course of making their claims.

Keeping this distinction in mind, let's examine some of the most common sites of evidence you are likely to use in your research.

You and Your Network. Let's start close to home: you and the people you know in your own life are a great, often-untapped resource for quality research. As we mentioned earlier in this chapter, your own life is a great starting point for selecting a topic that you care and know something about. Therefore, it is also likely a good place to find stories, examples, contacts, and ideas that might support the claims you want to make in your speeches. But don't limit your research to yourself. Consider the many people in your personal network that might be a resource for researching your topic. Your family, friends, colleagues, professors, acquaintances, even social media contacts all might have something valuable to tell you about your topic or know someone who can. Do keep in mind that just because people we know might have an opinion on a topic, they may not be a strong, credible source you want to use in your speech. But, if you do have credible sources of evidence in your life, don't be afraid to use them and cite them appropriately.

Unrestricted Online Research. The most common places most people begin their research process is on a general search engine like Google. We simply type our topic into the search bar and see what comes up. This type of research is what we might think of as unrestricted online research. By **unrestricted online research** we mean *online research through a generic search tool that gives the researcher access to free content on the Internet.* Unrestricted research is a great way to do research, particularly in the early stages of a project. These searches can help researchers identify the most obvious and direct information about their topic, help define basic terms about their topic, and assess whether their topic is widely discussed or relatively quiet on the web. However, unrestricted online research also comes with some significant limitations. In particular, search engines often do not return the most credible and reliable information on a subject; rather they tend to return to most clicked-on or most well-marketed information. In our current era of troll farms and propaganda campaigns by hostile nations, these vulnerabilities are disconcerting. But the challenges can also be more banal. Indeed, sometimes what seems to be a popular source for a speech ends up being something quite un-credible, like a high school student's paper or a blog by a disgruntled employee of a company. As such, researchers need to take steps to ensure they are conducting unrestricted online research wisely by:

- **Checking the URL**. The URL or link to a site can often tell us a great deal about its credibility as a source. URLs that feature .com, .org, or .edu tend to be the most credible, representing businesses, institutions, and schools and universities, respectively. However, note that there are few limitations on who can claim these URLs, so trust but verify who owns the site.

- **Watching out for advertisements**. On most major search engines, paid advertisements are returned and intermixed with your search results. Often, these advertisements are marked as such, but some are not.

- **Checking out the quality of the web design**. If you click on a site and you are underwhelmed by what it looks like, it might raise some concerns for you about the quality of the source. Most credible sources have the funds and expertise to put together a clean, clutter-free, and well-written and edited site to deliver their information. Sites that are cluttered, poorly written, and, frankly, ugly or outdated, are less likely to be a quality source.

- **Checking for an "About" section**. In addition, many credible sites have an "about" section where you can learn more about the credentials and career of the site's owner or operator. You'll want to read the "about" section to determine if this person is credible; however, not all sites with an "about" section will have a credible author. If there is not a way to learn more about the author or institution that runs the site, be cautious.

Restricted Online Research. While an unrestricted web search can pose some significant challenges as it relates to the quality and kind of sources it returns, restricted online research tends to return much more reliable results. By **restricted online research** we mean *online research conducted through libraries and databases that are not accessible to the general public for free.* Because libraries research, select, and pay for good-quality information databases, researchers are almost guaranteed to find quality evidence in these kinds of searches. As a student in SPCM 200, you have access to hundreds of excellent databases with academic and non-academic sources on all kinds of subjects. All that is needed to access these databases is an eID and password. In fact, your access to these databases is something every student pays for through their tuition at CSU; therefore, you are cheating yourself by not using them. You can see a full and updated list of the best databases for you to consider on your course's Canvas site.

The News Media. The news media is also an excellent source of evidence and research for public speakers. It is the job of news organizations to report on current events, offer analysis and insight into complex issues, and serve as a watchdog over powerful people, institutions, and corporations that might do harm to the public good. As a researcher, you might access information from the news media online in restricted and unrestricted ways, on television, social media, or even in print. Online, some news media sites are free whereas others have a pay-wall that restricts access only to those with subscriptions; however, almost every major news media site in the nation is accessible to you as a CSU student through the databases in the CSU Library.

As you review news media sites for research, there are two things we should keep in mind. First, while most news organizations do try to maintain professional objectivity in their reporting, journalists are also people. As such, most news sources have a degree of **political bias**, *a general slant in reporting that favors either the political right or left in implicit ways.* However, political bias need not be a detriment to our work as researchers. Instead, we need to know that biases exist in the news media, take that into account as we assess a source, and balance bias when possible or needed. Second, while genuine news organizations are a vital part of a democratic society, increasingly infotainment has entered an arena once held exclusively by journalists. **Infotainment** *describes online and TV personalities that use the news to produce content to entertain, enrage, or work up audiences for profit.* ***Infotainers are not journalists***; rather, they are performers that talk about and give their opinions about current events for an audience that often shares their political opinions. Some infotainers freely share that they are doing infotainment; however, some infotainment performers actively hide their role as an entertainment source and try to make people think that they are doing journalism. While infotainment can be entertaining, when infotainers fool audiences into thinking their commentary is actually true or legitimate news, they pose a serious threat to the public good. What's more: leaders under investigation by the actual news media now commonly try to make real journalists seem like infotainers to discredit accusations of actual legal and ethical misconduct (i.e., "that's just fake news"). As researchers, it is vital that we know the difference between journalism and infotainment and avoid the latter in our public speeches.

As a researcher in search of evidence to support your claims, you will almost certainly rely on the news media, databases, online searches, and people in your life to help you speak about what matters to you. However, while each of these potential sites of evidence is useful, their utility is directly linked to your ability as a public speaker to cite those sources correctly and effectively in your speech.

Researching Ethically: Plagiarism and Citing Sources

The final part of any good research undertaking is citing your sources. By **citing sources**, we mean *crediting the original ideas and expression of a speaker or author to that person.* In Western cultures, citing sources is a legal and ethical imperative. As researchers, we will be using a significant amount of other people's words and ideas in our own speeches. Therefore, it is essential that we learn how to cite sources correctly to avoid plagiarism.

Plagiarism is defined as *the act of representing the work of another person, persons, or institution as your own.* It is vital for a variety of reasons that public speakers do not engage in plagiarism. For one, plagiarism is a form of academic misconduct in college and university settings. Students who engage in plagiarism face severe consequences, including but not limited to failure of an assignment, failure of a class, and even expulsion from the university. Plagiarism also can have significant consequence in the professional world. Authors, screenwriters, novelists, politicians, and speakers have all been accused of plagiarism in the working world, resulting in lawsuits, firings, resignations, and public shaming. But perhaps the most important reason to avoid plagiarism is that it can have irrevocable consequence for your credibility in the public and private sphere. Even the accusation of plagiarism can lead members of the community to lose trust in the credibility of a speaker. As such, our effectiveness as a speaker, leader, and community member is all tied to avoiding plagiarism.

While avoiding plagiarism may be an obvious task to some novice public speakers, for others, considering the harm of plagiarism may be a new idea. Indeed, the harms of plagiarism are often misunderstood across cultural and generational lines. Culturally, the concept that ideas and expressions are strictly owned and controlled by a sole creator is a highly Western idea. In other parts of the world, more collectively oriented societies often place less importance on the creations of a single person; rather the community as a whole participates in the collective creation of an idea or concept. Therefore, if you come from a more collectivistic culture, you may be less familiar with the notion of plagiarism espoused in the U.S. Generationally, we have also seen changes in people's understandings of plagiarism. More specifically, with the creation of new technologies that make copying, pasting, and aggregating information simple and seamless, younger generations are often less likely to think critically about the legal and ethical needs to generate their own unique content in certain spaces. While these cultural and generational differences in thinking about plagiarism are important to know, they do not change the academic, legal, and professional expectations within the U.S. classroom. In other words, regardless of your familiarity with plagiarism, all students in U.S. universities will be held accountable for upholding the traditional expectations of avoiding plagiarism.

How then do we go about avoiding plagiarism? There are at least three vital ways to do so: knowing the types of plagiarism, using quote indicators, and citing sources. Indeed, as public speakers, we must do all three of these acts in order to be ethical and credible speakers.

KNOWING THE TYPES OF PLAGIARISM

One of the most important ways you can avoid plagiarism is by knowing the different kinds of plagiarism that must be avoided. In fact, there are four major types of plagiarism that you should know: global, incremental, patchwork, and self-plagiarism. Of the four types, global plagiarism is by far the best understood form of plagiarism. **Global plagiarism** is defined as *the taking of another person's complete work and attempting to pass it off as your own.* This form of plagiarism is the one we see in popular culture when a student takes a friend's essay, erases their name, and puts their own name in its place. It is such a clear form of cheating that most students understand it and most instructors can catch it easily. The other three forms of plagiarism, however, are more difficult to understand. For example, **incremental plagiarism** is *the taking of a short line or small amount of information from another person's work without appropriately quoting or citing that material.* Students often think that lifting a single sentence from another person's work is a minor offense and does not count as plagiarism. That assumption is wrong—particularly when a statement or idea is significant, notable, or famous; indeed, the inappropriate use of a single sentence or idea is enough to warrant and support a full plagiarism case. By contrast, **patchwork plagiarism** is *the taking of statements or ideas from many different people's work and combining them into your own without properly citing them.* Some students mistake patchwork plagiarism for research; however, there is a key difference: in research, a student draws from many other people's ideas, but credits those people with having those ideas. In patchwork plagiarism, a student collects many other people's ideas and statements and then takes credit for those ideas and statements themselves, whether they meant to or not. A final commonly misunderstood form of plagiarism is **self-plagiarism**—*the unauthorized reuse of one's own work in multiple places or publication outlets.* Self-plagiarism may not seem like plagiarism at first; how, you might ask, can I plagiarize myself? The answer here lies in the concept of double-dipping: trying to benefit twice from one original idea. In the professional world of writing and speaking, this kind of plagiarism is strictly penalized; if you write an opinion piece for one magazine, for example, you cannot legally get paid by a different magazine for that same piece. In an academic setting, the same is true: you cannot benefit for one speech or writing assignment in multiple classes. That means you cannot use a speech from a previous class for your speech class; instead, you need to write a new, original speech. Similarly, you cannot take text from a paper in a previous class and drop it into a speech for this class—this is also self-plagiarism. Ethically, a student could avoid these issues of self-plagiarism in two ways. First, they can seek authorization from their instructor to reuse earlier work. Second, they could use their earlier work as a starting point for a new original work that is substantively different from the first work.

USE QUOTE INDICATORS

As should be clear from this discussion, another way to avoid plagiarism is to always carefully quote ideas or expressions from others in your own work. This is a common theme in almost all of the descriptions of plagiarism above: the taking and use of another person's ideas or statements *without giving appropriate credit.* Part of the way speakers and writers give credit to others for their ideas and statements is using quote indicators. **Quote indicators** are *written and spoken cues to the audience that you are moving back and forth between your own original ideas and statements and those of another person.* In written discourse, quote indicators are called **quotation marks**, *an internationally recognized text symbol that the writer has moved from their own ideas to someone else's.* While quotation marks go a long way to avoiding plagiarism in written text, they do not help much in spoken discourse because an audience cannot see the quotes in your outline or manuscript (both of which we will address in Chapter 8). Therefore, in public speaking it is vital that we use *vocalized call outs to inform the audience that we are moving from our own original ideas to the ideas on another person*, what we refer to as **quotation notes**. To correctly use quotation notes in practice, a speaker should say the word "quote" every time they begin to quote another person's statements in their speech (or see an open quotation mark in their outline or manuscript). Similarly, the speaker indicates to the audience that the quotation is ended and that they are transitioning back to their own ideas by saying "unquote." For novice public speakers, getting comfortable using quotation notes in their speeches can be difficult; it can be awkward to say, difficult to remember, and often feel unnatural in the flow of the speech. However, using quote indicators is essential to giving credit fairly and avoiding plagiarism in public speaking.

Importantly, there are times as a public speaker when we will want to use the ideas of another person in our speech without quoting those ideas at length. In this case, we will want to paraphrase a source's ideas rather than quote them. By **paraphrasing** we mean *the restatement of another person or institution's idea in the speaker's own words.* Speakers often select to paraphrase a source in their speech for several reasons, including emphasizing a point, not having enough time to quote the source directly, needing to restate the original idea in a way that is clearer, or simply to improve the flow of the speech. However, while paraphrasing is an excellent way for a speaker to use the ideas of another person or institution in their speech, *it is still required that a speaker use a verbal indicator to mark the paraphrase in the speech.* Indeed, when speakers fail to use a verbal indicator to mark a paraphrase and to credit the speaker's original idea—even if the speaker puts that idea into their own words—the speaker is guilty of plagiarism. To avoid this charge, speakers must use a **paraphrase note** in their speech—*a vocalized statement that tells the audience that the speaker is restating the ideas of another in their own words.* While there are potentially many ways to use a paraphrase note, the most common is to simply say, "To paraphrase [the original source]" prior to restating your researched idea.

CITING SOURCES

The final essential way we avoid plagiarism—not only in public speaking but in most aspects of your academic and professional life—is by citing sources. By **citing sources** we mean *crediting the original ideas and expression of a speaker or author to that person.* As public speakers who cite their sources, we move to our most credible position in using evidence and argument by giving credit where credit is due and, in doing so, showing ourselves to be ethical participants in the public discourse.

There are many ways to cite sources in academic, professional, and public communication. Some forms of citation are only useful in certain kinds of communicative acts; however, in public speaking, we must cite our sources in three ways in order to be competent, credible, and ethical speakers.

The first way a public speaker must cite their sources is through in-text citations. An **in-text citation** is a *written indication in a speech text of who is the original source of an idea, paraphrase, or quotation.* In-text citations are one-third of a citation system that tells the reader or listener about where an idea or statement comes from and how to locate that original idea or statement themselves. The need for an in-text citation is easy to identify when you are working with quotations; in fact, anytime you use quotation marks in an outline or manuscript you need to pair those quotations marks with a corresponding in-text citation. However, even when a speaker is not quoting from a source directly—like in the case of a paraphrase—it is still necessary for the speaker to credit an idea back to its original source with an in-text citation. In-text citations come in many forms; in public speaking we use what are called parenthetical references. **Parenthetical references** *describe reference information placed inside parentheses at the end of a quote, idea, paraphrase, or paragraph.* It must contain two pieces of information: the author's last name and the page number of the quote or idea in the original source. So, for example, if I wanted to cite a quote by Rebecca Henderson on page 76 of her book, my parenthetical reference would look like this: (Henderson 76).

The second component of a complete citation of sources in public speaking is a Works Cited. A **Works Cited** is *a page (or a few pages) at the end of your outline that lists all your sources used through the speech and how to locate them.* It is a repository of information for you, the speaker, but more importantly for the audience. Using a well-done Works Cited, someone who heard your speech could find all of your sources and double-check all the information, paraphrases, and quoted materials you used in your speech. While the Works Cited page is the term used in MLA citations, other citation styles use other terms such as the Reference page or Bibliography. In SPCM 200, we prioritize MLA as our citation system; however, you might ask your instructors if you can use an alternate style in your own speeches. The formatting of a Works Cited page varies. The Modern Language Association regularly updates the format at certain intervals to reflect the most current thinking of how to cite sources appropriately. Therefore, you should consult with the most recent MLA Works Cited Forms link on your class's Canvas page when putting together your Works Cited. However, as a general rule, a Works Cited must:

- Start on a new page
- Include a title that says "Work Cited" on top
- Include all your sources listed alphabetically from A–Z
- Make sure each source starts with the author's name (when available)
- Includes a space between each citation in the Works Cited

The final component of a complete citation of sources in public speaking is verbal citations. **Verbal citations** are *vocalized cues given to an audience to inform them where a statement or idea in a speech originated.* Verbal citations are similar to quotation notes, in that they use an oral remark to provide the audience with information about an idea that is not original to the speaker; however, verbal citations are different than quotation notes because they indicate the *source of an idea* rather than *the idea itself.* As an audience member, you have probably heard a speaker use verbal citations in a speech when they said something like "According to the *Wall Street Journal*..." or "In Dr. Goodall's theory..." Both of these are good examples of verbal citations because they specifically and succinctly tell the audience about where an idea or statement originated. In addition, both statements aid the speaker's credibility by showing they did research on their topic and that they intend to share that research in an ethical way with the audience. Both examples also make clear to the audience that the ideas or statements to follow are not those of the speaker, helping the speaker avoid suggestions of plagiarism.

While many novice public speakers recognize the need for verbal citations in their speeches, they are often more unclear on how to do them well. Indeed, there are no hard and fast rules about how to do verbal citations well in every case; rather, each speaker needs to make decisions in their own speech about what information should be conveyed to the audience in the verbal citation in order for it to be successful. A good standard in thinking about what information to include in a verbal citation—one that we will enforce in this class—is that a speaker must include at least two (2) of these parts of a source for every verbal citation: the name of the speaker or author, the location of the speech or publication, the date of the speech or publication, and the title of the speech or publication.

PART OF CITATION	WHEN TO USE IT?	EXAMPLE
Name of the speaker or author	When the name or position of the speaker/author is recognizable to the audience and/or gives the source greater credibility	"Albert Einstein once said that..." "The great astronaut, Sally Ride, was quoted as saying..."
Location of speech or publication	When the location is relatable to the audience or gives the source prestige, credibility, or surprise	"When President Obama spoke on campus at CSU..."
Date of the speech or publication	When either the recency or historical nature of a source impacts its credibility	"In fact, a cutting-edge research project on this question published just last week shows..."
Title of speech or publication	When the title is famous or recognizable or imparts clarity to the audience	"In Malcolm X's 'The Ballot the Bullet' address, he addressed the question of violence and politics by..."

When combining two of these parts of a citation in a verbal citation, it is important for the speaker to integrate them succinctly and smoothly so that the verbal citation does not become verbal clutter. Examples of effective combinations include:

PARTS OF CITATION	EXAMPLE
Name + Location	"During the President Xi Jinping's speech in India, he remarked..."
Name + Date	"To quote Beyoncé and Jay Z's 2017 album..."
Name + Title	"According to David Brook's lecture entitled *The Road to Character*..."
Location + Date	"The *Wall Street Journal*'s editorial page has said little of the controversy all year..."
Location + Title	"When he delivered his *Remarks to the United Nations* before the General Assembly..."
Date + Title	"In the Pope's 2018 Easter homily..."

As we conclude this section, it bears repeating: to be an effective and ethical public speaker, you cannot simply avoid plagiarism for the most part or partially cite your sources. Rather, an effective and ethical public speaker avoids plagiarism by knowing the types of plagiarism, indicating the ideas and statements of others with quotations or paraphrase notes, and citing their sources fully—in-text, in a Works Cited, and with verbal citations. Anything less can radically undermine the credibility of a speaker and irrevocably harm their academic, professional, and public standing.

Chapter 7

SPEAKING AND ORGANIZATION

Organization is the root of all good and evil in public speaking. Well, that might be a bit dramatic. Nonetheless, there is ample evidence to suggest that both significant successes and tragic failures in speech can be traced back to the speaker's earliest decisions about how to organize their speech. Just consider how organization plays into the following examples of public speaking failures:

- Juan went over time. If he had better organized his speech in advance, he could have ensured he had plenty of time to get his important points across before time ran out.
- Kiara's delivery was a mess. More specifically, she couldn't deliver her speech effectively because she was trying to speak from jumbled notes and evidence.
- Paul's attempts at being funny failed. His jokes kept bombing because he stepped on his punchlines and referenced material out of order.

These are just a few examples of how poor organization might actually be at the root of other kinds of public speaking challenges.

But what do we mean by organization? **Organization** refers to *the inclusion and arrangement of key elements of a speech*. The ancient Greeks considered organization a foundational quality of a successful speech and the Romans identified it as one of the five canons every effective speech must have. It simply makes sense. If organization contains the vital parts and connections any speech needs in order to succeed, it would be a mistake to ignore them. Imagine trying to do any other task by leaving out a key component or doing steps out of order. For example, making chocolate chip cookies without chocolate chips just does not work. Similarly, pressing the accelerator without first turning on your car will never get you anywhere. As with all things in life, we need to be organized in our speechmaking if we want to do it successfully.

But the benefits of good organization are not limited to the speech itself; rather, effective organization also offers benefits to audience and speaker.

First, good organization is a positive for the audience. A speech that is well organized is easy to follow, clear in its application of reason, thoughtful and emotional without being too much of either one, easy to remember and recall after the event, and reassuring about the ideas involved. In other words, audiences respond to well-organized speeches better than to speeches that are not organized. If you need further proof, just think about the last time you heard someone give a speech without an effective organization. In short, if we are trying to get our audience to act on our messages, we need to give them those messages properly organized.

Second, good organization is also a positive for the speaker—and not just for their goals in persuading the audience. Rather, a well-organized speech helps speakers develop a well-organized mind. The connection between clear thinking and clear speaking is one that dates back centuries. Scholars have debated these connections, many drawing some different distinctions. However, most of these scholars share the belief that learning how to give a well-organized speech brings clear thinking to the speaker's mind. Some of us may feel that we already have a pretty well-arranged brain, but scholars argue that organization helps us do more than simply *place* ideas. Rather, it teaches us how to *pit ideas up against each other*, something we colloquially refer to as **thinking**. Constructing a well-organized speech trains the brain to identify new information, assesses it, define it, categorize it, compare it against existing information, render a final judgment, and then go through that process with others: all key component of a solid thought process. As such, we hope that this chapter will serve a larger role in training people how to consume and communicate information internally, not just to audiences.

Organizational Elements

There are many different elements relating to an effective organization of a speech; however, for our purposes, we will focus on two of the most important: the structures of a speech and the order in which those structures are arranged. The first is what we refer to as the structures of a speech. Speech **structures** are *parts of a speech that do particular tasks and work together to achieve the goal of the speech*. The second element of speech organization we want to consider is order. **Order** refers to *the manner in which the component structures of a speech are arranged to achieve a particular speech's goal*. Both speech structures and the order of those structures are necessary to achieve good speechmaking. In fact, an organized speaker knows that a speech that is lacking key structures or that does not have a well thought out order will almost certainly be unsuccessful.

To help better understand the different yet related way in which structure and order work together to make a successfully organized speech, think about your speech as a house. Like a speech, a house has structural elements that we are all familiar with: walls, floors, a roof, doors, and windows. Any house that was lacking one of these key structural elements would not be a very successful house—indeed it would not only be impractical and unsafe to live in, it might also not qualify as a house at all. But while houses have mandatory and voluntary structures, having those structures in a home is not enough to make a successful house either. These housing structures also need to follow a particular order. The walls must be arranged in a way to support the roof, which must sit on the walls if it is to function correctly. Likewise, the floors must be flat and even or else the entire building might become faulty. Therefore, just like a house needs both structures and order to be effective as a house, a speech too needs both to be a successful speech. It is not enough to say that a speech has its necessary component parts; rather, those parts must be placed in a meaningful and effective order for the speech to work.

To better understand structure and order in speechmaking, we need to understand the various parts of these larger terms.

Structures

While a speech can have many different kinds of structures, there are a few structures that are essential to almost any speech:

Introductions. The first structural element of a speech that we should know is the introduction. An **introduction** is *a relatively short opening to a speech in which the speaker prepares the audience to listen to and be engaged with the speech.* Introductions are not unique to public speaking. In fact, many forms of communication—including term papers, books, letters, even social interactions—feature introductions of some kind. Yet, introductions are especially important in public speaking because everything we say is **ephemeral**—*it is said and then disappears immediately, out of sight and mind, unless what we say leaves an impression.* As such, introductions are vital to effective speechmaking because, if done well, they create a strong first impression. As a general rule, each introduction has five key parts that do particular jobs in the course of the introduction. Knowing these five parts of an introduction is vital to doing an introduction correctly.

- **Attention getter**. The very first task in every introduction is to gain the audience's attention. The idea here is simple: if your audience is not paying attention to you as the speaker, you cannot in good faith start delivering your speech. If you did, your speech would fall on deaf ears and all your energy and effort in preparation would be wasted. While gaining attention has always been a challenge for speakers, in the 21st century, it is an even more difficult feat. Audiences are not only pulled away by conversations with others, their preoccupations of the day, their own feelings, and distracting sights and sounds; most of them also have very expensive and effective distraction machines in their pockets. Cellphones beep, buzz, friend request, comment, like, news alert, and selfie their way into our attention at an alarming rate, leading some researchers to say that attention—not food, water, or oil—is the greatest scarcity in human society in this century.[26] Therefore, we need powerful attention getters to cut through all the clutter. An **attention getter** is *a statement at the beginning of a speech to end audience distraction and draw their focus.* A good attention getter should be one or all of the following. It should be politely loud; a talking audience needs to hear you. It should be unexpected, either in content or delivery. It should surprise or shock the audience more than what they were focused on before. It might even be funny, clever, or entertaining. And it should always be relevant to your speech topic. Doing one or all of these tasks in a line or two is not simple, so be sure to spend some time working on this diligently in preparation for your speech.
- **Thesis statement**. An introduction is also wildly incomplete without a thesis statement. By now, we have discussed the purpose and forms of a good thesis statement several times; therefore, you should refer back to discussions of the thesis statements in Chapter 1, 5, and 6 before creating your thesis statement in your speech. However, we have not previously addressed the place of a thesis in the introduction. While the placement of the thesis can vary in an introduction, as a general rule it should probably be expressed before the relevance statement and credibility statement and certainly must be expressed before the preview.
- **Relevance statement**. As much as speaker may be excited for their topic in a speech, not all audiences will be equally as excited. Therefore, it is important for the speaker to make sure the audience knows that the speech they are about to listen to has meaning and a connection to each individual audience member's life. Doing this work is the job of a relevance statement. Typically phrased as "This speech should matter to you because…" the **relevance statement** *tells the audience that the topic under discussion will have consequence for their lives.* While it is vital to make sure the audience sees the relevance of the speaker's topic, it is also important that speakers not rely on exaggerated assumptions to do this work. For example, while many people in your audience may have or want children, for most audiences, it would be inappropriate to

say that "We should all be concerned with this topic since we all want or have children." The speaker simply does not know this and, in fact, may offend audience members who do not hold those views or beliefs. Rather, the speaker can acknowledge a diverse audience while still demonstrating relevance by saying something like, "As a society, we are all invested in the lives of children, whether they are our own or others."

- **Credibility statement**. Just like the relevance statement tells the audience what the topic of the speech has to do with them, the credibility statement tells the audience what the topic has to do with the speaker. In other words, a **credibility statement** is *a way for the speaker to show the audience that she knows about the topic she will speak on through research or experience.* An example of an effective credibility statement might be, "As someone who has struggled with taking standardized tests myself, I deeply believe it is important for us to reconsider the role of standardized testing in college admissions." For many novice speakers, a credibility statement does not seem important. However, consider: would you want to take advice or action based upon a speech from someone who did not know what they were talking about? Hopefully, the answer is "no." Audiences are always more likely to be moved to action by someone who they believe knows their subject and can be trusted to talk about it in an ethical way. And the only way an audience will know that person is you is if you say so in your introduction.

- **Preview**. A preview in a speech is a lot like a preview or trailer for a new film. This set of short images of a full film gives the audience a taste of a film that will be "coming soon" and gets the audience excited about what they have to look forward to. Similarly, a preview in a speech is the "coming attractions" of public address. In a single sentence, the **preview** *tells the audience what the speaker will be talking about in the next few minutes to give them both a sense of what is to come and to get the audience excited about what follows.*

While it is essential that your speech contain all of these different elements in order to maximize its effectiveness, it is also important that the speaker keep their introductions short and to the point. Indeed, the introduction is exactly that: introductory. That means it should be just a sample of what you will say. Rather than have a lengthy introduction, speakers are best served by having a brief introduction and saving the bulk of their evidence, explanations, and arguments for the body of their speech.

Body of the Speech. The longest and most substantial structure of a speech is the body of the speech. The **body of the speech** is *the bulk of a speech in which the speaker makes arguments, presents evidence, and develops claims to move the audience.* Depending on the kind of speech you give and the different goals you might have as a speaker, the body of a speech can vary significantly. Indeed, unlike other structures of a speech, the body is the most likely to look different in its size, parts, and features. Nonetheless, there are common elements of a speech body that are a part of almost any speech.

- **Main points**. Most speech bodies are organized into sets of main points. We defined and discussed main points in depth in Chapter 5. Organizationally, most main points appear as a single sentence in which the speaker presents a single line of argument. While there is never a mandatory number of main points that determines whether a speech is successful or not, most speeches have between 2 to 4 main points that work together to prove the speaker's thesis statement.

- **Sub-points**. We also know from Chapter 5 that underneath each main point is a series of smaller points called sub-points. On their own, sub-points are not particularly helpful to a speaker. They often consist of a single statistic or a quote or an interesting question; however, when a series of related sub-points are clustered together underneath a main point, they serve as an essential ingredient to building a good argument.

Transitions. Transitions are essential for the public speaker in aiding the flow of their speech as well as letting the audience know that you are moving from one point or idea to the next. While there are dozens of transitions at the speaker's disposal, some of the most common transitions used in public speaking are:

On one hand...On the other hand...	Whereas
My first point is...my second point is...	Likewise,
However,	Particularly,
Otherwise,	Surprisingly,
Regardless,	Then again,
Nonetheless,	While
Rather,	In reality
Furthermore,	By the same token,
Similarly,	Even though
Additionally,	As a result,
In addition,	As a matter of fact,
In order to	In effect,
In fact,	In conclusion,
For example,	In short,
Since,	Therefore,

Now that we understand _____ we can turn to _____

- **Transitions**. Between each main point in a speech should be a transition. **Transitions** are *words or phrases that connect one main point to the next main point in a fluid and clear way*. To go back to our house metaphor, a transition is like a nail or a screw holding different beams of argument together—sure, a set of beams are the large, most noticeable pieces of a house, but without small joiners keeping them together, those beams cannot do anything. So it is with transitions: these little statements make clear to the audience that your main points are not disconnected pieces, but different kinds of argument that when put together make something meaningful and substantial.

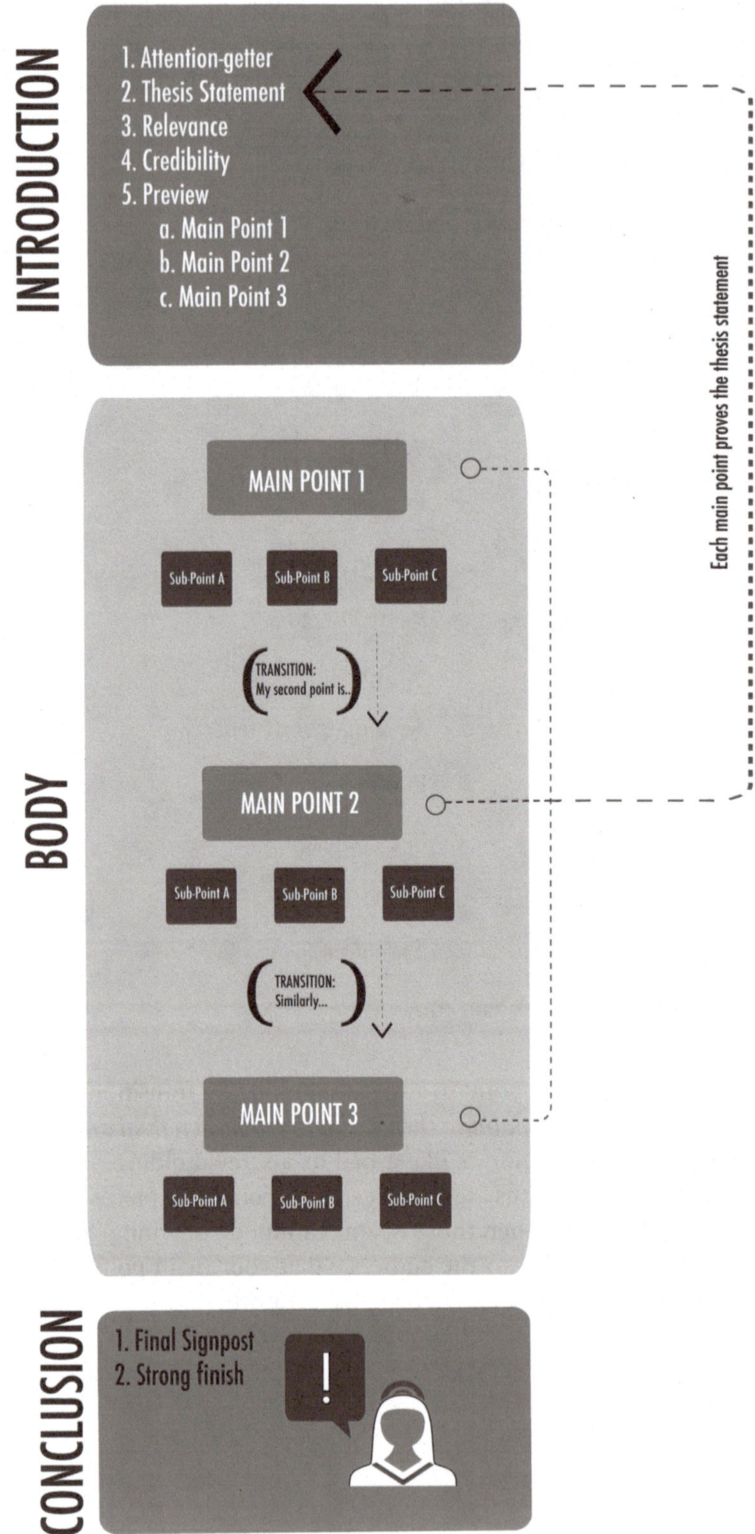

Figure 7-1. Speech Structures

Conclusion. The final important structure in a speech is the conclusion. A **conclusion** is *the intentional ending of a speech that prepares the audience to think about the speech one last time before it is complete.* When many novice speakers think about the end of a speech, their focus is often on simply getting to the finish. Because they are happy to finish their speech, they tend to often leap to that finish with a quick, relatively pointless conclusion. The most common examples are phrases like "That's it!" "Thank you for listening," or "Thank you." However, ending a speech with these short and simple statements is a major missed opportunity for a public speaker. By the end of a speech, an audience may have forgotten some of the earlier points you made in your address or their attention may be wandering to something else. In that case, an effective conclusion must regain the attention of the audience, remind them of what you have said, and set the tone or direction for the audience after you stop speaking. Therefore, our conclusions need to feature some key elements as well.

- **Final signpost**. It's good practice in the creation of a conclusion to a speech to include a final signpost. **Signposts** are *rhetorical tools that let the audience now where we are in the course of a speech.* Examples of signposts might be, "As we conclude this speech..." or "In my final summation…" The final signpost, then, tells the audience that the end of the speech is near and that they should reengage with the speaker if their mind has wandered. Including a final signpost into your conclusion is a highly effective way of getting your audience's attention back as the speech comes to a close.

- **Summary**. Somewhere in your introduction, you need to remind your audience of the good points you made during the course of your speech. This *short reminder of your thesis and main points* is what we call a **summary**, also known as a review. It should be relatively brief and most good summaries succeed if they simply recount the main points of a given speech. But without this summary, it is common for an audience to quickly forget anything they've been told in the speech up until that point.

- **Strong finish**. Lastly, every good conclusion needs to end with a solid finish. Any of us who have heard a great speech are familiar with this concept: we want to end our extended commentaries with a zingy, catchy, or even quotable final phrase that emphasizes our thesis statement and sticks in the audience's mind. Think, for instance, of Winston Churchill, in concluding his speech to inspire the people of the UK during World War II saying, "Let us therefore brace ourselves to our duties, and so bear ourselves that if the British Empire and its Commonwealth last for a thousand years, men will still say, 'This was their finest hour.'" While we might not be as eloquent or dramatic as Churchill, each of us will want to end our speech with a strong finish. Doing so identifies the end of the speech, cues the audience to begin its applause, and hopefully leaves a mark with the audience. Therefore, it serves very clear functions in every kind of speech. However, if we are delivering a persuasive speech, we often want to end our address with a particular kind of strong finish called a call to action. A **call to action** is *a strong finish that lays out what the speaker wants the audience to do at the end of the speech.* Typically calls to action, for example, ask audiences to vote a particular way, give money to a certain charity, or simply change their mind about a topic. Calls to action are vital kinds of strong finishes for persuasive speeches that we don't find in other kinds of speeches.

Order

How a speaker chooses to order her points is also a crucial consideration in designing a successful and effective speech. When thinking about ordering the structural components of a speech, there are some aspects that simply must proceed in a particular order. For example, an introduction must always come first, and a conclusion must always come last; doing anything otherwise would certainly lead to a failed speech. Similarly, within an introduction, some points must come in a certain order. The attention getter, for example, must always come first because gaining your audience's attention is always necessary to be a successful speaker. To put it another way, there is no reason to get your audience's attention later in the speech, because everything you've said up until that point would be wasted.

Yet, while there are some places in a speech where order is simply non-negotiable, there are other places in which the speaker can make decisions about order more directly. In making these decisions, speakers should follow two guides: ordering principles and ordering patterns.

Ordering Principles. One factor a speaker might take into account when making decisions about order are ordering principles. By **ordering principles** we mean *general rules about order that are shaped by human psychology and experience.* In this class, we will focus on two principles in particular:

- **The primacy principle.** The primacy principle states that *whichever point or idea in your speech is the strongest or most important should go first.* The logic behind this principle is simple: people retain information at a significantly higher rate earlier in a speech. Therefore, if you know your audience will lose attention as the speech goes on, it makes sense to ensure they hear the most important information early.
- **The recency principle.** The recency principle states that *whichever point or idea in your speech is the strongest or most important should go last.* Like the primacy principle, the recency principle is based on theories of human attention. In particular, it recognizes that people pay attention toward the end of the speech, much like they do toward the beginning. As such, to make sure your audience hears your best arguments, consider putting them at the end.

Obviously, while both of these principles are generated from the same research, they pose a tricky challenge for the speaker: where do I place my best piece of evidence? There is no clear answer here; the evidence suggests either last or first will work well. Where these principles matter most is with the remainder of your arguments. Once you've placed your strongest argument, you should probably place your second strongest argument at either the end or beginning (depending on what is still vacant). Your weakest point, by process of elimination, will then end up in the middle of your speech's body.

Ordering Patterns. In conjunction with ordering principles, speaker can also use ordering patterns to make decisions about ordering the information in their speech. Like ordering principles, ordering patterns are derived from the research and practices of communication scholars; however, **ordering patterns** are different in that they are *prefabricated methods of ordering points that are applied to the entirety of a speech.* In public speaking, we regularly see certain kinds of ordering patterns that you might consider in designing the order of your own speech. The most common of these patterns include:

- **Chronological pattern**: *ordering your main points by time, step, or process.* If your speech includes main points that only make sense if they proceed from first to last, earliest to latest, or step 1 to step 3, the chronological patterns makes a great deal of sense. In fact, depending on the topic, you may have no choice but to order your points chronologically if the speech itself will make logical sense.
    - **Example**: In order to counteract foreign meddling in our elections, we need to first admit the problem, second identify our weakness, and third develop strategies for combating these attacks.
- **Spatial pattern**: *ordering your main points by location, juxtaposition, or hierarchy.* Some speech topics lend themselves particularly well to being organized spatially. When your speech touches on an issue occurring in different parts of the nation or the world, experiences from different places in society or culture, or even different positions in an organization, spatial patterns can bring to light how location alters perceptions and reality.
    - **Example**: To better explain how the new corporate policy affects employees, I will talk about its effects for upper, middle, and lower management.
- **Circular pattern**: *ordering your main points as proceeding through a cycle or by returning to the beginning.* Few speeches in Western cultures employ a circular pattern of organization. From a cultural perspective, we presume things proceed in a straight line and that no new moment is like the moment that came before. But in other cultures, much of life can best be understood by thinking of it as a circle, with ends returning us back to the beginning. These cycles can be virtuous or vicious. In virtuous cycles, certain decisions lead to good outcomes, which lead to good decisions, and onward from there. In vicious cycles, poor decisions lead to poor outcomes, which lead to poor decisions, and onward from there. If your speech deals with issues that move cyclically, whether at the level of the individual or the society at large, you might consider a circular pattern.
    - **Example**: In today's speech, I will discuss how smart micro-lending policies can not only empower women in rural communities but also prompt broader and more inclusive micro-lending in the years that follow initial investment.
- **Narrative pattern**: *ordering your main points as a story.* Some scholars argue that most of human communication is actually storytelling in action. Others have been so bold as to say that there are actually only a few types of stories in human experience that are simply told and retold with different characters and in different settings. Both of these viewpoints would lead us to believe that organizing our main points as a story makes great sense. Indeed, some speech topics are particularly suited for storytelling, including biographical speeches, stories of struggle with a disease, the growth of a movement, among others. If you select a narrative organization, be sure that your speech still has several main points rather than a single narrative; otherwise, you are likely to lose any real structure in your speech. And keep in mind that some topics can become trite and thereby flawed when told in a narrative form.
    - **Example**: The story of Helen Keller is quite popular but is actually more complex than you know. In this speech, I will share Keller's life story, not ending at her discovery of language but on her deathbed as an advocate for social and political change.

These four ordering patterns are not the totality of all ordering patterns you might use in your speech. In fact, many speakers identify particular ordering patterns of their own making that work quite well for specific topics and particular audiences. Therefore, you should not feel constrained by the ordering patterns above; rather you should feel assured that there are always certain ways of organizing your ideas that have been proven through time to be highly effective at your disposal.

Likewise, there are other patterns of ordering that are specific to particular kinds of speech goals. We will not address these ordering patterns here but will discuss them in depth in the speech-oriented chapters in Unit III.

Chapter 8

SPEAKING AND MEMORY

How do I remember what to say? For the novice public speaker, the question has almost certainly popped into your mind during your preparation for a speech. It's a good question: how we commit to memory the words and ideas we wish to express in our public speaking has been a concern since the very founding of the art form. In ancient times, where written languages were still in early development and the cost of parchment and ink was exorbitant, memory was an especially significant concern. Nor was it unusual during this time for speakers to be responsible for telling stories and giving speeches that were three, five, or eight *hours* long! It might seem impossible to us today, but speakers in the ancient world gave these long, complex speeches from memory regularly for centuries. This was made possible through the development of what they called the ***ars memoriae***—the arts of memory—*a system of mental tricks, maps, and other mnemonic devices that allowed for the compartmentalization and recall of complex ideas.* In fact, many of the people who you might know as having a great memory are likely not particularly gifted with profound memory skills; instead, they have simply spent significant time studying and practicing how to use their memories effectively in ways similar to how the ancients did.

Unlike the ancients, however, most of us today spend very little time working on our memory skills. It is a reflection of the fact that, over the last several centuries, we have developed significant and affordable tools that make recalling information much easier than it used to be—one of the most significant being the widespread adoption of the written word. As people acquired these easier routes for recalling (rather than retaining) information, our societies simply stopped valuing training in memory the way our ancestors did.

Public speaking, in its modern form, has also become far less reliant on the *ars memoriae.* Contemporary public speakers now have at their disposal an assortment of different tools and techniques that they can deploy in order to bring something to mind, to remind us of what we want to say, or to make our exact wording present to us in the moment of speaking. Not all of these memory tools are appropriate for every kind of speech or speech situation; instead, public speakers rely on different memory tools to help them achieve their goals in different speech situations. In this chapter, we will familiarize ourselves with these different memory systems so that you can bring them to bear on your next speech.

Impromptu Speaking and *Topoi*

One of the first kinds of speechmaking situations in which you might find yourself relying on memory skills is when you are asked to say a few words unexpectedly and on the spot, what we can impromptu speaking. **Impromptu speaking** refers to *giving a speech with little or no preparation.* It should come as no surprise that impromptu speaking is one of the forms of speaking and memory that new speakers are the most concerned about. Many people get anxiety even with days to prepare for an upcoming speech. When speakers are given no time to prepare at all, the anxiety can be even more immense. But impromptu speaking is a good skill for people to master. Realistically, few of us give long, prepared speeches on a regular basis; however, it is common for people to be asked to "say a few words" on the spot, whether they are about a project you've been working on at work or during a celebratory meal with friends. If you find yourself in one of these unexpected situations, you'll be much better off if you don't sweat it, take a deep breath, collect your thoughts, and then use one or all of these memory tools.

Speak on the Basics for a General Audience. Most people worry about impromptu speaking because they expect to be asked to speak about something intimidating and complex. But realistically, most people will not be asked to speak casually or off the cuff on a serious subject. More often, when you're asked to speak in an impromptu manner, your audience wants to know basic or elementary information about something you know much more about. If the audience wanted more than that, they would probably ask for a formal presentation. Or, they might ask you to elaborate more once you've given them a taste of the subject. Either way, delivering a short speech that offers basic details to a general audience will largely satisfy most impromptu speaking occasions.

Speak about Your Experience. One of the best tools for impromptu speaking is to focus your speech on what you know best: yourself. While you might not know a lot about a given topic, you almost always have your own impressions, run-ins, or opinions with that topic. What are your initial thoughts? Do you have experiences with the topic under discussion? If so, use yourself as a jumping off point from which to explore the topic with your audience.

Speak from the Heart. You've probably heard someone say something like this to a person who finds themselves caught unprepared to speak at an audience's request. It can be good advice. By speaking from the heart, we mean actively avoid fretting over eloquence and style in the moment. Instead, the speaker should just seek to answer the question or address the issue under discussion in an honest and authentic way. That might not always be easy to do. Speaking from the heart might mean we need to be vulnerable, exposed, or even demonstrate our ignorance of a subject. But if an audience perceives a speaker as trying to address the moment authentically on the spot, they're likely to give the speaker a great deal of latitude and even root for their success.

Use Common Topoi. Another tool for impromptu speakers dates back to the early formalization of speech education in ancient Greece. In his lectures on rhetoric, Aristotle codified the use of *topoi* (toe-poy) as an impromptu speaking tool. **Topoi** are best understood as *common lines of argument that a good speaker can go to that are applicable for almost any topic or subject matter.* In other words, by learning and remembering key topoi, a speaker should never be caught with nothing to say; rather, they can quickly apply their given topic to a common line of argument in the moment. Consider some of these key topoi that you might apply when speaking impromptu:

- **Possible/impossible**. Is the policy or event under discussion possible to do? Or is it impossible?
- **Cause and effect**. What caused this topic of discussion? Or what effect might it have if implemented or constrained?

- **Past fact/future fact.** Does our past experience with the topic of conversation tell us something about its current experience? About how we should handle these issues in the future?

Speech in Action: Topoi Races

As a class or in small groups, review the three common topoi described previously. Then break up the class into two teams. One team will be assigned the task of topic generation: the team will come up with as many general topics as possible and list them on the board as they do. Meanwhile, the other team will be assigned topoi generation: this team will try to produce a line of argument appropriate for each topic the first team places on the board. After a few minutes, the team can switch roles. Once both teams have gone, compare the percentages of each team: which team was able to generate the most number of arguments per topics on the board?

Extemporaneous Speaking and Outlines

By far, the most common way in which speakers engage their memory in public speaking is through extemporaneous speaking. **Extemporaneous speaking** is defined as *a speech delivered with preparation from a loose set of notes and ideas.* In other words, extemporaneous speaking asks the speaker to research a topic and share information and arguments with an audience in a relatively casual way. In 21st century U.S. cultures, extemporaneous speaking is often the most desirable form of speaking because it encourages speakers to be both an expert in their topic and relatively casual in their delivery. Contemporary U.S. audiences want to feel like they are hearing a speech from a real, relatable person in a format that resembles a conversation in tone. Extemporaneous speaking, with its combination of preparation and innovation, is the best method for hitting that mark.

Since extemporaneous speaking is considered the most desirable method of speaking in U.S. culture today—and as a result, in much of the Western professional world—nearly all of our speeches in this class are extemporaneous speeches. In fact, when in doubt, a speaker is probably safe in assuming that, if they are asked to speak or present, whether in a professional or personal setting, they are likely being asked to prepare an extemporaneous speech.

There are two particularly common memory tools for extemporaneous speaking, which you have probably engaged with at some point in your earlier academic career: outlines and notecards.

Outlines. An outline is a *written, page-sized document that organizes information and ideas for the delivery of an extemporaneous speech.* As we will see, an outline is different from a manuscript, which more closely approximates a speech in essay form. Rather an outline is a stylized representation of ideas, argument, and evidence that a speaker can dip in and out of over the course of a speech to deliver their address well.

All outlines have several common features. Any outline that is lacking these features is not an outline.

- **Section headers.** Clear and specific headers are given to every section of an outline to convey where each section begins and ends and what kind of content it includes. Common headers in a speech outline include "Introduction," "Body," and "Conclusion."
- **Points and sub-points.** Within each section of a speaking outline are numerous points and sub-points that need to be articulated by the speaker. Every successful outline includes multiple points or sub-points for each section. If you can only generate one point per section, it is likely the point you are trying to make is either underdeveloped or under-researched.

- **Coordinating numbers and letters**. To keep each point and sub-point distinct and easy to follow as a speaker who is giving a speech, every point needs to be designated with its own letter or number, all of which must correspond in the appropriate order. By convention, this system of coordination begins with Roman numerals (I, II, III...) for all your major sections headers. Then, each main point within each section should be marked with uppercase letters (A, B, C...). For sub-points, we return to numbers, this time with lowercase Roman numerals (i, ii, iii...) and then lower-case letters for sub-sub-points (a, b, c...). Again, it would be unusual for a successful outline to require a greater degree of depth than these four levels of coordination.

- **In-text citations and a Works Cited**. Both of which we discussed in Chapter 6.

While all of these dimensions are vital to an effective outline, it is also important to know that there are two common types of outlines that differ in important ways. The first is called a **preparation outline**, *an outline that includes a complete accounting of all the information the speaker wants to provide in his or her speech, in full and complete sentences*. The utility of a full-sentence preparation outline is it helps the speaker prepare their text and practice what they want to say in the course of giving a speech. The preparation outline—which details your thought process and research for your speech—is what you will turn in to your instructor. However, once a speaker has developed and fully practiced their speech, most speakers will move to a keyword outline. A **keyword outline** is *an abbreviated version of the preparation outline that includes key words, phrases, ideas, and evidence that can jog the speaker's mind and facilitates a truly extemporaneous speechmaking delivery*. In an ideal speech preparation, speakers would use both forms of outlines, starting with the preparation outline and moving to the keyword outline; however, speakers sometimes use only one or the other, often to problematic effect. Speakers who use the preparation outline to deliver their speech often end up overly reliant upon it, read too often, and suffer significantly in delivery and connecting with the audience. By contrast, speakers who only develop a keyword outline can often find themselves searching for words and expressions in their delivery, not completing their speech on time, and undermining their credibility and the perception of their research. As such, speakers are highly encouraged to use both forms of outlines during the complete speechmaking process. A side-by-side comparison of a preparation and keyword outline are available for review on Canvas.

While having the key components of a good outline is vital to speechmaking success, it is also important to use an outline effectively. When delivering a speech with an outline, remember to:

- **Use a large, readable font**. In particular, no outline should have font smaller than 14 points if the speaker wants to have any hope of reading it from a distance.

- **Keep your pages unstapled**. That way you can avoid the spectacle of turning a page, which is distracting both visually and audibly. Consider using a paperclip to keep your pages together instead.

- **Number your pages**. That way, they can easily be put in the proper order should you drop your outline by mistake.

- **Keep the outline on the podium**. Podiums are designed to hold outlines and provide speakers with the maximum use of their hands.

- **Don't fiddle with the pages**. Outlines can provide an easy object to fiddle with if a speaker becomes anxious; however, doing so can create noise that will undermine your speech.

Becoming an expert at creating an effective outline is a skill every public speaker needs to learn. To help you in the development of your preparation outline, you can refer to the course's Canvas site, which features sample outlines for each extemporaneous speech in the class. You should also review Dr. Carl Burgchardt's addendum on Canvas on *How to Create an Outline.*

Note Cards. Besides outlines, notecards are the other primary tools speakers use to deliver an extemporaneous speech. Just like outlines, notecards break up evidence, arguments, and claims in a structured way to facilitate the extemporaneous delivery of a speech. However, while outlines do this work on one or several pieces of standard size paper, a speaker using notecards breaks up their points so that each notecard represents a single idea within the speech. When the speaker has delivered an idea expressed on one note card, they turn to the next notecard to make an additional point. As such, a successful extemporaneous speech will consist of multiple notecards, typically in a stack that the speaker holds while speaking. Why use notecards? Proponents of notecards prefer them to outlines for several reasons, including that they are smaller and easier to hold, better permit the use of gestures, facilitate moving away from the podium, and keep a speaker focused on one idea in the speech at a time. In SPCM 200, students are welcome to use notecards to deliver their extemporaneous speeches; however, they must ***also*** produce and turn in a preparation outline in order to earn full points on their speech.

If you are considering using notecards for an upcoming speech, make sure to:

- **Write on your notecards clearly and legibly**. Otherwise, it might be difficult to read in the course of delivering a speech. You can either write on the notecards by hand or consider printing out text for each notecard and taping the text onto the card itself.

- **Number your cards in the proper order**. Since most speeches have more than 10 notecards, it can be easy in the course of a speech to mix up the cards and, therefore, present your speech out of order. Numbering your cards will make sure you can always put them back in proper order in a short amount of time.

- **Use smaller cards.** Notecards can come in large sizes as well as standard, smaller sizes. The small cards are preferable.

- **Use key words**. Notecards are designed to be small and discrete, so they do not provide much space for full sentences. As such, use key words on your notecards to present your information efficiently.

- **Keep notecards out of your face.** Just as with outlines, makes sure that your notecards do not become a distraction. Keep them down, don't let them block your face, and do not fiddle with them!

While everyone in SPCM200 must submit a preparation outline to their instructor, you can choose whether you prefer to use keyword outlines or notecards for your memory aid. You might try different ones for different speeches to see which one works better for you. Whatever your preference, you should create them based off the preparation outline. Read your preparation outline several times before creating your keyword outline or notecards. Practice with your memory tools and be aware that you might need to add more key words or take some away to make your notes more effective. Creating several drafts of speaking notes will help you figure out what works best for you as a speaker.

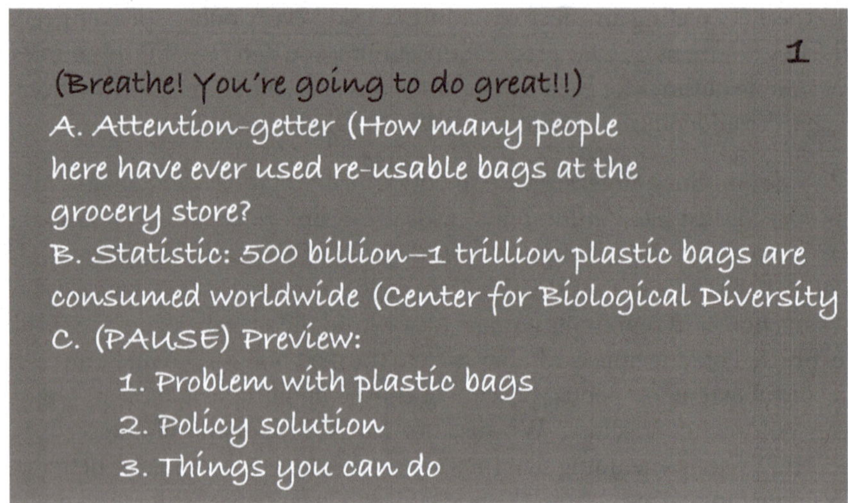

Figure 8-1. Example of a Well-Written Notecard

Manuscript Speaking and Other Prepared Texts

The final area in which we must prepare our memory to speak is manuscript speaking. **Manuscript speaking** consists of *delivering a speech from a text that is written out word for word in advance.* While manuscript speaking might sound like simply reading a speech aloud, it is actually something quite different (see the distinction between oral and written style in Chapter 3). In fact, when you speak from a manuscript, it is even more important that you look up, make eye contact with the audience, and deliver your speech with zeal; otherwise, a manuscript speech is almost guaranteed to bore your audience. But if the risk is so high, why use a manuscript? While there might be several reasons to use a manuscript, the most meaningful is that the speech is so important, vital, or consequential that every single word needs to be accounted for.

In the popular imagination, the most common way in which audiences encounter a manuscript speech is when we listen to a prepared speech by the U.S. President or other world leaders. To be sure, not every speech a world leader delivers qualifies as manuscript speaking; in fact, "speaking from a teleprompter" has recently become a popular way to attack politicians on the campaign trail in the United States for being inauthentic. But, for particular kinds of speeches—think the State of the Union address or a speech at the United Nations—all presidents resort to the power of manuscript speaking. And that just makes sense. When the words of powerful people in the world can ignite wars, betray state secrets, or start a worldwide economic downturn, every single word matters, and manuscript speaking is the most surefire way to make sure every single word is just right.

To most novice speakers, manuscript speaking might appear to be the easiest way of remembering your prepared remarks. After all, all the words you will need are literally right in front of you! However, speaking from a manuscript can actually be quite challenging, particularly for speakers who do not have a lot of experience doing so and in cultures in which a more casual speaking style is often favored. An ill-prepared manuscript speaker might sound robotic, disingenuous, or disinterested in their topic or audience. But a practiced manuscript speaker can often do just the opposite. Armed with a well-conceived text, a manuscript speaker can move their audience with eloquence, tackle complex issues with poise, and rouse a crowd with a dynamic oration. However, to succeed with a manuscript speech, a speaker needs to harness several memory tools to their advantage.

Preparation in Writing. Unlike an impromptu speech or even an extemporaneous speech, a manuscript speech cannot be put together successfully without lots of good preparation. Indeed, preparing a manuscript for a speech is much like writing a paper: since the speaker will say every word that is written down, each word must be the best word for conveying the intended meaning with clarity and decorum. In an impromptu or extemporaneous speech, a weak portion of an outline can be made up for in the moment; but in a manuscript speech, deviating from prepared remarks is rare. Therefore, it pays to get it right with lots of preparation.

Practice, Practice, Practice. Practice is, of course, necessary for all good speaking. Yet, with manuscript speaking, practice takes on a different meaning. It becomes less about knowing your content so well that you can speak relatively off the cuff; rather, practicing a manuscript speech is like rehearsing for a play. To be successful, you need to know your lines inside and out so that you can deliver them correctly and give a performance that feels to the audience like you are sharing it with them in the moment.

Oral Style. As we discussed in Chapter 3, there is a major difference between reading and speaking. Since manuscript speaking is a form of reading aloud, it is critical the speaker prepare her manuscript for that purpose. That means that even though the document is written, it should be more casual and conversational in tone, rely more extensively on repetition, and provide greater ways of citing sources orally, among others.

The Manuscript Itself. Just like an outline is a tool for extemporaneous speaking, a manuscript—often on paper—can be designed and formatted to help the speaker succeed at their rhetorical undertaking. How, then, might you design a manuscript in order help you succeed? Consider:

- **Font size**. Since you will be reading word for word, make sure you can comfortably see and read the text. In particular, ask: will I be able to see the text clearly enough if it is placed on a podium two feet away from my eyes? As a general rule, when preparing a manuscript on 8½ × 11 paper, the text should be no smaller than 14 pts.
- **Numbered pages**. Manuscripts almost always have multiple pages, so it is important to number each page.
- **Phonetic spellings**. If your manuscript will contain words that you are not comfortable saying correctly, consider noting the phonetic spelling of that word in parenthesis near the actual word.
- **Delivery notes**. Remind yourself in the manuscript to continue to pay attention to delivery. For example, you might remind yourself to "pause" during a particularly dramatic section of the speech. Or, you might tell yourself to "look up" at the end of a page to connect with your audience. Make sure to put delivery notes in your manuscript somewhere where they won't be misconstrued as part of your speech text (you might, for example, put them in italics or in the margins of your document like stage directions in a play).
- **Identify stylistic devices**. In SPCM 200, you are required to identify your stylistic devices in your manuscript text to demonstrate your intention to use style appropriately in your speech (for more on stylistic devices, see the next chapter in this book). The easiest way to do this is with a parenthetic reference. As opposed to a parenthetical reference for citing sources, using a parenthetical reference to identify a stylistic device should simply state the types of stylistic device inside parenthesis immediately following its usage in the text. For example, a use of parallelism would be identified by (parallelism) in text. For further examples, see the sample preparation outlines for the Commemorative speech on Canvas.

Teleprompters. A relatively rare tool public speakers use to deliver a manuscript speech is a teleprompter. **Teleprompters** are *screens positioned near a speaker but out of sight of the audience that scroll through the speech text as the speaker delivers their address*. These digital tools are commonly used by politicians and newscasters but are expensive investments for most public speakers. They can also create their own problems. For example, President Bill Clinton once delivered 40 minutes of a State of the Union address from memory because an aide loaded the wrong speech into his teleprompter! However, in high stakes, professional settings, a teleprompter can be a useful tool for a speaker who needs to give a long speech with confidence and aplomb.

These various methods of using memory in the execution of a great public speech are wonderful resources for today's public speakers. While we may no longer rely on the *ars memoriae* to underpin our own speech success, it should be clear to us that memory remains a vital aspect of speechmaking that we cannot ignore.

Chapter 9

SPEAKING, STYLE, AND LANGUAGE

What do we mean when we tell someone, "I like your style"? Typically, we are referring to another person's manner, choice, or approach to the world. And while we most often use the word "style" today to refer to the way people dress, style is also a term with significant meaning in public speaking. Indeed, the choices we make about the manner of our speech often tell an audience much more about us and what we want to achieve than the aesthetics of our appearance.

In public speaking, **style** refers to *the ways in which a speaker uses language to advance their message.* It is one of the two ways in which we often describe how a person speaks in forms of public address: delivery, as we will see in the next chapter, refers to how we speak using our body, while style refers to how we speak using our words through language. You might be thinking: doesn't organization or topic selection or even memory also involve our use of words? Absolutely. Organization involves the arrangement of words, topic selection is often achieved through listing and considering different words, and memory is about knowing our words well. But in a meaningful way, style is about a very different focus on words: how the selection of different words conveys different meanings and different understandings about the speech situation.

Language and Style

To better appreciate the importance of style, we need to better appreciate how language works. For many novice public speakers, language is a relatively simple term referring to the particular national or ethnic language we speak in our homes, our schools, or at work (i.e., English, Chinese, Spanish, etc.). Yet while this is by far the most colloquial understanding of language today, language is also so much more.

Language *should be understood as one of the most prevalent symbolic systems human beings use to create and share meaning about their world and, ultimately, to change it.* Embedded in this definition are some key concepts that we need to unpack to fully appreciate the power of language:

- **Languages are systems.** Just like other forms of systems—transportation systems, electrical systems, political systems—language is a complex web of activity guided by knowledge, rules, expectations, and interactions. To successfully use this system, you need to be well-versed in the many aspects of the system. Think about transportation systems as a metaphor. If you want to ride the public transit system from your home to school, you need to know where to pick up the bus, how much your fare will cost, when and to whom you pay that fare, where to transfer within that system, and ultimately how to get off at the right spot. Similarly, to use language you need to know which language rules are in effect in your location, what other expectations about language are present in that setting, how to use language to meet or disrupt those expectations, and on and on. When thinking about the systemic elements of language, we might need to know things like proper grammar and spelling, rules for addressing others, how to order words though syntax or to make them fit together correctly through conjugations, among countless others.

- **Languages are symbolic systems**. Symbols are one of the primary aspects of what makes up language systems. By **symbols** we mean *written, spoken, or visual representations that stand in for or represent something else.* The most common symbols in language systems are words. While we use words every day, most of us don't spend much time thinking about what words actually are. On one hand, words can be quite insignificant. Anyone who has spent time with a young child speaking gibberish knows that simply stringing together a bunch of sounds or letters only creates babble and babble is of little use to other people in the world. We simply can't do anything with a child's babbling other than laugh at it and think it is cute or funny.

  On the other hand, when letters and sounds are strung together in a meaningful way (i.e., in a way that makes sense to another person) words can become extremely useful. To understand how language works to make meaning between people, we need to understand what C. K. Ogden and I. A. Richards called the **semantic triangle of meaning** (Figure 9-1). The semantic triangle of meaning challenges the idea that words have fixed and easily defined meanings. Rather, it argues that the meaning of a word in language is fluid and based in the "the relations of words to ideas and of ideas to things."[27] As Figure 9-1 shows, meaning is actually made in language when one person uses a word (or "**symbol**") that represents a **thought** about a thing that exists in the world (or "**referent**"). For example, if I pointed to furry, brown, four-legged animal (i.e., the referent) and said the word "dog" (i.e., symbol), the word "dog" only has meaning if you hear the word and in your mind imagine something similar to the furry, brown, four-legged animal I intended (i.e., thought). When people's symbols, referents, and thoughts are closely aligned, language can then become a powerful basis for communicating about the world.

  Yet, while language is an excellent way to build meaning between people through symbols, it is not a perfect system. In fact, when I say the word "dog," you probably pictured a very particular breed of dog that was familiar to you—a breed that is probably different than the one to which I was referring. For me, "dog" might bring to mind the thought of a Chihuahua while for you "dog" might signify a German Shepard. Neither of us is wrong in that case; both a Chihuahua and a German Shepard are, in fact, "dogs." And depending on what we're talking about this minor difference in meaning may not matter. If, for instance, I say "I love dogs, don't you?" it probably does not matter what type of dog each of us is imagining in order to produce meaningful conversation. If, on the other hand, I said "I love bringing my dog on an airplane when I travel, don't you?" the fact that we were imagining very different types of dogs does matter a great deal. In this case, the imprecision of meaning inherent in the symbolic use of language is problematic; in fact, it will probably lead to confusion, misinterpretation, and the need to clarify our symbol's meanings with each other before we can continue the conversation. Simply put, language is an imperfect system of communication. As such, when our words convey meaning between people, they become the foundation for conversations, debates, and public speaking; when, on the contrary, people do not share the same meaning for a particular word, it becomes difficult for us to communicate with each other about the thing in question.

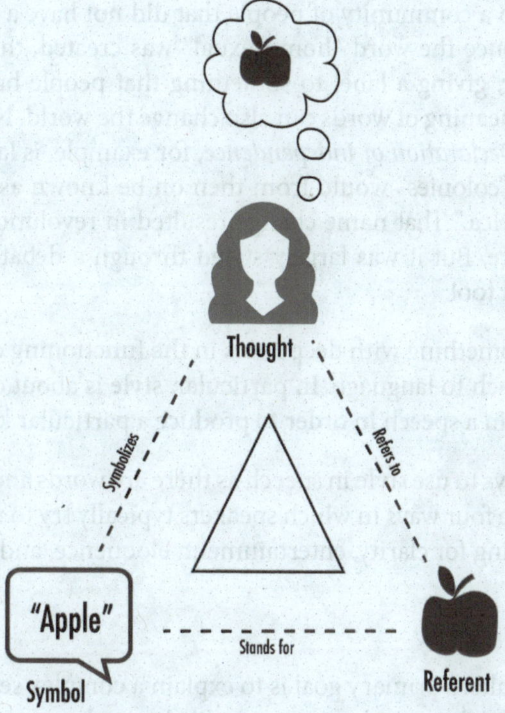

Figure 9-1. The Semantic Triangle of Meaning

- **Language is used to create and share meaning about our world.** In its more sophisticated form, language is not simply about having one or two symbols in common that two people can point at; rather, language is about millions of people sharing billions of words in common. With these many shared symbols, people can do amazing work together as groups, families, societies, and cultures. In fact, our communal forms of relating to each other are only possible thanks to language. Without language, it would be difficult to imagine people doing too many sophisticated tasks together. By contrast, with a rich and deeply shared set of words and a system for regulating how those words are made and processed, people actually build the world in which we live. Shared symbolic systems make it possible to call ourselves "Americans" or "Chinese"; shared symbolic systems allow us to think of ourselves as "educated" or "hardworking." Indeed, all our religions, laws, cultures, values, and social lives require language systems. In other words, as stated in the famous theories of Kenneth Burke, human beings live a world made of their own symbolic language.[28]
- **Language is used to change the world.** Because we live in a world created and sustained by shared understandings of word and language, we can then use language to change the world in which we live. It is this belief that is at the very core of public speaking: through language, we can move people to think and create the world differently than it currently exists. There are numerous different ways in which we use language to change the world. Sometimes that act is as simple as saying the right words at the right time. J.L. Austin, for example, demonstrated how two people can change the very nature of their relationship by simply saying the words "I do" during a wedding ceremony.[29] Other times, we use language to change the world by creating new words, for good or bad purposes. Think, for instance, about how different labels for communities of people can radically shift our societies. The scholar Michel Foucault shows, for example, that the word "homosexual" was created in English for the first time in the late

1800s, giving a name to a community of people that did not have a word to identify them previously. Interestingly, once the word "homosexual" was created, the word "heterosexual" was created soon thereafter, giving a label to something that people had rarely thought of previously.[30] Changing the meaning of words can also change the world. Names are particularly good examples of this. The *Declaration of Independence*, for example, is largely a long explanation of how the 13 American "colonies" would from then on be known as a "nation," later called the "United States of America." That name change resulted in revolution, war, death, destruction, victory, and much more. But it was largely stated through a debate about a word. Language, then, can be a powerful tool.

While language is clearly something with deep roots in the functioning of all human societies, style is about a particular approach to language. In particular, style is about choosing the most effective word, term, or set of terms in a speech in order to produce a particular kind of change in the world.

While there are as many ways to use style in speech as there are words and symbols in our languages, in public speaking, there are four ways in which speakers typically try to use language in order to advance their message: speaking for clarity, entertainment, eloquence, and inclusion and affirmation.

Speaking for Clarity

In many cases, a public speaker's primary goal is to explain a complex set of ideas or information to an audience. In those cases, public speakers are most likely to rely on speaking for clarity to achieve their goal. **Speaking for clarity** is *a style of speech in which the speaker uses simple words, basic sentence structure, and ample definitions in order to teach the audience about something they do not know.*

Common situations in which a speaker might need to speak for clarity include:

- A college lecturer introducing a new theory to their class
- A military leader briefing his commanding officer on the current battlefield situation
- A manager explaining a new corporate strategy to their team

Because speaking for clarity is all about speaking simply and understandably to an audience, many novice public speakers wrongly assume that it does not involve any style; however, it is a *choice* to use little extravagance or detail in a speech, just as it is a choice to use excessive stylistic devices. Therefore, speaking for clarity is just as much a style choice as any other speaking style.

While speaking for clarity is generally marked by the absence of tropes and figures common in other styles of speaking, there are some terms we should keep in mind if we want to teach, explain, or inform.

- **Definition.** One of the most important tools for speaking for clarity is definition—the act of explaining each significant term in the course of a speech in order to make sure it is understood in the same way by everyone in the audience. If our goal as speaker is to inform, then making sure our audience shares common definitions is crucial to our task. As speakers, we should be sure that we not only define complex and new terms for our audience, but also that we define terms that our audience might think everyone understands in the same way, but that in reality, may have many different meanings or interpretations. Refer back to Chapter 5 for more on definition.

- **Directness**. Speaking for clarity also involves directness or speaking to the point at hand without evasion or digression. A direct speaker gets to the point without haste and has no time for diversions or undue complexity.
- **Simplicity**. When a speaker speaks for clarity, they keep things simple. They use simple words, use simple sentence structure, and explain ideas and concepts in simple terms.

Speaking for Entertainment

While many novice speakers are focused on clarity in their speechmaking, we should not ignore another vital and power speaking style: entertainment. **Speaking for entertainment** is *a speaking style that uses complex word play and ambiguity in order to give an audience a sense of joy.* In some ways, speaking for entertainment is one of the oldest traditions of public speaking. Indeed, in the ancient world—long before cell phones, movies, and streaming services—it was common for audiences to gather in fields, halls, and amphitheaters to listen as great speakers delivered speeches that were clever, frightening, or hilarious. While today new art forms have come into being whose major aim is to entertain, there are still numerous occasions and events in which a public speaker might choose to use an entertaining style. Consider:

- A wedding toast, where the speaker not only wants to be heartfelt but also funny
- An end-of-the-year address at a formal dinner or company picnic, where the boss wants to not only say "thank you" but do so while putting a smile on everyone's face
- A roast on the retirement of a colleague, where funny and tongue-in-cheek speeches are the expectation

We should also note that speaking for entertainment is not limited to events where our primary aim is to entertain. Rather, speakers who are trying to inform or persuade their audience will also find that humor, storytelling, and sarcasm can be powerful speaking tools in achieving these non-entertainment-focused goals.

Speakers who wish to entertain their audience through their speaking style may rely on any number of tropes and figures in order to do so; however, some of the most common include:

- **Ambiguity**. We often think of ambiguity—*the undefined, unclear, a vague description of a situation*—as a problem in language. In many cases, we are urged to be precise, specific, and as we saw above, clear. But when trying to entertain an audience, ambiguity can be a valuable stylistic tool. In particular, ambiguity is essential to being funny. Much of how humor works is about leaving out information or misleading an audience's expectation before ultimately clarifying the situation in a surprising way. A speaker can ruin a perfectly good joke, for example, by being too forthright and stepping on the punch line. As such, thoughtful ambiguity can be a powerful tool in making our audience laugh.
- **Irony**. Like ambiguity, irony is also used by speakers to entertain by playing with the audience's understanding and interpretation of the situation. Irony is *a trope in which the speaker implies a meaning different or opposite of the literal meaning.*[31] Unlike ambiguity, where meanings are kept vague, irony is clear about its meaning—only that meaning is quite unexpected. Another way to think about irony is that it is a tongue-in-cheek expression of an idea: the saying of something we don't mean for entertaining effect. In public speaking, its value lies in cleverness, mild put downs for humorous effect, and, in some cases, calling out hypocrisy. An example of irony might be when, in the middle of a tropical storm, someone says "What nice weather we're having!"

- **Self-deprecation**. One of the greatest friends of the public speaker seeking to be entertaining is what we call self-deprecation. Self-deprecation refers to *the mocking or poking fun at oneself in order to make a larger entertaining commentary about the world.* A self-deprecating public speaker is highly self-aware and confident in themselves, so much so that they are comfortable being the butt of a joke in front of their audience. However, this vulnerability reveals the power of self-deprecation. On one hand, the power comes from the fact that if it is the speaker who is making fun of themselves, they still retain all the power over that humor (hence, it stays safe). On the other hand, by focusing the ridicule at oneself, the speaker avoids mocking the audience (and all the risk that comes with it), while still being able to make a broader point about people, the community, or society at large.

A final note about speaking for entertainment: it is an old adage in public speaking that you can't go wrong by starting with a joke. This is horrible advice. Know yourself and your strengths as a speaker. If you are a funny person, start with a joke. If you don't come off as particularly funny, stay away from joke telling and use an assortment of other tropes and figures to your advantage.

Speaking for Eloquence

Perhaps the most familiar kind of style in speechmaking is speaking for eloquence. While speech and eloquence are often misunderstood as synonyms, eloquence is actually a very particular kind of speaking style. **Eloquence** can be understood as *a style of speaking in which the speaker uses beautiful, poetic, and complex language in order to inspire the audience to action.* This inspirational quality is often deeply connected to the immediate goals of a speech. In particular, eloquence is frequently used in order to ask the audience to take a difficult action and to risk much in service of something other than themselves. In this way, eloquence is not for small things, but the big and important events of each of our lives.

Some classic examples of speaking for eloquence include:

- A politician urging voters to the polls
- A president preparing her country for war
- A religious leader urging his followers to believe and have faith

The list of tropes and figures at the disposal of someone speaking for eloquence is vast; however, for our purposes in this class, we should know these terms for sure:

- **Metaphor**. A metaphor is *a comparison between two things with similar qualities in order to explain or simplify one of those things.* Winston Churchill provides a good example of a metaphor when he describes the complex geopolitical occupation of Eastern Europe by the Soviet Union by saying "an iron curtain has descended across the continent." Because metaphors are often used to explain something complex, you might think of metaphors as key to speaking for clarity as well as speaking for eloquence. However, when metaphors are used numerous times in a single speech or form the foundation to how a speech unfolds, they are more likely to be at work in the search for eloquence rather than clarity.

- **Simile**. Closely aligned with metaphors are similes. Similes are *another form of comparison between two distinct things, this time with the explicit use of the words "like" or "as."* By using "like" or "as" in a simile, a speaker is avoiding a gentle or understated comparison; rather, the speaker wants the audience to know that they are making an explicit and direct connection between two things. An example of a simile might be, "Exercise is like brushing your teeth; you have to do it every day in order to stay healthy." While both metaphors and similes are powerful stylistic tools, speakers must take care that they are comparing things with actual shared qualities; otherwise, they might find themselves making a false equivalency that is unethical.

- **Alliteration**. Alliteration is *the repetition of an initial sound across a set of words in a sentence.* This trope is easy to see in tongue-twisters like "She sells sea shells down by the sea shore." By intentionally repeating this sound in a condensed and compact sentence, alliteration aids the speaker by (re-)gaining the audience's attention and making a statement of emphasis.
- **Parallelism**. While alliteration is the repetition of a particular sound in a single sentence, parallelism is *the repetition of a particular wording across multiple, adjacent sentences.* When done well, parallelism can give a speech a particular cadence or rhythm that is particularly noticeable. That cadence can also be a tool for attention or emphasis; in addition, it can also serve to build the speaker's point, like an argument building to a conclusion.

Speaking for Inclusion and Affirmation

A final goal of public speaking that can be immensely improved with the right style is speaking for inclusion and affirmation. By this, we mean *speaking in a way that makes all the members of our diverse, pluralistic audience feel acknowledged, welcomed, and valued by the speaker.* Speaking for inclusion and affirmation is highly related to speaking across difference, which we discussed in Chapter 2. Some students easily confuse speaking for inclusion and affirmation with being politically correct, but the truth is that all effective public speakers must speak with a degree of inclusion and affirmation if they want to be successful. As we have already discussed, our audiences are complex with many forms of visible and invisible difference. Therefore, if the goal of our speech is to get the audience on our side, aggravating or attacking our audience by being divisive, narrow-minded, or making false assumptions is simply counterproductive. Frankly, a speech that offends part or all of an audience will more likely than not be ineffective.

With the goal of speaking for inclusion and affirmation in mind, speakers will want to make a series of stylistic choices, including:

Avoid Offensive Terms, Names, and Phrases. The English language is rife with old words and phrases that are meant to hurt, attack, or cause violence toward other people and communities. These words can be racist, derived from centuries of slavery, segregation, and faux-scientific terms; they can be anti-Semitic or anti-Muslim; they can be sexist and misogynist, passed down in both formal or informal conversations; they be classist, anti-military, anti-immigrant, homophobic, anti-trans, ageist, or contain any number of discriminatory feelings or activities. As a society, many of us know these terms as soon as we see or hear them and actively avoid them. Sometimes, however, these terms are more colloquial or implicit, containing the seeds of discrimination that we did not even know about until it was explained to us. An excellent example is seen in recent debates about the Washington NFL Team, the Redskins—a name that is derogatory to Native Americans yet has been used without much real thought or intent by fans for decades. As public speakers, our job is not to ignore these words or make believe they do not exist. Neither is it the role of the public speaker to spread these words or the anti-person language they contain. As public speakers, we choose our words wisely, respect all people as people—even if we disagree with them—and avoid the words that keep our society locked in the prejudices of the past.

Avoid Social Justice Elitism. At the same time public speakers must avoid offensive terms, we must also avoid the elite use of terminology around the work of social justice. **Social justice**—*the struggle for equal treatment for all people across all kinds of difference*—is a worthy cause, one that Colorado State University holds as central to its *Principles of Community*. However, sometimes *in our efforts to show how open-minded and committed to justice we are, speakers can pack their speeches with highly selective, overly-complex, and unexplained terms about social justice.* We call this practice **social justice elitism**. A good example of social justice elitism is a speaker who advocates for LGBT rights to an audience with little knowledge or interaction with the LGBT community by saying: "In troubling gender and sampling the spectrum of sexual identity, I became a strong advocate for those who identity as cis-, trans-, questioning, queer, gender non-conforming, and those who practice polyamory." There is nothing wrong with the content of the speaker's words; nor is the speaker's claim contrary to the work of social justice. Nonetheless, the speaker choice to use these advanced social justice terms with this particular audience is problematic. In this example, the speaker might feel good about themselves for their advanced vocabulary in this realm of social justice work; however, the audience might simultaneously find themselves lost, confused, or even hostile to the ideas of social justice because none of these terms were explained to them by the speaker. Indeed, the choice to *not* define these terms for this audience could be interpreted as a slight by the speaker, implicitly denigrating the audience for not knowing as much as the speaker from the outset. Simply put, this is counterproductive. Therefore, as speakers, we hold a joint responsibility in the struggle for social justice: avoid offense *and* avoid elitism that willfully disinvites others from the work of making the world a better place.

Use Gender-Neutral Language. A good hallmark of a speech for inclusion and affirmation is the presence of gender-neutral language. By using gender-neutral language, *a speaker intentionally uses a diverse set of differently gendered or gender-less pronouns, phrases, and examples to make their claims.* A classic example of moving from gender-exclusive to gender-neutral in speech is to use the term "humankind" instead of "mankind." The idea behind gender-neutral language is simple: in the English language, we have long relied on terms and expressions that suggest women and gender non-conforming people are unable or incapable of being powerful and important individuals in our public life. By rooting out and removing that gendered-language, we show that we understand our world is impacted by many different kinds of people and we invite those people to join us in our rhetorical endeavor.

Use Ability-Inclusive Language. In addition, public speakers should be sure to avoid ableist language in their speeches. **Ableist language** describes *words or phrases that consciously or unconsciously disparage people with disabilities.* A term like "stand up for yourself" is a good example of ableist language because it relies on a physical act a person in a wheelchair, for example, might not be able to complete to signify what is "right" or "valuable." Like gendered language, ableist language is a remnant of a time when only certain kinds of people were invited to be a part of our public lives. Instead of ableist language, we want to use **ability-inclusive language**—*words and phrases that do not discriminate on the basis of ability*—in our speeches. In academia, the move from "blind review" to "anonymous review" is a good example of the transition to ability-inclusive language.

Use Community-Preferred Terminology. It is also valuable for public speakers to use community-preferred terminology. Using community-preferred terminology simply means *referring to people or communities that may be different from you by the names or terms that that community has identified as acceptable or preferred.* As we now know, the terms communities use to talk about themselves are powerful and U.S. culture in particular has long used terms to ridicule, mock, and discriminate against certain communities of people. As speakers we don't want to propagate the latter and should empower others to refer to themselves as they see fit. Community-preferred naming can be a challenge as a public speaker because the preferred terminology of different communities has changed rapidly as our society has become more diverse. However, a good practice is to use the term that members of a community use in their own speeches to refer to themselves (as long as that term is not controversial). It is also important to listen; only by paying attention to others' self-description can we be sure we are addressing them as they want to be addressed. For some examples of current community-preferred terminology, see the chart below.

Use Preferred Names and Pronouns. A good public speaker in the 21st century will always recognize that individuals have the right as human beings to be called and referred to by the names that they choose. This is basic manners: would you ever respond well to someone who called you by a name that was not your own? Choosing to abide by the naming conventions of people is a way to show respect for other people. In public speaking, this expectation means the public speaker should take several steps if they will be speaking about or to someone in their speech, including: 1. Being aware that names and pronouns are fluid and not always obvious, 2. Asking politely and without judgment how a person would like to be referred to in a speech (or researching this question if speaking about someone you don't know personally) and, 3. Following through by using the name and pronouns expressed by the person in question.

Examples of Community-Preferred Terminology

The terminology we use to refer to people of different communities in a pluralistic society is important and constantly changing. As a member of our pluralistic society, it will be important for you not to rely on terms you grew up with (for better or worse), but to be constantly mindful of the changing nature of appropriate forms of address. With this limitation in mind, the following are some examples of acceptable community-preferred terminology, partially produced by Kathy Castania and promoted by the Anti-Defamation League. See "The Evolving Language of Diversity," Cornell Cooperative Extension, 2003, https://www.adl.org/sites/default/files/documents/Evolving-Language-of-Diversity-The.pdf.

African American or Black

Asian American/Pacific Islanders (or more specific national iterations such as Japanese American, Chinese American, Korean American, Indian American, etc.)

European American (or more specific national iterations such as Irish American, German American, Polish American, etc.)

Latina(o)(x) or Chicana(o) or Hispanic (or more specific national iterations such as Mexican American, Colombian American, Cuban American, etc.)

Native American, Indian American, First Nation, or Indian (or a more specific national iterations such as Cherokee, Navaho, Pueblo, etc.)

Person or People of Color

White people or person

Differently abled or person with a disability

Young person or people

Older person or people or elders

LGBTQ community (additional letters that represent different parts of the community are included and excluded at different times for precision and inclusivity)

Gay (man, woman, person, or community)

Lesbian (or lesbian community)

Bisexual (man, woman, person, or community)

Straight or heterosexual

Transgender

Cisgender

Gender non-conforming

Working Class

Middle Class

Wealthy

Person or people of faith (or more specific faith iterations such as Christian, Hindu, Muslim, etc.)

People experiencing homelessness

People without documents

Chapter 10

DELIVERING A SPEECH

In September 2010, Phil Davison—a former council member and deputy mayor for the city of Minerva, Ohio—became famous for a reason most public speakers fear: the absolutely horrible delivery of a speech. Davison was speaking before a meeting of the Stark County Republican Party of Ohio where he sought the position of Country Treasurer. In the speech, Davison wanted to convey his passion, enthusiasm, and genuine excitement for his candidacy and what he thought he could do for the county…but, in doing so, he let his poor delivery get the better of him. Instead of speaking with power, his speech appeared more as a man yelling and screaming. Instead of showing himself to be reasonable and someone meriting the support of his party, his erratic pacing and confused facial expressions suggested just the opposite. Instead of a speech that conveyed confidence and preparation to lead, Davison's delivery threw off both the audience and himself. In fact, he got so frazzled by his own out of control delivery that he lost his place in the speech, made a number of grammatical mistakes, and even yelped out in frustration. All of this is a shame because, if we look at Davison's speech as an outline, it is actually a pretty strong speech. But, ultimately, Davison's well-written and well-prepared speech was undone by his poor preparation in the area of delivery.

By **delivery**, we mean *how a speaker uses their body to emphasize or enhance the words of their speech.* It is often talked about as the execution of a speech, the bringing of a prepared outline or manuscript to life in the moment. However, delivery is best understood as two sides of the same coin. On one side, delivery can be a form of *emphasis*. Much like *italics*, underlining, or **bolding** in text, delivery is a means by which the speaker can draw greater attention to a particular facet of their speech. As such, the rising volume of the voice, the quickening of rate as the evidence piles up, the unexpected silence just before the revelation of a shocking fact: all of these are embodied versions of emphasis made possible by delivery. On the other side of the coin, however, delivery can be a form of *distraction*. When delivery is done poorly without much thought or attention, it can draw the audience's focus away from the speaker's major point, undermine her credibility, or challenge his authority. Much like with Phil Davison as mentioned above, beautiful words or careful research can be completely wasted by a speaker who turns speech into yelling, gestures into erratic swatting, or takes eye contact from genuine to creepy. As an audience member, how could you possibly focus on what a speaker is trying to say when the delivery is so overwhelming? As such, good delivery is less about having it or not; instead, it is about finding just the right amount of delivery for your speech and doing it effectively.

Because it is the most visible part of public speaking, delivery also happens to be the most angst-inducing part of the public speaking process. Novice speakers in particular tend to be worried about their delivery to an extraordinary degree—Will I sound nasally? What if I stutter? How will I look if my knees are shaking? Given our previous discussion, it is only natural that a speaker who wants to succeed would have some concerns about their delivery. Yet, despite this perception among new speakers, it is not an accident that delivery is Chapter 10 in this book. That is because, while many first-time speakers put delivery at the top of their list of concerns in public speaking, we know that it should actually be less disconcerting for most people. In reality, delivery is just one component of the process, can be managed well with practice, and—in the context of the United States—is often less formal than we might presume. Putting delivery in perspective, then, and helping speakers to deliver great speeches is the aim of this chapter.

The Body and Public Speaking

To better understand public speaking and our anxieties about delivery, we need to start with the source of delivery in public speaking: the body. While bodies are something we all have as human beings, our understandings, experiences, and use of the body can be quite different. Therefore, before we go any further, let's set some ground rules for thinking together about the body in public speaking. In particular, we need to remember three things:

First, delivery is a full-body experience. As described above, the body is the chief vehicle through which we deliver our speech. While this certainly makes sense in the context of the role our eyes play in making eye contact or way our hands work making hand gestures, it is also true that our bodies play a key role in less obvious aspects of delivery like the volume or rate of our voice. Indeed, to do delivery successfully, we need to avoid thinking of our bodies as simply the surface or canvas on which we see delivery; rather, great public speakers recognize that their whole bodies are also instruments that perform the delivery of a speech, on the inside and outside. As such, when we think about the role of the body in delivery, we need to keep in mind that it is a full body experience that includes not just our hands and eyes but also our lungs, our heart, our diaphragm, our feet, our blood flow, and much, much more.

Second, we are more than our bodies. Philosophers, scientists, and faith leaders have debated this topic for centuries, but many seem to be in agreement: our bodies do not fully—or even nearly—constitute the full person. Whether you want to think of our personalities, our ideas and thoughts, or our relationships with others, most people recognize that the human experience is only partly dictated by our bodies. However, particularly in the 21st century, the body has taken up an undue amount of space in our culture, conversations, and sense of self. At a cultural level, we obsess about our bodies: our looks, our clothing, our hair, our weight. Nor are we simply concerned with how we see our bodies; how others see our bodies preoccupies a great deal of our time. And while bodies do matter, our preoccupation with the body has become unhealthy, generating calls for changes in our advertising, our representations, our policies, and even our values. Given all this, it should not be surprising that delivery in public speaking causes some undue stress: it is just another example of how our bodies are put on display for others. However, while our ideas about bodies may give us psause, we need to know that an effective delivery is not about fashion, weight, hair, skin, or looks. Rather, it is about using our bodies to emphasize our ideas, our arguments, our evidence, and our convictions. So, in this chapter, yes, we will be talking about bodies. But always remember: just how your body only represents a small percentage of all the amazing, interesting, and complex things that do constitute you, your delivery only represents a percentage of you as a great public speaker.

Third, different bodies love different approaches to delivery. As a final point, we need to acknowledge something that science, culture, and society often ignores: there are many different kinds of bodies in this world. And that's great! Tall, short, large, small, thin, heavy, round, narrow, conventionally abled, and differently abled: no body is alike. Moreover, because nobody is exactly like every other body in the world, there can be no hard and fast rules for using our bodies effectively in delivery. In the history of public speaking, we have not always followed this rule. We treated bodies as if they were all regimented and that they could be choreographed in a single way to produce a universally-recognized meaning. But we soon found that was folly: the diversity of human bodies is numerous and amazing ideas and great speeches have never been limited to any particular body type, regardless of what we might have told ourselves. That said: there are expectations about delivery that most people should keep in mind when they give a speech—not because they are iron-clad law, but because they have some general application to large numbers of speakers. However, each and every speaker needs to make choices about their delivery that make sense for them. As such, the general rules we will examine in this chapter are simply a menu of options that each of us will have to select from smartly in order to fit our own speeches and our own bodies.

With these ground rules established, let's look at the various ways in which our bodies interact with our speeches to raise consideration of delivery.

Dimensions of Delivery

Delivery provides the public speaker with numerous challenges and opportunities. Below, we'll examine the challenges and opportunities that you are most likely to encounter. Yet, it is important to note that you almost certainly will not have to or want to tackle all of these dimensions of delivery in your speech; rather, you'll want to identify which are challenges you face and work on them while looking for dimensions you think you can do well and selecting them. While most of us will have some delivery challenge to overcome as we become more effective public speakers, each individual might have a very different challenges than our classmates, colleagues, or friends. It is even possible that a delivery challenge you face in one speech might be replaced by a different challenge in another speech. For all these reasons, it is important for us to know all the most common challenges of delivery and to be able to recognize them in ourselves and others.

Let's look at the challenges and opportunities that delivery offers to a public speaker, addressing each one from the head down.

Eye Contact. One of the most important dimensions of delivery starts at the top of our bodies: our eyes. Eyes play many key roles in execution of a successful speech. For many speakers, we use our eyes to examine our speaking situation, to check our time, to gauge the audience's response to our speech while it's in progress, and to follow our outline as we deliver the speech. Yet, while all of the functions of the eyes in public speaking are vital, they are not necessarily elements of delivery. In other words, they don't enhance or emphasize our words intentionally. But there is a way in which we can use our eyes to enhance the delivery of our speech: eye contact. As the name suggests, **eye contact** describes *the visual connection we make with individual audience members in order to enrich our verbal messaging.* At its best, eye contact is a resource for making a connection with audience members and expressing to them that we want their attention, interest, and participation.

Given the many benefits that good eye contact can provide to a speaker, it should not be surprising that poor eye contact works in just the opposite way. Speakers who only look at their notes or outline, who spend the entire speech reading their visual aid, or who look over or past their audience are all common examples of poor eye contact. As audience members, when speakers engaged in these poor eye contact practices, they're not just missing out on an opportunity to better connect with their audiences; rather, they are actively doing harm to the speaker-audience relationship. By refusing to make eye contact with an audience, speakers are conveying one or more negative messages to the audience, including: that they are unconfident in or unprepared for their speech, that they are lying or being deceitful, or, perhaps worst of all, that the speaker has no interest in or concern for their audience.

While failing to make eye contact is by far the most common delivery mistake speakers make, there is also such a thing as *too much eye contact.* A speaker who makes eye contact for too long with a single of several audience members can often be read by speakers as singling out a particular audience member, actively avoiding other audience members, or even intimidating and threatening a person in the audience. What qualifies as too long? Like many dimensions of delivery, the answer is often culturally-contingent; in other words, different cultures have different expectations for the appropriate amount of eye contact. However, in professional and civic settings in the United States and most of the Western world, if you count to one "Mississippi" (M-I-S-S-I-S-S-I-P-P-I), that is about the appropriate amount of time to make eye contact with any one person before moving onto the next person.

Facial Expressions. Of all the dimensions of delivery in public speaking, the one people most often forget are their facial expressions. The reason why is pretty straightforward: while we are speaking, it is not uncommon to forget about what your face is doing because we can't see it! We can see if our arms flail or if our toes tap; but in a room before an audience, we're the only ones who can't see our own faces. That can be problematic because our facial expressions have a lot to add to our speech.

By **facial expressions** we mean *the ways in which we contort, shape, or keep at ease our faces to convey contextual cues to our audience.* Of all the dimensions of delivery, we know the importance of this dimension without much work because, frankly, we read faces every day. When we see a friend smile, we feel good about them and ourselves. When they wear a stern scowl, we might assume that they are upset and question whether we did something to upset them. When our friend has tears running down their face, we suspect that these are tears of sadness but hope they are tears of joy. For most human beings, the expressions that we wear on our face come to us as a natural reflection of our inner experience in that moment—and people read and interpret our current mood through our face. For most public speakers, our facial expressions work exactly the same in the course of delivering a speech. If our topic is happy, we tend to smile; if our topic is sad, we tend to frown. If this is the case with you and your public speaking—great! Don't overthink it and let your facial expression continue as they are.

However, you might also be a person whose facial expressions are sending your audience the wrong message. You might be speaking about great places to go on Spring Break...but your face is very serious. Or you might be wrapping up a speech with an assurance that the problem you're discussing can be solved...with an expression of deep anxiety on your face. Or you might even be delivering a eulogy for someone who has recently passed away and who you miss deeply...while you are struggling to hold back a hysterical, laughing outburst. If any of these people are you, you can probably understand why an audience might be confused. Your facial expressions are out of sync with the tone and tenor of your speech topic and message. And when that happens, audiences tend to be confused and suspicious of what a speaker is trying to say.

But why would our faces ever do something like this to us? It actually makes a lot of sense. If our faces are visual reflections of our inner state, they can reflect our inner feelings at the moment whether or not those feelings correspond with our speech topic. The serious-faced speaker talking about Spring Break is determined to get a good grade, so of course they appear serious. The anxiety-faced speaker who is trying to reassure us also happens to be experiencing extreme communication apprehension on the inside. And the speaker laughing through their eulogy? Grief and sadness often get processed in unexpected ways, including nervous giggles. The point is that even facial expressions that do not match with our speech topics are natural; but they also happen to be counterproductive for being successful speakers.

What then can we do about it? If you fall into this latter category, your best bet is to spend some time in front of a mirror. You want to double check what your face is doing while you speak, and the mirror will help you see what the audience sees. If everything looks good, keep moving forward. If your facial expressions look off, consider practicing your speech enough so that you alleviate your inner turmoil. Also, work on being mindful about your facial expressions as part of your preparation. If all else fails, considering changing topics.

Articulation, Pronunciation, Rate. It should come as no surprise that one of the most important parts of our body for successful delivery in public speaking resides in our mouths: our tongues. While we don't often think about the anatomy of successful public speaking, there is no doubt that our ability to use muscles and tendons in our mouth and face play an instrumental role in the words we speak. Therefore, we need to be mindful of three important dimensions of delivery relating to those body parts: articulation, pronunciation, and rate.

Of the three, articulation is the most closely associated with delivery as an embodied experience. That is because **articulation** is concerned with *the ability to harness our tongues, throats, and mouths in different ways to make crisp, clean words that are understandable to our audiences.* On one level, articulation deals with saying our words crisply and distinctly. If you've ever said a tongue twister, then you know what we mean. Whether you're trying to clearly emphasize the start of each new word when you say, "She sells sea shells down by the sea shore" or to get your mouth quickly reset for new phrases as you describe "Big black bugs bleed blue brown blood, but baby black bugs bleed blue," you know that articulation is essential to effectively communicating your message. On another level, articulation is not just about making the right anatomical configuration to say succeeding words distinctly; it is also about learning how to make those anatomical shapes and sounds in the first place. Indeed, learning a new language is often the first time that people discover that they don't just need to learn new words, but that they need to learn to do new things with their mouth, face, and tongue in order to make the sounds necessary to say those words. For some English speakers, you might have discovered, for instance, that you either can or cannot roll your tongue to make the double "rr" sound in Spanish words like "burrito." By the same token, students for whom English is a second language (ESL) may discover they have some different challenges with articulation when delivering a speech in English. If this is you, please be sure to speak with your instructor about how you might agreeably sort out differing expectations for articulation in your class.

Often confused with articulation is another dimension of delivery somewhat related to the mouth: pronunciation. **Pronunciation** is defined as *the proper saying of a word or words according to the established norms of a given language.* While saying a word correctly is the subject of good pronunciation, it differs from articulation in that poor pronunciation does not have to do with a failure of our body, per say. Rather, in pronunciation, we fail to say a word correctly because we may not *know* the proper way to say it. As someone who spent his entire life growing up on the East Coast, I remember vividly the first time I mispronounced Tucson, Arizona, when I moved out West. In front of a huge class, I very intently pronounced "Tucson" (two-son) as "Tucson" (tuck-son). It was pretty embarrassing when the class burst out into laughter, but I learned an important lesson: if you come across a word you don't know in a public speaking setting, it is good not only to get its definition in a dictionary, but also to learn the proper pronunciation. Luckily, most online dictionaries now offer a pronunciation guide that will say the word out loud for you. You should also practice the proper pronunciation and consider spelling the word out phonetically in your speaking outline, manuscript, or notecards. Taking these steps is essential to maintaining your expertise, authority, and credibility as a speaker before an audience.

Another dimension of delivery that can greatly impact both pronunciation and articulation is rate. **Rate** simply means *the speed with which a speaker delivers their speech.* It is among the most common challenges speakers face before an audience because communication apprehension can often lead people to speak more quickly than they would in everyday life. This can be a large challenge for speakers because a very high rate can result in significant misunderstanding or missed information by the audience and seriously debilitate an otherwise effective speech. In other cases, speaking too slowly is also an issue of rate, making a speaker painful to listen to and their audience potentially bored. But issues with rate can also cause cascading problems like going over or under a time limit, forgetting to say or breezing past oral citations, and making challenges with articulation and pronunciation even worse. Therefore, it is essential that speakers take challenges related to rate seriously.

What constitutes an effective rate for a public speaker? While rate also varies from culture to culture, in most cases a good rate in public speaking is the same as a good rate in everyday conversation. Indeed, in most Western societies, speakers who adopt a **conversational style** in their speaking are lauded as some of the most effective speakers. To put it another way, if *a speaker attempts to speak to an audience in a manner and pace that mirrors the way they would talk about a similarly important issue with a friend or colleague in an interpersonal setting*, that speaker is likely to be practicing a good rate of speaking. Of course, some people are just naturally or culturally fast talkers, even in everyday conversations. If you are one of those people, you will want to be extra conscious of trying to slow down in your speech. For more advanced speakers, rate might also be a place in which speakers can add not only clarity but emphasis to their speech. For example, if a speaker is delivering a speech at an effective, conversational rate, but then intentionally slows down her rate on one key sentence, she will almost certainly draw added attention from the audience to that point in her speech. Good rate, then, is not just about avoiding the problems of speaking too fast or too slowly, but about modulating the speed with which one talks within a conversational rate to add emphasis where it is desired by the speaker. With practice, proper pronunciation, articulation, and rate can be highly valuable tools for successful speaking.

Vocal Variety. Before we move on to other parts of the body that can enhance our delivery, we need to say a few words about another dimension of delivery controlled by the mouth. **Vocal variety** is *the pleasing modulation of tone in a speaker's voice during the delivery of a speech.* While vocal variety is difficult to explain with written words like this textbook, you'll understand better what vocal variety is if you think about speaking with someone who does not practice vocal variety. Have you ever spoken with a person whose voice never meaningfully changed in tonality or tenor? If the human voice is like music, the equivalent would be like sitting at a piano and hitting the same key over and over and over again. You might change the speed or frequency or even the strength which with you hit the key…but no matter what you do, if you can only hit the same key the sound emanating from the piano rarely makes anything approaching what we think of as music. When a speaker does the same thing as that single piano key, we refer to that person as speaking in monotone. To speak in **monotone** means *literally to speak with one, unchanging tone throughout the course of a speech.* While some people generally have a monotone voice and others only dip into it in certain communication situations, monotone can be very problematic for a public speaker. Like our musical analogy earlier, a monotone speaker is often unpleasant to listen to. It is boring and repetitive and offers none of the energy or variation we craze in extended social interactions.

Contrast a monotone voice with a speaker who has vocal variety. In our musical metaphor, a speaker with vocal variety is like listening to a symphony where all the instruments have all the notes at their disposal. It is melodic, with notes building together, and then dropping, only to build again in a different way before weaving in and out of each other in an exuberant musical dance. Speakers who practice vocal variety do something similar. As they proceed through their speech, the voice changes throughout: sometimes it goes up at the end of a word, other times it goes down, and often it zigzags within a word itself. For many of us, this is how we speak in our everyday conversations and it is something we want to transport into our public speaking voices as well. A speaker with vocal variety, much like a symphony, can add energy, vigor, and distinction in their delivery in ways that make listening to the speaker both enjoyable and enticing.

Posture. Moving down the body, we come to the neck, shoulder, and back, which cues us to think about posture. Posture simply refers to *the manner in which we arrange our upper body in a communication situation*. Many of us have probably heard of posture before in conversations about the right way to sit or stand at a desk, at the dinner table, at the gym, or in the military. In these conversations, posture is often raised in the context of manners, decorum, health, or training. For our purposes, we are concerned about posture in public speaking in two ways.

First, posture matters to the public speaker in the context of effective speech. That is because a speaker with appropriate posture will be positioned for optimal projection, breathing, and eye contact. Consider for a moment what it would be like to deliver an 8-minute speech while lying down looking at the ceiling. Not only would it be nearly impossible to make eye contact, but the position of your body would make your speech difficult both to hear and deliver. By contrast, a speaker who is standing (or seated) with their spine aligned as straight up and down as possible, their chin up, and shoulders back will be optimally situated to speak loudly and clearly and see everyone.

The second reason posture matters in public speaking is professionalism. Simply put: in the Western world, a professional speech is expected to be given with good posture. Less than optimal posture is often interpreted as laziness, a lack of seriousness, or the absence of preparation. While a conver sational style might be ideal in the words we choose, a conversational posture is often counterproductive. As such, a good speaker will want to use posture to her advantage in conveying ethos and credibility. Of course, these connections between posture and professionalism are largely based on conventionally abled assumptions. Therefore, it is important to recognize on the part of speakers and audiences that not every speaker will be able to perform posture in ways conventionally considered "professional." But that fact should not impact our interpretation of the speaker's work. If you have concerns about posture as it relates to speaking, please consult with your course instructor.

Breathing and Volume. Connected to posture are the series of delivery techniques associated with the upper body: breathing and volume. Breathing is essential for a good speech delivery, particularly when we think of delivery as a full body experience. In most cases, there is no audible or visible dimension of breathing in good delivery; however, the proper flow of oxygen consistently through the body is necessary for consistent speaking, for making fluctuations in tone, and for projection. Good breathing also helps blood flow, which can prevent that pins and needles feeling in your fingers or toes. Volume is also critical to good delivery and derives much of its power from this part of the body. By **volume** we mean *the capacity to speak with increasing and decreasing projection during a speech*. Volume is directly connected with the lungs and diaphragm and is something a speaker must be mindful of. As we have already discussed, slouching or bad posture can collapse or constrict the lung-capacity of the speaker or their diaphragm, significantly undercutting their volume. A speech delivered with volume taken seriously will be adjustable to a small or large room, to audience members that have different hearing needs, and to speech technologies (i.e., microphones) that might assist the speaker in being heard.

Gestures. One of the most commonly recognized dimensions of delivery is what we refer to as gestures. Gestures are *meaningful and often intentional arrangements of the hands, arms, and fingers in the course of a speech to add value to the words with which they correspond.* While almost all speakers use gestures, one of the best places to see the power of gestures is by watching U.S. presidents. Because the presidency has long been among the most filmed positions in the entire world, it should come as no surprise that most people have watched their fair share of presidents speaking at a podium. And because they do so much speaking, we as audience members can start to discern different gestures that our presidents rely on their speaking engagements. Over the last couple of presidencies, each president has had very notable gestures. President Bill Clinton, for instance, regularly placed his thumb between his index and middle finger to emphasize a point; President George W. Bush preferred a chopping motion with his hand. Meanwhile, President Barack Obama took a two-handed chop approach, and President Trump favors a sideways swat with his hand. For all of these leaders, they have found that, rather than let their arms lay limp or useless at their sides, they can use their hands to bring emphasis to their words through the power of gestures.

When considering gestures, we should think of them as two different kinds. One form of gestures is what we might call an **emphatic gesture**. An emphatic gesture is *a relatively benign use of the hand to motion or signal that a point in the speech merits the audience's attention.* In other words, the gesture is relatively meaningless in and of itself; it only gains meaning when used in conjunction with the speaker's words as an underline or bolding of their assertion. Examples of emphatic gestures include waving, pointing, or gesticulating. The other form of gesture is an **illustrative gesture**. Unlike an emphatic gesture, with an illustrative gesture *the form of the gesture itself has a meaning that is distinct from the speaker's words.* To put it another way, the gesture serves to do work on its own above and beyond the speech itself. You've almost certainly seen illustrative gestures as an audience member: the speaker who raises his clenched fist in the air in a show of strength and defiance, the speaker who points intently at the horizon and the hope it promises, or the speaker who squiggles his hand in the air as if to sign a document that does not yet exist. These gestures have meanings that audiences recognize themselves. In fact, if you watched a speaker using these gestures online while on mute, you will still gain valuable messages about the speech even without the words.

As speakers, both emphatic and illustrative gestures can be important tools for a more successful delivery for either emphasizing a speech's words or making a visual argument all their own. However, not every speech calls for an elaborate gestural design. In fact, for some speakers or some speeches, keeping gestures at a minimum is the fitting approach. This is largely the case when a) the occasion of the speech is somber or peaceful and excessive gesturing would appear over the top or b) when the speaker is prone to let their gestures get out of hand, to the point that they become distractions from the speech. Your instructor will be sure to let you know if your gestures are inappropriate or distracting, but a general rule is that all gestures should be both appropriate for a G-rated audience and kept below the speaker's neck.

Proxemics. A final dimension of delivery vital to speaker success is **proxemics**: *the ways in which speakers use space to advance their speaking situation.* You might be wondering what we mean by the speaker's use of space during a speech. That makes sense because, for most us, when we picture a speaking situation it seems as if the space is already predetermined. There is often a podium where the speaker stands at the front of a room facing an audience several feet away. Indeed, this is the traditional, Western image of a speech situation in space that many of us have seen so many times that it is almost impossible to imagine otherwise.

However, as with most dimensions of delivery, speakers have a great deal of latitude in moving through space or even changing space when they are the speakers. Consider two examples. In the

1992 election, then-Governor Bill Clinton made national headlines by breaking with the tradition that all speakers must stay at their podiums during a presidential debate with President George H.W. Bush and Ross Perot. In particular, Clinton earned people's respect when, during a very personal question from the audience, Clinton walked around the podium to the front of the stage within a few feet of the questioner. For the viewing American public, Clinton's unconventional use of space as a speaker signaled something important: this was not some run of the mill politician who just said he cared about us and our problems; in fact, he actually did, and he showed it by physically being closer to the real people seated below him. In 2000, at the Republican National Convention, then-Senator Elizabeth Dole took it a step further. During her keynote address, she took the unprecedented step of leaving the podium behind and walked into the gathered crowd to give her speech. Over the course of a 20-minute address, she roamed the hallway, smiled at individual voters, and made real connections with people in the crowd. Both of these examples demonstrate that great speakers don't need to be held captive to a podium; instead, speakers can put their feet to work and use the space of their speaking environment to make real connections with the audience.

What might you, as a speaker, have at your disposal when considering space in a public speaking situation? Like Clinton and Dole, you might also decide to ditch the podium and walk meaningfully and intentionally in front of the class to show both your confidence and your interest in the audience. You might also ask if you can rearrange the room, so that everyone sits in a circle and feels like an equal part of the speech-driven conversation. If you're speaking in front of a group of children, perhaps you'll decide to "take a knee" to get down to their eye level to tell them what's on your mind. All of these are inventive and valuable ways a speaker might enhance their speech through attention to proxemics.

While we would encourage you to think hard about how proxemics might work to your advantage, it is also important to consider how proxemics can go wrong in public speaking. Culture, for instance, is always an element to consider and different cultures have different norms of acceptable proximity between people that you should know in a globalizing world. Isolated proxemics decisions can also go wrong. You should not make the choice as a speaker to be nearer or farther away from a particular person or group of people but should give proximity to an audience as evenly as possible, much like you would with eye contact. Finally, it is important to remember that while closeness can be valuable, that is not the same thing as touching. *As speakers, we should never touch another person without their express permission to do so, even if it is well intended and seems harmless to you.* While some people may appreciate a genuine feeling of interest that closeness can convey, touching has wildly different cultured and gendered meanings, some of which are harmful or even threatening. So, make sure you remember that proxemics is always about space, not about touch.

As we have already noted, delivery is often a major source of public speaking anxiety for novice public speakers; however, as this chapter has shown, a speaker who uses delivery effectively has the capacity to significantly improve the quality of their speaking.

Chapter 11

SPEAKING WITH SPEAKING AIDS

While we often think about public speaking as a verbal exercise, in reality, successful public speaking is a whole person experience. An effective public speaker not only says the right thing at the right time, but supports those words with powerful images, illuminating examples, and recognizable enthusiasm. While we have spent significant time in these pages considering the ways that we use delivery, style, and memory to provide these appeals to the full human experience, we can also recognize that the speech itself cannot do all this work alone. Therefore, this chapter addresses what else we can use to assist us in this rhetorical enterprise: speaking aids.

Speaking aids refer to *a wide array of artifacts and tools at the disposal of the speaker to aid her in amplifying the message(s) of her speech.* Public speaking classes and textbooks have long discussed a particular set of speaking aids, what we call visual aids, and we will in this chapter as well. However, visual aids only provide assistance to the speaker in one sensory dimensions of the human experience. As we will see in the following pages, there are a number of other human senses that can serve as resources to the public speaker if we are only willing and able to consider them.

Why Use a Speaking Aid?

Before providing an account of the many different kind of aids available to the public speaker, it would be helpful to examine the various different reasons why speaking aids should be considered by anyone about to step up to a podium. There are several reasons why speaking aids can be a useful tool for the public speaker. For example:

- **Speaking aids amplify your message to the whole person**. As our introduction suggests, while the bulk of the work we do as public speakers is achieved orally, we do not want to leave a single stone unturned in trying to deliver our message effectively to our audience. Therefore, we can look beyond speech alone to assist us in this process.
- **Orality does not convey all messages equally well.** While speech is one of humanity's most vital tools for conveying messages, the nature of orality makes it less well equipped to convey all kinds of messages to an audience. In particular, because speeches are ephemeral and language based, they have limitations in communicating certain information types. For instance,

speeches are not a great way to convey to an audience a comparison between large amounts of data. Think about it: before a speaker could even begin to compare the data, they would have to spend significant time listing all the different data points for the audience. However, if the speaker provided the audience this data in a handout or a chart where it could be absorbed visually, the speaker could save significant time and energy and focus on the implications of that comparison.

- **Speaking aids can emphasize key points.** While some information is poorly presented in oral form, other information benefits from being emphasized or repeated in non-verbal formats. As a speaker, it is easy for me to remind an audience not to forget to register to vote; however, it is much easier to forget this information as an audience than it is to say it as a speaker. Speaking aids, then, do not need to take the place of the speaker's message here; rather, it can add emphasis to this easily forgotten point through visual assistance.

- **Speaking aids can facilitate action beyond your speech.** While speeches can do important work during the course of the speech, they have limited reach once your audience leaves the immediate space and time of the speech. A week after the speech, it is impossible to reconstitute the speech to continue to push for action. Speaking aids, however, can go where the speaker cannot. For example, handouts can follow an audience home and provide a gentle reminder to the audience to take action!

- **Speaking aids create a more inclusive experience.** Finally, another good reason to use speaking aids is to ensure different kinds of people in your audience can participate more fully in your communication. As a verbal form of communication, speeches tend to reach a relatively high level of audiences, but nowhere near 100%. In a pluralistic society with people of all kinds of ages and abilities, we need to do better. That's where speaking aids come in. Through the use of a variety of speaking aids, a speaker can reach an audience member who does not hear well or whose memory is not as strong, an audience member who has a different first language than the speaker, or an audience member who responds to and retains information more efficiently through sight or experience. As such, speaking aids can be just as much about being an ethical speaker as an effective speaker.

A Speaking Aid Is Not a Speech

Before we dig deeper into understanding the various speaking aids we might draw from in our own public speaking, it is important to make an important distinction: *a speaking aid is not a speech.* There are, of course, stark differences between the series of spoken words that make up a speech and the handout that goes with it. Yet, far too often, novice speakers blur the line between speaking aid and speech, sometimes intentionally and sometimes not. Consider this scenario: a speaker develops an elaborate, text-heavy PowerPoint presentation that he projects in front of the class. With his main ideas projected for the entire room to see, the speaker reads aloud each of these points, one at a time, until his audience is exhausted and his "speech" is done. Is this a speech, in the proper sense? No! All this person has done is turn his outline into a PowerPoint and read it to the class. It demonstrates that the speaker does not have a good understanding of what a speaking aid should do and has likely harmed his relationship with the audience and his ability to achieve the goal of his speech. As such, before you plan your speaking aid, make sure you are not treating the aid as the speech itself!

Kinds of Speaking Aids

While speakers have been using speaking aids since the earliest era of public speaking, the diversity of speaking aids available to the public speaker in the 21st century is greater than it has ever been.

VISUAL AIDS

Of all types of speaking aids, most of us are familiar with the visual aid. A **visual aid** is *a speaking aid that appeals to the audience in visual forms in order to convey, emphasize, or amplify the verbal message of a speech.* That the visual is our most common go-to for speaking aids is not surprising. Significant research in the 20th and 21st century suggests that we increasingly live in a visual culture that prioritizes the speed and attention-getting power of visuals as a means of explaining our world. To put it another way: in a world where we are surrounded by screens, most of us instinctually expect any serious form of address will include some visual dimension. As such, the public speaker who ignores visual aids does so at her own peril.

Given that we occupy both a visual and a screen culture, by far the most common way of using visual aids in recent years have been what we might think of as visual aggregation tools. **Visual aggregation tools** are *software programs that gather, collect, and modify different kinds of visual information and mediums into a single stream for displaying to an audience.* These tools have changed dramatically over the years, from slideshows to projector displays; however, today the most common form of visual aggregation tools we see in speechmaking are software like PowerPoint, Prezi, or Keynote. Each of these programs, in its own way, gathers together images, photographs, text, videos, web-content, and other mediums with a visual component into a single file that the speaker can proceed through with the audience. In this chapter, we will not cover how to use each of these pieces of software; however, resource guides for using this technology are available for you on your course's Canvas site.

While visual aggregation tools are the most common way speakers use visuals to aid in their speeches today, it is important to note two factors about these visuals.

First, while a visual aggregator tool allows you to synthesize a number of different visual artifacts into one, **not every speech or speech situation benefits from these tools**. We often forget, but any of the individual visuals that can be placed in a PowerPoint slideshow can also serve as a standalone visual aid. Consider, for instance that one of the most powerful speeches I ever saw was a speech celebrating the life of a freed slave that included nothing other than a single photograph—the only remaining image of this women. The speaker did not augment the image with animation or text but simply provided a full-size poster of the women's face that starred into the eyes of the audience as the speaker spoke. The key takeaway then is that, not everything needs to be placed into a visual aggregator to be effective. A single photograph, video, graph, chart can all, if done well, meet the needs of a powerful visual aid.

Second, while audiences may be increasingly comfortable with screen-oriented visual aids and speaking venues are ever-more likely to provide technology to facilitate the use of screens in speech presentations, **that does not mean that the screen is the only visual format we should consider in preparing our visual aids**. Some visual aids, in fact, do not translate well into a visual aggregator tool, particularly because a live, in-person visual act performed by the speaker is more meaningful, engaging, and affecting than anything on a screen. Consider these other forms of visual aids that may be more effective in-person and, frankly, in the flesh:

- The sight of an original artifact or objects
- Costumes or other cultural artifacts
- The performances of a dance, gesture, or sign language
- A tour of a space or place
- An impressive view
- An unusual trick or performance
- Body art on the speaker
- The live creation of a work of visual art

AUDIO AIDS

While a speaker typically provides all the audible sounds in a speech, certain speech topics may also lend themselves to additional kinds of audio aids in the act of public speaking. **Audio aids** are *speaking aids that appeal to the audience's sense of hearing in ways beyond the speaker's voice.* We often overlook audio aids as a tool in public speaking: they are not as flashy as visual aids and we already feel overly-reliant on asking our audience to listen to us as speaker. But audio aids can provide an invaluable addition to messages and evidence of certain kinds of speeches. Consider:

- A speaker on the life of Senator Robert F. Kennedy who ends the speech by playing the sound of the recorded screams, yelling, and conversation of bystanders in the crowd after he was shot
- A speaker who informs his audience about the benefits of listening to vinyl records by playing a segment of track on digital and vinyl against each other
- A speaker on the power of meditation who asks the audience to sit silently at their desks for a minute to fully illustrate how disconnected and unfocused our everyday lives can be

Each of these speeches involves very different topics and uses an audio aid for very different effect: to convey a sense of horror and loss, to demonstrate a difference in technology and experience, and to reframe the understanding and experience of the audience in real time. Yet, in each case, the addition of an audio aid into the speech proves a dramatic assistance to the speaker's aim, in a way that an image or graph simply could not.

HAPTIC AIDS

The sense of touch can be particularly powerful for a public speaker who wants to be sure to engage their audience. **Haptic aids**, *speaking aids that rely on touch, textures, and the ability to encounter the authentic and genuine*, can be a significant resource. As with all speaking aids, the utility of haptics aids depends on the subject of the speech in question. Certain topics—for example, speeches about highly abstract ideas or philosophical issues—may not lend themselves well to haptic aids. In addition, bodily exposure to some subjects—like toxic waste or viral organisms—can be quite dangerous for the speaker's audience and should be avoided at all costs. But, for other topics, the ability to touch and feel something real with your own hands is a compelling experience that can go a long way to winning over an audience. Anyone who participated in "show and tell" in grade school should be able to see the benefits of this approach.

Some examples of the power of haptic aids:

- A speaker interested in archival research was given permission to bring the class a document from the early 1800s and allowed the class to touch the decomposing document properly.
- An Animal Science major brought in a set of different toad species to show differences in their shading and the texture of their skin.
- A fashion design student passed around different swatches of material as he explained how selecting the right fabric is crucial to effective design.

NOTE: As we mentioned in the previous chapter, while the sense of touch can be a powerful tool in public speaking, a speaker should *never touch an audience member* in any way without their express stated permission.

OLFACTORY AIDS

A largely overlooked type of speaking aid is an **olfactory aid**—*a speaking aid that relies on the audience's sense of smell to advance the speaker's message.* We might be quick to think that the sense of smell has little role in the processes of informing or persuading, but we would be wrong. Smell is a powerful human sense and can often lead us to make snap decisions about a person, place, or thing. Smell can be subtle but gives us a general impression that shapes everything else we hear or see. And smell is the sense that research shows is most directly connected with memory, capable of transporting us back to another time, place, or state of mind.[32] While public speakers may not have been quick to figure out the power of smell, business has: next time you walk into a large corporate storefront, stop and sniff mindfully. It is now common practice for businesses to invest millions of dollars into creating branded scents that will give customers just the right kind of sensory experience the businesses want them to have. But, how might public speakers use olfactory aids in their public speaking?

- A student brewer might pass around a handful of hops for his audience to smell as he explains the intricacies of the beer-making process.
- A speaker painting a vivid image of a landscape might ask her audience to imagine not just what they see, but also the rich noticeable smells common to that scene, like the smell of freshly cut grass.
- A speaker commemorating her grandmother's love of cooking might bring in a small sample of her favorite meal for the audience to smell and sample during the speech.

ENVIRONMENTAL AIDS

A speaker need not always bring an aid to a speech in order to be successful; sometimes, a speaking aid is located in the space of the speech itself. These *kinds of speaking aids that can be pointed to or invoked in the space a speech is delivered in* are called **environmental aids**. Depending on where you give your speech, the value of an environmental aid may not be clear. A college classroom, for example, may not be particularly rich in views, artifacts, or spaces that promote inspiration or understanding. Or do they? As an instructor, I once witnessed a student in Education show her audience how the architecture and design of the contemporary U.S. classroom employed subliminal messages about authority, participation, and inclusion. However, we might not all be so lucky. We don't all get to pick the place in which we speak.

But sometimes we do. Particularly in professional public speaking, the selection of a venue is a crucial part of the process precisely because it can amplify or illustrate the value or message the speaker wants to impart to the audience. Dr. Allison Prasch, for example, has shown in her research how U.S. presidents regularly use the environment they select for their speech as rhetorical fodder in their persuasion.[33] But how might we as professional public speakers, use our environment to our advantage to aid in our speech? Consider:

- The history of the space: which might convey an authenticity, a feeling, or reveal an unknown truth.
- The sights of the space: what does the environment show us? What's missing? What's present?
- The function of the space: what goes on in this place? Can the place tell us something about that process, for better or worse?

DIGITAL AIDS

A still relatively contemporary set of resources for the public speaker are digital aids. Digital aids are *speaking aids that call upon the power, resources, and interconnectivity of the Internet to advance a message or position in public speaking.* As we will discuss in the last section of this book, digital aids are different from speaking in a digital environment. The latter is much more about speech in cyberspace whereas the former is, like our other speaking aids, about using a small slice of the non-verbal world to help our oral presentation. So, what exactly do digital aids help us do as public speakers? While the possibilities are as rich as the wealth of information online, digital aids tend to do several things well in public speaking situations. For example:

- **Digital aids can gain attention and participation**. Speakers might choose to ask the audience to find, confirm, or participate in the speech using their individual digital devices.
- **Digital aids can illustrate**. A speaker might have their audiences learn from an Internet search what information is out there or what public opinion online is.
- **Digital aids can connect**. Using special software, speakers can have audience members participate anonymously and quickly in polls and surveys during the speech to get a quick snapshot of the room.

One of my favorite examples of using digital aids in a speech was as an illustrative attention getter. In this case, the speaker asked the audience to raise their hand if they think they have a diverse group of friends and family. Then, he asked the audience to take out their cell phones and scroll through their text messages and asks themselves: how many times have I texted with someone different from me in race, class, gender, or sexual orientation in the last month? The digital aid demonstrates for some people the compelling disconnect between our values and actions in relating across diversity.

Using Speaking Aids Safely and Ethically

While you have an array of excellent speaking aids at your disposal as a public speaker, it is important to remember that those aids need to be used in ways that are effective, safe, and ethical. As such, you should follow these general rules to make sure you avoid any issues:

Timely Use of Speaking Aids. Make sure that your choice to use a speaking aid does not negatively affect your time management. This is particularly true if you are under a tight time constraint.

Space and Occasion Appropriate. Similarly, as an aid to your speech, you will need to make sure that the aid you select is appropriate to the space and/or occasion in which you will be speaking. For instance, while an olfactory aid might be extremely effective, many speaking occasions are too formal to provide food to taste and smell.

Distraction-Free Speaking Aids. Public speakers must be mindful that their speaking aids cannot become distractions. If your speaking aids pulls focus from you the speaker or your argument and ideas, you should reconsider using that speaking aid. Alternately, you might brainstorm ways to remove your speaking aid from the speaking situation immediately after you have used it.

Safe and Legal Speaking Aids. It is vital that public speakers take appropriate steps in advance of using a speaking aid to make sure that the speaking aid they are considering for an upcoming speech is both legal and safe. Public speaking is full of discussions about controversial issues, regulated products and items, exotic creatures and foods, among others that can cross the boundaries of legality and safety (illegal drugs, weapons, banned practices or substances, etc.). As such, a novice public speaker might incorrectly think it wise to expose their audience to a speaking aid that illustrates these topics. That is a mistake. A public speaker should never expose their audience to objects, devices, creatures, substances, and—in some rare circumstances—images or information, that might harm them. Doing so wildly undermines the credibility of the speaker, the effectiveness of their speech, and may make the speaker liable to legal and administrative penalties.

No matter the occasion or the speaker, when we are asked to give a speech in public, our most important resources are always our self, our ideas, and the words we use to express them to others. However, just because our words take on the starring role in public speaking does not mean that we don't also need to rely on other tools to make our speeches great. Speaking aids are those tools—valuable tools that offer us important ways to expand our message, engage our audience, and make sure our messages reach across the many ways difference is inflected in our 21st century pluralistic society.

Unit 3

COMMON SPEECHMAKING TYPES

Chapter 12

A QUICKSTART GUIDE TO SPEAKING

So, you need to make a speech and you need to do so quickly? This is not an unusual situation for a public speaker; however, if you are a novice public speaker with little experience in giving speeches, how to start that process can be quite confusing. This chapter is designed to remedy such a situation. In particular, over the next few pages, this chapter will identify the key things that almost any public speaker should do in any speech in order to be successful. And, if you have time to develop your speech more fully for another occasion, this chapter will allow you to build a foundation upon which that editing and revising can take place.

A QuickStart Guide to Public Speaking

Much like a new phone or laptop has a QuickStart guide to help you get started using your new device without reading the full manual, this chapter is designed as a QuickStart guide for doing a short two-minute speech on a relatively simple subject. Bear in mind: this guide is simply that, a guide. Depending on the nature of your speech, you may have additional responsibilities than this chapter discusses; or you might have less. And, if you need to give an hour-long lecture, this chapter will not be nearly enough material to get you through to the finish. However, it is a place to start.

That said, what does every speaker need to know to succeed in a brief speech?

1. **Know what you need to do**. All speeches are goal-oriented undertakings; every speech has a goal that it is trying to achieve. No one stands up and gives a speech without trying to achieve something. As such, before you do anything else, figure out what your speech has to do in order to be successful. Are you speaking to introduce yourself? To introduce someone else? Do you need to explain something? Do you have to argue for something? Are you saying some nice words about someone? These are all common types of speech goals. Figure out which one of these (or another) is yours. Then start writing your speech with that goal in mind.

2. **Have a single, central argument**. Because all speeches have a goal, every speech needs to have a simple sentence in which the speaker tells the audience what that goal is. In a more developed speech, we call this the **thesis statement** (see more on thesis statements in Chapters 1, 5, and 6); however, for our purposes in this chapter, let's keep it simple. With your goal in mind, write

a single sentence that expresses what your speech will be about. It can be as direct as "Today, I want to tell you why my friend Dave is such a great guy" or "In the next two minutes, I want to raise the three keys issues we need to think about as a team this year." These sentences are not complex or eloquent, but they do tell us what the speech will be about. Having this sentence will also keep you on track as you add more detail.

3. **Jot it down**. However you can, put some key ideas you want to cover on a sheet of paper. In a pinch with no preparation, a sticky note or even the notepad on your phone can work. If you're comfortable putting together a brief outline, do that. If not, think of it as a checklist: what things do I need to say in my short speech in order to achieve what I need to do? You might not need these notes as you speak, but you'll be glad to have them if your mind goes blank or if you forget something.

4. **Know how much time you have**. A common error for a quick and little-prepared speech is to either say too little or too much. If you have been asked to speak by someone, they almost certainly have an idea of how long they would like you to speak. So, simply ask them. This will give you a sense of how much time to fill. Most formal presentations and speeches will come with a very specific time constraint. In less formal settings where someone asks you to "say a few words," you probably want to keep your comments to no more than two minutes.

5. Use the **I + 3 + C pattern**. This book is filled with complex ways of elaborating and organizing your speech. For now, let's stick with the classic. Just like almost every novel or TV show or movie has a basic formula, most speeches do as well, what we call the I + 3 + C pattern. The name of the pattern tells you what you need to complete it: an "I" for introduction, a "3" for three main points, and a "C" for a conclusion. Most good speeches have these components, no matter if they are an hour long or 45 seconds. Start with the introduction: say who you are, why you are here, what your central argument is. Then provide some depth to your central argument by elaborating about it in three ways. If you can't find three different ways to say more about your argument, you probably need a different argument. Then, finish with a concluding thought, something that wraps it all up. Be sure to end with something meaningful; "Thank you" or "That's it" are not good ways to end a speech.

6. **Keep it casual**. In this moment, forget all the bad advice you've ever heard about how to give a good speech. Instead, tell yourself one thing: keep it casual. While there are times and places for a speech to be highly eloquent with soaring language and stirring oratory, those speeches happen less often than you expect. Particularly in the civic and professional settings in the United States and most of Europe, people have come to expect a speech to sound like someone is having a conversation with the audience. Keep it relatable, but professional. No need for fancy words; just be clear. Delivery is simple: look at your audience, stand up straight, and don't fidget.

These six things to know to put together a short speech quickly are *far removed* from the art of public speaking. In fact, a great speaker almost certainly needs to do more than these six things in order to be effective. Luckily, the remainder of this book covers all you would want to know to be a great speaker. Feel free to jump around the textbook if you have more time to develop your speech. Alternately, you might develop your short speech using the suggestions above and then revise that speech with the lessons of the other chapters in mind. But for a new speaker with no experience who is just trying to get through this speech while looking thoughtful and poised, these six steps are what you should prioritize. Good luck!

Chapter 13

INFORMATIVE SPEAKING

One of the most basic functions of human language is giving information. The ability to provide information to others is essential to our everyday personal and professional lives but is also necessary for some of the most foundational aspects of human society. Without the ability to convey information effectively, we could not govern ourselves, we could not educate ourselves, and we could not resolve differences between ourselves. As such, providing information to others in speech is an underappreciated but wildly important skill for human civilization.

As you might have guessed, in an informative speech our primary goal is to persuade the audience to *learn* important information about a new topic. But informative speaking is about more than just information transmission; rather, it is information transmission for a reason. In most cases, people do not want information for the sake of information. People want information so they can *do something with that information*. In this way, informative speaking is a way of facilitating action.

For the purposes of this book, when we think about **informative speaking**, we should think of it as *the form of speaking that empowers others to decide or act*. This definition includes two aspects worth elaboration. The first we have already mentioned: that informative speaking makes possible decisions or actions. But the second part of this definition is just as crucial: "empowering others." As we will see in the following chapters, in different ways, all public speaking is about action. But what distinguishes informative speaking from other kinds of speaking is that the decisions and actions taken after our speeches are not done at our behest as speakers. Informative speakers, while not objective, do not speak with an explicit agenda other than to encourage their audience to be attentive and open to new information; they are not advocating a position nor are they talking down an alternative. Rather, in informative speaking, our job as speakers is to provide the very best information to others, to encourage them to consume that information seriously, and then to step back and allow those others to do what they think is best with this information. It is a strange position to be in, one that many novice speakers have difficulty figuring out at first. But as we will see, in our contemporary society, there are many reasons and places a reliable and credible provider of information is simply essential.

In the pages that follow, we'll investigate the challenges of informative speaking, how we use informative speaking in the real world, and what we need to do in order to make our own speeches successfully informative.

Is It Possible to Only Inform?

A question that inevitably follows the topic of informative speaking is whether it is possible to only be informative. Another way of getting at this question is to raise concerns about objectivity. In public speaking, **objectivity** refers to *the belief that speakers can address a topic without allowing their personal viewpoint and beliefs to shape or interfere with the information they provide an audience.* Informative speakers may then find themselves asking whether they can or should be truly objective in their speeches.

The debate about language and objectivity goes back centuries; however, our contemporary concerns about objectivity in speech comes out of the Enlightenment and the Scientific Revolution when followers of the scientific method began to question the need for eloquence in the discussion of ideas. Thinkers like René Descartes, who studied and practiced rhetoric in school, were particularly concerned that most discussions and debates—in science, politics, and everyday life—were best done through the application of reason and the rejection of the human senses, which might warp our understandings of the world. The argument went that, if our sense could not be trusted, our speech should always be objective: cold, clear, logical, and devoid of emotion. This view became ascendant with the rise of science in the 17th, 18th, and 19th centuries in the Western world and significantly curtailed the study and practice of rhetoric, oratory, and public speaking for a time.

However, scholars in the 20th century pushed back against this idea of objectivity. In particular, thinkers in speech, communication, and language demonstrated how essential language was to all human decision making. Human beings think, act, and live *in* language and it is an unavoidable part of ourselves that we can't put aside. In addition, these scholars questioned whether it was ever possible to be objective. Indeed, even the expectation to be objective is actually a value-judgment: it makes some things able to be discussed and other things not. How then could scientists say that they were being scientific when they actively denied parts of the world? What's more: the 20th century illustrated over and over again the horror that can occur when we put aside feelings and ethics in pursuit of objective knowledge. From poison gas to genocide to nuclear weapons, we learned the hard way that objectivity can often become an excuse to argue for horrible acts.

In this class, we answer the objectivity question as such: "No, it is simply impossible to be *completely objective* as a public speaker (or as a human being!)." All of us use language, have senses, and have conscious and unconscious drives that shape what we think, what we say, and what we do, even if we don't believe we're being particularly persuasive at the time. However, while we can never be wholly objective in our speeches, we can, as speakers, make the decision to limit our human instincts to advance a particular world view in certain circumstances. This means, as we have seen in previous chapters, being aware of our biases, emphasizing logos, and speaking for clarity, among others. Informative speaking is by far the most common place we choose to make these decisions and, while we can never be entirely objective, being more objective than not can be a valuable choice in achieving our ends as public speakers.

Examples of Informative Speaking in the Real World

While informative speaking is a staple of most public speaking classrooms, many students do not tend to think of informative speaking as a particularly common form of speaking in the real world. What's more: today, the transmission of information is commonly achieved through written discourse more often than spoken discourse. But novice speakers would be wrong to think that informative speaking does not happen regularly in the real world. Let's consider the following examples:

Briefings. One of the most common forms of informative speeches in business and government are briefings. **Briefings** tend to be *relatively short summations (hence the root word, "brief") of the key points or findings from a broader body of information.* Individuals in positions of authority and importance are regular recipients of briefings. This makes sense: if you are running a multimillion dollar company, directing a massive military force, or leading a government, you have little time to dive deeply into thousands of pages of information on any given topic, especially when your position requires you to know what is important about hundreds of topics at once. Briefings, then, allow experts to simplify and convey only the most pertinent and most up-to-date information to their superiors so that they are equipped with the best information at all times.

Public Advisories. Another place we commonly see informative speeches in the real world are **public advisories**, *speeches that provide the public with information during events that threaten public safety.* It is typical to hear public advisories before, during, or after natural disasters, terrorist attacks, riots, or mass shootings, among others. In these dangerous situations, the public at large desperately needs sound and reliable information about how they should or should not act in that situation. As such, public advisories are not about beautiful talk, emotional appeals, or long and complex ruminations. Rather, a good public advisory provides facts in simple and easy-to-understand language that is direct and useful and, most importantly, sober. Hysteria is the enemy of public safety; as such, the cool, calm, and collected delivery of information to the public is essential.

Testimony. As we saw in Chapter 5, **testimony** is *public statements made by a witness that describe and event, idea, or situation.* When citizens are asked or compelled to testify in a court of law, the officers of the court have little interest in that person's opinions. What they want are the facts and only the facts. And while lawyers on each side will use testimony to try and establish the facts, as the person testifying, all you can do legally is give honest, direct answers about what you know, saw, or did. Good testimony from a witness is clear, logical, credible, and understandable. In short, testimony is informative speaking at its best.

Lectures or Talks. On a college campus, you commonly come across lectures or talks as a form of informative speaking. A **lecture** is *the presentation of new research to the public in the form of a speech.* Sometimes, when these lectures are more casual or speculative, they are called **talks**. When sharing research with the public or with colleagues, researchers are invested in being believable and credible. This is particularly true when their findings can impact public policy or decision-making. Since they are almost always presenting some form of new information, it is crucial for a lecture to be clear and understandable to the audience. Hence, most lectures are primarily if not exclusively informative in nature.

Tutorials. A final example of informative speaking in the real world is tutorials. **Tutorials** are *detailed speeches that teach an audience how to do something, often on their own in a do-it-yourself style.* Some people might think of a tutorial as a "how to" speech; however, this genre of speaking is common for small children and often deals with simple tasks (how to make a peanut butter and jelly sandwich, for example) that are inappropriate for a college classroom or professional setting. However, tutorials are significantly more advanced in subject matter and often teach people skills or knowledge that is challenging or specialized. While tutorials can happen face-to-face, increasingly the Internet is the primary space in which tutorials are most widely available to the public. When tutorials are effective—clear, knowledgeable, easy to follow—the audience acquires valuable information. But we all know that trying to explain something online is not always easy. YouTube, for example, is full of tutorial fails where the speaker obviously does not know enough or cannot communicate it effectively.

These five examples from the real world are only some of the ways in which people use informative speaking on a daily basis in their careers or everyday lives. As we will see, each of them shares many characteristics that make them notably informative in nature.

Characteristics of an Informative Speech

Like all of the major types of speeches, informative speeches have distinctive characteristics to help the speaker attain their primary goal—in this case, persuading an audience to learn important information about a new topic. To make sure we are actually giving an informative speech, as opposed to another type of speech that is simply masquerading as providing information, it is important for public speakers to recognize these characteristics and make smart choices about including them in their speeches.

Be Genuinely Informative. To say a speech is genuinely informative is to say that the speaker is providing the audience with information that they really do not know. To put it another way: an informative speech should never be a recitation of common knowledge or a regurgitation of long-established facts. Rather, a genuinely informative speech should be cutting edge, offering the audience information that is new, recently uncovered, a radical rethinking, still in its early stages, esoteric, or highly technical or specialized. In addition, just because your speech is genuinely informative does not mean the speaker doesn't have a responsibility to make it interesting! Ask yourself: at the end of my speech, will your audience be able to honestly say "Wow, I didn't know that!" If so, you have found an excellent topic for an informative speech.

Speaking for Clarity. If our informative speech is genuinely informative, it is highly likely that our audience will be learning something new and potentially complex. As such, it is vital that an informative speaker is speaking for clarity. As we discussed in Chapter 9, speaking for clarity is about simple speaking. An informative speech is not the place to be eloquent, overly technical, or highly emotional. Rather, teaching others new information demands speaking with clarity in language and expression. Refer back to Chapter 9 for more information on speaking for clarity, knowing that most informative speakers will emphasize the following in their speeches:

- Definition
- Directness
- Simplicity

Informative Organization. As we will see in the following chapters of this book, when speakers are trying to persuade an audience on policy or engage them in a deliberative dialogue, there are an assortment of organizational styles that can be brought to bear to assist them in this act. However, informative speaking is quite different. In informative speaking, the main function of organization is to provide information in a simple, straightforward, and clear way. As such, organizing an informative speech is best done through a simple organization. This means, an informative speech should:

Contain the basic components of *structure* expected in most speeches, including a(n):

- **Introduction** with an attention getter, thesis statement, credibility and relevance statement, and preview
- **Body** with clearly distinguished main points, sub-points, and transitions
- **Conclusion** with a final signpost, summary, and strong finish

and

Order those structural components in one of several clear ways. In particular, informative speeches tend to use the following kinds of ordering patterns:

- Chronological
- Spatial
- Narrative
- A distinctive pattern that makes sense for your particular topic

For more detailed information on these organizational components and how to use them correctly, see Chapter 7 in this book.

Significant and Explicit Evidence. Let's be clear: nearly every speech you will see in this book will require substantial research and evidence in order to be successful. However, informative speaking has a particularly high expectation for evidence and citation. Indeed, since the primary goal of this speech is to persuade the audience to learn important information about a new topic, your speech needs to have significant and reliable evidence. In addition, in informative speaking it is essential to demonstrate the credibility and quantity of your evidence to the audience in the course of your speech. Indeed, since most audiences will not see your outline during an informative speech, the only way to know that your information is good is if you describe it. As such, in informative speaking, speakers should:

- **Have multiple, high-quality sources.** While the particular number of sources you should have in an informative speech will vary by topic and length, a speaker should never give an informative speech with one or a few sources. Nor should an informative speaker ever rely on opinion alone or one kind of source to constitute the entirety of their evidence.

- **Have corroborating sources for each piece of information.** Ideally, an informative speaker should have more than one source for each key point they are sharing with their audience. Doing so demonstrates that their first source can be corroborated and is, therefore, more trustworthy. If a speaker cannot offer a corroborating source for each piece of information, the information might be wrong, partial, or simply opinion.

- **Should provide three (3) points of attribution for each of their sources.** Unlike other speeches, informative speaking benefits from stating explicitly in the speech more information about the sources than might be needed otherwise. Therefore, the speaker should identify three of the most salient facts about a source to name while giving their speech. To determine which facts about your source might be most prevalent for your given topic, consult with the chart in Chapter 6.

An informative speech is an often-under-appreciated form of speaking. However, as we have seen in the previous pages, the ability to provide your audience with credible and reliable information is one of the most essential skills a speaker needs in the 21st century.

Chapter 14

SPEAKING FOR PUBLIC DELIBERATION

In the last chapter, we examined providing credible and reliable information as a common reason for public speaking. In the chapters ahead, we will discuss the most typical forms of speaking we encounter in a democratic society: speaking for policy and commemoration. However, in this chapter, we will discuss a form of speaking that exists somewhere between informative and policy speech and is focused on encouraging an audience to consider the various, credible ways we as communities must talk through difficult problems together, what we refer to here as speaking for public deliberation.

There is a good chance that you have found yourself in a situation in your personal or professional life in which you had to talk through a difficult problem with others. Whether discussing how different people interpret a situation, considering all the possible options for responding to the situation, or simply trying to give yourself the "big picture" of what you are facing, talking through a difficult problem with others can be a wildly informative, challenging, and helpful exercise.

However, talking through a problem is not just a valuable exercise in our personal or professional lives; indeed, learning how to productively talk through a difficult problem is also incredibly necessary in public life as well. The facts are clear: as a society, we are not particularly good at seeing, let alone reasonably considering, the many points of view that exist in our community on contentious public issues. In recent decades, community members have increasingly locked ourselves into knee-jerk partisan perspectives, isolated ourselves from people and communities different from us, and narrowed our sources of information to those that simply confirm our pre-existing worldviews. These trends have made it gradually more difficult to effectively discuss problems that affect us all in a meaningful way because we simply do not know or care to know about the various perspectives of the community on these problems.

This situation is discouraging to anyone who values public discourse and well-run communities; however, it has also prompted action. In particular, communities have turned to the deliberation movement as one of several possible avenues through which people can learn to speak with each other in clear and credible ways about difficult public subjects.

In this chapter, you will be introduced to some of the basic tenants of speaking for public deliberation by giving a public deliberation speech. In this speech, you will talk through with your peers the various sides and competing values present within a particular public problem. In doing so, you will learn how to look at an issue through many different perspectives, to recognize how others engage those perspectives, and to lead a discussion on these various perspectives. By the end of the speech, you should have acquired not only a basic sense of deliberation, but a more holistic appreciation for public problems, which will serve you well in your policy speech in the next round.

What Is Public Deliberation?

Deliberation is an old term that has acquired some new meanings in the realm of communication and public speaking. Since some of the earliest theorizations of rhetoric in Ancient Greece, **deliberation**—*the mindful and thorough investigation of public problems and policy solutions through speech*—has been a goal of speech in the civic realm. Traditionally, this deliberative goal was sought and achieved through combative debates and pointed policy speeches—something we will try our hands at in the next unit of the class.

However, the 21st century has prompted the need to consider additional ways of having productive deliberations on public issues. One of these is public deliberation. According to CSU's Center for Public Deliberation, **public deliberation** is *a form of communication that features "open spaces for citizens to come together, good and fair information to help structure the conversation, and skilled facilitators to guide the process."*[34] Unlike more traditional forms of deliberation, public deliberation sets up a process that encourages a genuine exchange of ideas and actively avoids the more common pitfalls of contemporary public discourse. A key feature of this process—good and fair information—is an expectation for all public speakers and public speeches. However, the active choice to provide a place for the audience to engage the speaker and each other on an issue and to have a speaker prepared to facilitate that engagement are additions to the more traditional models of public speaking that make speaking for public deliberation distinctive.

In this book and this class, we will take a small, tentative step into the realm of public deliberation with the public deliberation speech. Yet, there is no way we can possibly go in-depth into these skills, let alone provide you the many hours of experience needed to become an advanced facilitator of public discourse. As such, students interested in learning more about developing public deliberation skills or even becoming a facilitator of public deliberation should consider taking coursework in Communication Studies like SPCM 207: Public Argumentation or applying to be a facilitator with the Center for Public Deliberation—both of which are opportunities offered to students regardless of major or minor.

Deliberating Wicked Problems

While deliberation is a goal common to many issues, some public issues are particularly prone to benefit from a public deliberation approach. These issues are what we call wicked problems. Dr. Martín Carcasson, one of the leading experts on public deliberation, defines **wicked problems** as *"problems [that] have no technical solutions, primarily because they involve competing underlying values and paradoxes that require either tough choices between opposing goods or innovative ideas that can transcend the inherent tensions."*[35] As this definition shows, wicked problems are often among the most controversial and challenging issues to discuss in public settings. That is because these are not simply problems with a "right" or "wrong" answer; rather, wicked problems are public issues where different public values are pitted against each other, making building consensus on how to choose and make priorities among them—and even to discuss them!—difficult.

An example of a wicked problem can be found in public debates around the privacy of personal information on social media. Over the last few years, there have been great debates over what, if anything, to do about these concerns, with very little action at either the national, state, or local level. We might argue that is because the issue is one in which a variety of competing values intersect, including:

- **Communication and community**. We value being *able to communicate* with others about all aspects of our lives; therefore, we do not want to be limited in what we can say or do on social media sites.
- **Convenience**. We value *the convenience of access* (less time, less hassle, less cost) made possible by sharing private information with social media companies; therefore, we want to be able to provide as much personal information as possible to social media companies.
- **Safety and security**. We value *knowing that our personal information will be protected* from public scrutiny, invasion, and abuse by hostile outside forces; therefore, social media companies need to be held accountable for breaches of private information.
- **Business**. We value the fact that *social media companies are businesses* that make money and employ thousands of people; therefore, we do not want to overly constrain or regulate them.

The examples above illustrates why acting on the issue of protecting privacy on social media is so difficult: in offering solutions, our values are frequently at odds with one another. We want access and convenience, but we don't want our data to be compromised. We want these companies to grow, but we don't want them to abuse our data that we provide freely. These are just some of the different values in conflict with one another when we debate these issues in public.

Activity: What do you value most?

Martín Carcasson, Director of the Center for Public Deliberation at Colorado State University, often asks his students to consider the many values that are promoted in our culture, including: Freedom, Safety, Equality, Justice, Care for future generations, Community, Self-Responsibility (individuality), Consistency, and Progress. As an individual, rank each of these values from most to least important (1 = most important, 9 = least important). Then, get into groups of 3–4 and explain why you ranked your values the way that you did. Next, try to make an argument for why someone might rank their first choice as the bottom choice and their bottom choice as their top. After each person has had a chance, return to the whole class and try to identify common policy debates in which these values are in competition.

However, in many traditional debate formats, we do not enter the debate with all of these values in mind. Many of us and our leaders attack these issues through a single perspective; but this approach can be counterproductive. If one side only sees the issue through the lens of "safety" and the other through the lens of "business," we will never make any progress on the issue.

A public deliberation speech, by contrast, provides a way of moving forward. Rather than asking us to advocate for a single position—as we will in the policy speech—it asks us to show the public the many different perspectives and values at stake in a given policy discussion. In doing so, each position is given a fair hearing and presented regardless of the feelings of those in the room. It is also supported with credible and well-supported research. However, once the many perspectives on the issue have been presented to the community, the speaker becomes a facilitator who asks the community to talk through which of these values matter more to them. As such, by the end of the speech, the community should know which values at stake matter most to them at the moment, which can be used to encourage informed advocacy for a policy solution later. In this way, public deliberation speeches fall somewhere between an informative and policy speech: providing a particular kind of information so that a productive persuasive case about policy can be made later.

Characteristics of a Public Deliberation Speech

Because the public deliberation speech may be new for both you and your audience, it is important to make sure that you are actively adopting the key characteristics of public deliberation in giving your speech. These characteristics include:

- **Choose a controversial problem.** A public deliberation speech needs to address a wicked problem; therefore, you should not select a speech topic on which there is wide agreement. Instead, focus your considerations on challenging topics where there is a lot of disagreement.
- **Be audience-focused.** In all speeches, it is vital to be focused on the audience of your speech in order to be successful; however, in a public deliberation speech, it is especially important that you recognize the speech should serve your audience by treating them equally, encouraging their participation, and providing them with useful information.
- **Be the honest broker.** Remember that in this speech, you will need to fairly and equally present the many values at issue in your public problem. As in the informative speech, this can be challenging for some novice speakers and even for advanced speakers who have strong feelings about the topic under discussion. In fact, some of us may even subconsciously push a particular agenda in the speech without knowing it. Therefore, make sure that when you select a topic, you pick something you are confident that you can be an honest broker for in your speech. Remember: a public deliberation speech is not really about what you think; it is about what *the community* thinks about a public issue broadly.
- **Use multiple perspective ordering patterns.** Since the aim of your speech is to present the audience with an assortment of different values and perspectives on a public issue, you need to organize your speech in a way to help you do so. In particular, you will want to make sure you do not fall into the habit of laying out your speech with two main points (i.e., a pro/con speech, a liberal/conservative speech, or simply a two-sided speech). Rather, you want to make sure your speech has a main point for each of several different competing values. If your speech does not identify at least three (3) competing values, you should consider a different speech topic. If your three competing values include "for," "against," "undecided," or "doesn't care," you are not doing the multiple perspectives pattern correctly! You can find an example of an outline featuring the multiple perspectives pattern on Canvas.
- **Use appropriate language.** As with the informative speech, language is again a vital consideration in the public deliberation speech. Language appears as an issue in this speech in at least two ways. First, because this speech is in part about giving information to an audience, it is important that the speaker speaks for clarity. Second, language is important for the speaker in that they must be sure their language fairly and equitably presents all values under consideration. Be sure your language is not implicitly or explicitly favorable or unfavorable to one value or another value. You will certainly have your opinions on these issues; however, those are best saved for the end of the speech or the policy round.

Tips for Facilitating a Dialogue

As part of the public deliberation speech, speakers will be asked to facilitate a dialogue among the class at the end of their speech where individuals can share their perspectives on which values and/or perspectives matter most to them in the current situation. Facilitating a dialogue is often a new experience for many novice speakers; therefore, it is important to follow some basic tips on how to do so productively. The tips we recommend to all novice speakers are:

- **Prepare dialogue questions in advance.** It can be quite difficult to come up with good questions in the moment without preparation and speakers who fail to do so can radically harm their credibility in the process. Therefore, come to your speech with a set of questions prepared for your audience in advance. You need not use any or all of the questions you prepared if the conversation takes off on its own; however, you will be happy to have them if the conversation is slow to evolve organically.
- **Ask open-ended questions.** In a discussion, **closed-ended questions**—*questions that can be answered with a single one-word response or choice from a list*—can quickly limit conversation. They are most commonly started with the words, "Do," "Are," and "Is." Try to avoid these kinds of questions in your dialogue. Instead, to prompt conversation, use **open-ended questions**—*questions that can be answered with complete sentences and thoughts*. These questions typically begin with the words "What," "How," or "Why." The latter works much better at getting the group to explain, question, reconsider, compare, and rank their views and often sparks input from others.
- **Pause for participation**. Audience members may need a moment or two to actively think about your questions and your speech before they can offer a contribution to your dialogue. Therefore, after you ask your question, be sure to give the audience a few seconds to respond. If the room remains quiet for some time, consider asking your same question in a different way before moving on to another question.
- **Encourage wide participation**. A good dialogue will feature comments and participation from a diverse group of community members. As such, you will want to call on different people in your audience and people with different perspectives over the course of the dialogue. This might also mean politely cutting off an audience member who seeks to monopolize too much time in the dialogue to ensure others get to speak as well.
- **Encourage the audience to use the language of the speech**. During your speech, you will have laid out several values and/or perspectives that you find in opposition around your public problem. In the dialogue afterwards, encourage your audience to use these same values and/or perspectives in expressing their own viewpoints. This will allow everyone to stay focused on the same issues and have a more productive conversation. When in doubt about what value or perspective your audience member is addressing, consider restating the participant's case to connect it back to the discussion.
- **Actively ask for opposing viewpoints.** If your dialogue seems to lead to wide agreement on how these values should be ranked, look for those who might offer a different perspective. It is OK if everyone in the room agrees, but only if a fair chance has been given for opposing viewpoints to be presented.
- **Actively seek out values that you did not mention**. While you may think you have fully presented the most important values at issue in your topic, be open-minded that there might be other values you did not address that motivate the audience. In order to be open-minded with your audience, seek out those unstated values during your dialogue.

Concluding After the Dialogue

Once a speaker has completed their facilitated dialogue with their audience, it is vital that the speaker take a moment to conclude their public deliberation speech. Indeed, as we have seen in previous chapters, conclusions are vital elements of all public speeches and do important work that contributes to the success of a speech. As such, failing to provide a conclusion at the end of a public deliberation speech is a significant lapse in speaking effectivity.

The challenge, of course, with concluding a public deliberation speech after a dialogue is that your audience will likely introduce new information into the speech during the dialogue. As a speaker, you cannot ignore that information in your conclusion, but you also cannot anticipate everything that will come up in your dialogue either. How then do you conclude your speech after a dialogue? In short, you should be sure to:

- Remind your audience of the topic of your speech and the primary goal of the speech: to persuade your audience to consider different perspectives on a public issue.
- Summarize your own main points from your prepared speech.
- From memory or from notes you jotted down during the dialogue, briefly mention ideas, questions, or perspectives raised by your audience in the dialogue.
- Conclude your remarks with a note of appreciation for the audience's participation in the dialogue and encouragement to continue considering the complexity of the issue you discussed.

Being an Ethical Audience Member in a Dialogue

While the speaker has significant responsibilities to encourage a fair and ethical discussion of the many values around their selected topic, the speaker is not the only participant in the dialogue that has obligations. Audience members, too, have an obligation to act in an ethical and deliberative way if the public deliberation exercise is to be a success. While those obligations will vary by topic and potentially even by each individual person in the class, overall, each audience member in a public deliberation speech should:

- Listen to the speech with an open mind, even if you have or believe you have strong feelings on the topic of the speech.
- Make note of the various perspectives and values presented by the speaker.
- Note additional perspectives or values on the issue that the speaker did not address as the speech continues.
- Participate in the dialogue by raising questions or offering alternative perspectives or values.
- Use language and delivery that demonstrates a genuine desire for conversation rather than language that attacks the speaker or another audience member. Similarly, you will want to use language and delivery that encourages people to participate and make their own judgments about the issue.
- Be mindful to not take over the dialogue and to allow others to participate.

Remember: Since all members of the class will participate in the dialogues as audience members and speakers, you will want to be the kind of audience member for others that you will want to have as a speaker.

Real-World Public Deliberation Speaking Examples

Unlike some other aspects of this class, the real world is not yet rife with numerous examples of public deliberation speaking. Nonetheless, there are many places in your life where you can use the skills and goals of the public deliberation speech. As a public speaker, you might use public deliberation speaking in community meetings, business meetings, and meetings of civic organizations, among many other places. Luckily, for the purposes of this class, you can also find examples of real-world public deliberation speaking on Canvas.

However, if you are interested in other ways in which public deliberation is used in the real world, you need look no farther than CSU's Center for Public Deliberation (CPD). The CPD is a group of students trained in facilitating public deliberations who work with local community entities and organizations to assist them in discussing wicked problems they face in making public decisions. Faculty members in the Communication Studies Department here at CSU lead this effort. To learn more about the work of the CPD, including opportunities to become a trained student facilitator, visit their website at https://cpd.colostate.edu/.

Chapter 15

POLICY SPEAKING

When most people think about public speaking in the United States, more often than not, they are imagining the kind of speechmaking we will examine in this chapter: policy speaking. A **policy speech** is *a speech in which the speaker identifies a problem of public concern and advocates a particular course of action to resolve or minimize that problem.* While policy speeches are not unique to democracies, there is something highly democratic about the idea of a policy speech. It presumes that, as a people, we are best positioned to identify the problems that exist in our society and to debate amongst ourselves how we should collectively address these problems. Policy speaking, more so than most of the speeches in this book, is an excellent example of citizenship in action.

However, policy speeches can be among the most difficult speeches we give as speakers. Unlike informative speaking, we need to do more than just share information with an audience; rather, we need to advocate for a particular position. Unlike a public deliberation speech, we tend to have strong personal feelings about an issue when we give a policy speech; indeed, typically, we are not seeking out opinions, but trying to move and shape public opinion in a specific way. As such, policy speeches represent a new order of complexity for the novice public speaker.

Nonetheless, while policy speaking is challenging, it can also be among the most rewarding of the speeches we give. Policy speeches ask us to be informed and involved in our community, to witness the suffering and challenges of others in our world, to think seriously about a set of ways those people might be assisted, and to advance a particular solution that we think will work best. If we succeed, we can proudly say that we made a difference in our society. But even if we fail, policy speaking is an exercise in citizenship: an example of people being active members of the public in search of its best self.

Persuading People on Policy Is Hard

While speaking effectively in any situation is a complex task, research in the fields of Communication Studies, Political Science, and Psychology have shown over and over again that speaking with someone about policy issues can be particularly challenging. That has not always been the prominent view. Indeed, for centuries, speakers worked under the assumption that while people were hard to shake from their pre-existing position on difficult issues, most of us were naturally open minded, willing to listen to others and to admit that we were wrong, and open to changing our minds when presented with sound, logical evidence to the contrary.

More recently, however, it has become clear that people do not always act as the ideal audience in an argument. Frankly, many people do not like to be wrong, they are not always open to other positions, and people can disagree wildly about what counts as logical evidence. On top of all these issues, consider the following challenges to persuasion identified by psychologists, political scientists, and communication scholars[36] that can aggravate the policy speaking process:

Confirmation Bias. Research illustrates that when people have strong views or beliefs on a particular issue, they are unlikely to interpret new information about that topic in a fair and objective way. This psychological process is called **confirmation bias** and has been defined as *people's tendency to take evidence that confirms their existing views at face value while being highly critical and suspicious of information that challenges their existing view of an issue*.[37] As such, public speakers (among others) should not expect to persuade their audiences simply by providing them with new information; rather, they should expect the audiences that disagree with them to doubt or even disbelieve their research, even if they only do so at a subconscious level.

Partisanship. Today, in the United States and many other parts of the world, people's views on policy are heavily influenced by **partisanship**—*the knee-jerk belief that the best policy is whatever policy is advocated for those who share my political affiliation*. Implicitly, this also means that strong partisans regularly assume that the best policy is almost never those advocated for by people with other political affiliations. Therefore, public speakers who advocate for a policy as a known partisan can potentially be met with higher levels of doubt from audience members who strongly identify as a member of a different political party.

Policy as Identity. Contemporary research also illustrates the increasing degree to which people view particular policies as a core part of their identity. In particular, theories of **identity-protective cognition** show that *people process information about the world so that it confirms their own ideas about who they are*. More specifically, thanks to identity-protection cognition, people easily remember information that confirms our self-image and forget information that questions our self-image.[38] Therefore, a public speaker who argues to change a policy because it is racially biased might meet resistance from an audience, not because the policy is *not* biased, but because the audience does not want to think of themselves as having previously supported a policy that was racist.

Intolerance and Security. Related to issues of identity, scholarship over the last decade has demonstrated that, while people are generally open minded about other people, cultures, and ideas, they become less so when they feel their own way of life is under threat. Researchers call this the **authoritarian dynamic**: *people's psychological tendency to demand strict traditionalism, security, and limitations of permissiveness and change in the face of perceived risk to themselves and their values*.[39] This means that public speakers may have a more difficult time persuading an audience that feels at risk because of changes in society.

The "Backfire Effect." Recent research in political science and psychology has found that sometimes *correcting a person's misperceptions about a policy actually leads them to believe that misperception more deeply*. This finding is called the **backfire effect**. While researchers continue to study the backfire effect and its causes, a leading explanation is that when people find themselves in positions that require them to defend their beliefs, it actually raises that person's stake in that belief. As such, the person in the wrong tends to dig their heels in even more when questioned on a topic.[40] Consequently, audiences that have the wrong facts about an issue may be even more difficult to persuade if a public speaker asks the audience to defend or reconsider those views.

These challenges to persuasion are notable; however, none of this is to say that persuasion is impossible. Indeed, most research that casts doubt on our ability to persuade others on policy simultaneously suggests that there are limits to how far people will stand by their anti-persuasive impulses. However, the existence of these low-level impediments to persuasion suggests that policy speakers need to be strategic in how they argue their case if they wish to be successful.

Persuasion That Works

It might seem like the deck is stacked against us in being persuasive in policy speeches. However, the same research that tells us why it is difficult to persuade an audience also illuminates strategies that can be most effective in persuasion, particularly around politics and policies. Many of these theories are examined at length in Communication classes like SPCM 437: Studies in Persuasion. For our purposes here, though, some useful theories and strategies for persuasion include:

Relevance and Engagement. A now long-established fact about human persuasion is that people are more likely to listen to, consider, and potentially support policies when speakers present those policies in ways that motivate the audience. The Elaboration Likelihood Model, first conceived in 1980, established this point by noting that audiences hear speakers in one of two ways: through either central or peripheral processing. When audiences hear a speaker's arguments through the peripheral processing route—marked by sporadic attention and the passive or uncritical consumption of ideas—they are less likely to engage the speaker's argument or act upon them. Meanwhile, when speakers invite audiences to listen to them through the central processing route, audiences engage the speaker's ideas, actively consider them, and are more likely to act on them.[41] In order to urge an audience to engage their speech through the central processing route, speakers need to show their audience that their topic is relevant to their lives, in explicit ways and regular intervals. At a practical level, this means the speaker must select a genuinely interesting and meaningful topic, use effective attention getters and relevance statements in the introduction, connect the speech to the audience throughout the body, and deliver the speech in compelling and engaging ways.

Repetition. We often find repetition to be annoying. Indeed, most of us have probably felt annoyed by the never-ending onslaught of political ads that emerge every election season on our televisions, phones, and other devices. However, while these ads might be annoying, they also work, and a major reason they do is repetition. In fact, researchers in many fields of study have confirmed that repetition is one of the most effective strategies for moving an audience to think about a policy in a particular way.[42] Nor is repetition unique to political advertisements; a good public speech also has structural elements that remind the audience of key arguments in order to produce a persuasive effect. These structural elements include introductions, previews, reviews, internal summaries, and the conclusion. In addition, a speaker might use stylistic elements like alliteration, parallelism, or rhyming to do repetition. An old public speaking mantra perhaps best summed up the value of repetition in persuasion: "tell them what you're going to tell them, tell them, and then tell them what you told them."

Empathy and Perspective-Taking. A long line of humanities and social scientific research also suggests that speakers can persuade audiences to reconsider or change their views on policies when they are asked to see the world from the perspective of another person or community. To put it simply: many people find it can be harder to support a policy that harms or is unfair to a community different from their own once they gain knowledge of that community and identify with them. This idea has appeared in various forms through time: as appeals to empathy, calls for identification, and interactions that encourage perspective-taking. Likewise, it has been foundational to political strategies like "coming out," which has played a part in significantly increasing the acceptance of the LGBT community in the U.S. more broadly. While scholars and researchers continue to investigate the ways these appeals do or do not work on audiences, a recent study found that even relatively short face-to-face interactions can lead to diminished animosity toward communities of difference and greater acceptance of political support for those communities in audiences that had not previously felt that way.[43]

Moral Reframing. In policy speeches, we tend to seek to persuade others through *our own perspectives* about why something is right or wrong, what we might call our **moral frameworks**. However, research shows that public speakers and other policy advocates can be more successful at persuading others to adopt their position by advocating their policy through the audience's moral framework rather than their own. This process of *using the audience's moral perspectives to persuade them to adopt a different policy position* is called **moral reframing**. An example of moral reframing from a 2015 study showed that political conservatives were unlikely to support accepting increased numbers of Syrian refugees into the United States if asked to do so by moral appeals to "fairness" (namely, that it is unfair to treat Muslim refugee requests with more skepticism than those of non-Muslims), a moral framework often coded as more liberal. However, the researchers found conservatives were persuaded to accept more refugees from Syria when they were approached with arguments that appealed to traditionally conservative moral frameworks like "patriotism" and "loyalty" (i.e., these refugees want to come to this country just like our ancestors; they want to become Americans and, as Americans, we should welcome them, as is our tradition).[44]

Anticipating Counterarguments and Disadvantages. As speakers, we often feel that our audience must perceive us as entirely correct to be successful; that to admit that our speech has limitations or weaknesses would be to show a fatal flaw that threatened our entire speech. Yet, research tells us something different. In particular, audiences often respond favorably to a speaker who proactively admits the limitations of their position before the other side raises these deficiencies. The *preemptive admission and refutation of limitations to our policy* is called **anticipating counterarguments and disadvantages**. There are many ways this approach can contribute to persuasion. For one, it demonstrates that the speaker is confident enough in their proposed policy to acknowledge its limits. For another, it provides the speaker the opportunity to poke holes in the opposition's perspective before their opponents can even make them. Finally, according to inoculation theory, speakers can actually thwart the persuasive appeals of their opposition by providing audiences a small and measured sense of your position's weaknesses prior to that side making their own claims.

These strategies for effective persuasion are just a few of the many tools at your disposal as a public speaker; however, each strategy is so effective that it is not unusual to see each appear in numerous places throughout the world's most successful public speeches.

Examples of Real-World Policy Speeches

Anyone who pays attention to politics and government even tangentially should be experienced in watching examples of policy speeches in the real world. But you might be surprised to learn that policy speeches are not limited to government and politics. In fact, policy debates take place in all sorts of social formations in which rules and procedures need to be established to make the organization work. As such, policy speeches and debates can be found in organizations as diverse as businesses, non-profits, social organizations, campus clubs, athletic groups, leagues, fan clubs, children's groups, and many, many more. While these examples of sites for policy speaking are quite broad, we'll offer a few classic examples below to make the utility of a policy speech clear.

- **Campaign policy speeches**. When politicians run for office, many of their campaign speeches focus—in entirety or in part—on the particular policies that they would seek to enact if elected.
- **Legislative debate speeches**. In legislative bodies, like Congress or state legislatures, legislators are responsible for debating policies that reach the floor in the form of legislation.
- **Comment periods in local government**. In more local settings, governments often provide citizens the opportunity to express their opinions in speeches about proposed laws or upcoming decisions by local leaders.
- **Advocacy group speeches**. Outside of government, non-profits and advocacy organizations use policy speeches at public events and news conferences to make arguments for the kinds of polices they would like to see enacted by government leaders.
- **Speeches at annual retreats, business meetings, or orientations**. In the corporate world, there are often annual gatherings of employees and business leaders in which executives relate and explain key changes in how the business will work in the new year.

Characteristics of a Policy Speech

Policy speaking is one of the most complex types of speechmaking we participate in as citizens and professionals; therefore, it is crucial that we recognize the many characteristics of policy speaking necessary to advance a persuasive case. These characteristics include:

Focusing on Fixing Public Problems. A policy speech is a particular kind of persuasive speech focused on identifying and fixing a public problem. Sometimes, novice public speakers go astray in policy speaking by focusing on the word "persuasion" rather than "policy." Instead of discussing how to address an issue that affects the public good, the speaker calls into question a social value or what they see as a moral failing in society and seeks to attack or criticize it. Speakers who do the latter are certainly engaging in persuasive speaking, but not policy speaking. If your speech does not offer a solution to a problem that affects the public, it is failing to meet the primary goal of this speech.

Challenging the Status Quo. An essential element of policy speaking in this class is to argue against the status quo. By **status quo** we mean *the current way in which we deal with a public problem*. As such, to give a speech against the status quo means that we must argue that the current way in which we deal with a public problem is inadequate, ineffective, or immoral (among others). And, if we think about it, it makes sense that this is the position we need to take. How often, for example, do you hear someone give an extended detailed speech about why everything is great, and we should keep it up? Usually, the only time someone speaks for the status quo is when someone else first seeks to challenge it. So, in this class and in most of your real-world speaking, you will be expected to advocate a policy that challenges the status quo and thereby will take on the **burden of proof**—*the expectation to show that continuing to do or not do what we are already doing will be problematic.*

Identifying Policy Experts. Once the speaker has identified a public problem and is prepared to challenge the status quo, the speaker will want to identify policies they agree with from reputable experts. As members of the public, we are all entitled to demand change; we might also have strong feelings on how those changes should be made. However, few of us are actual policy experts or policy makers. While we know what we want to see happen, we don't have the knowledge or experience about how to put those changes in place. Therefore, turning to policy experts who have drawn up precise and tested plans of action is our next best bet. By finding policies we approve of and advocating for them, we remove the need to be policy experts or to craft policy ourselves. Instead, we advance credible policies we have researched.

Need/Plan/Practicality. Any good policy speech must address three issues in order to make a successfully case: need, plan, and practicality. AnnaMarie Adams Mann outlines these points in the *SPCM 200: Speech Coursebook*, which was modified for the description below:

- **Need**. Every policy speech must demonstrate that there is a need—a public problem that currently exists, needs fixing, and relates to the specific audience at hand. While the need might be apparent to the speaker, not all audience members may inherently recognize the need the speaker wants to address; therefore, the speaker must explicitly raise and explain the need their policy will address in the beginning of their speech by explaining:
    - The problem
    - The population that is affected by the problem
    - The severity of the problem
    - The dangers involved if the problem is not solved
- **Plan**. For a policy speech to be successful, it must also advocate a particular plan. A policy speech that simply rails about a need but offers no direction for action will not be successful. Meanwhile, a policy speech with a plan tells the audience that there is a way to solve or mitigate the stated need. For a plan to be effective in a policy speech, it must:
    - *Be explained clearly and plainly*. What does your plan entail? What are the specific courses of action you advocate implementing?
    - *State who will enforce the plan*. What person(s), organization, agency, or government will execute the plan? How will they do so?
    - *Discuss funding, if necessary*. Where will the money to pay for your plan come from if it requires new funding? Remember: funding need not come from taxes but could also come from reallocating existing funds.
- **Practicality**. Once the speaker explains the plan in full, they should also discuss the practicality of the plan—whether or not the plan is feasible given the current situation. It is easy for a speaker to offer a plan without discussing practicality; in fact, we often hear our leaders make grand statements about how to fix an issue without describing how to address issues of cost,

risk, time, politics, or many other considerations. Meanwhile, a policy speaker who voluntarily discusses practicality is more likely to be taken seriously and more likely to win approval of her plan than those who do not. To describe practicality effectively, a speaker must:

- *Describe how or to what extent the plan cures the need.* Not all plans need to cure a problem completely in order to be practical; however, for your plan to be practical it should have a meaningful impact on the problem you identified in the need.
- *Weigh advantages over disadvantages.* All plans bring with the disadvantages. As a speaker, you must show how the advantages/benefits of the plan outweigh the disadvantages/cost. Remember that costs can be monetary but also include the loss of liberty, ethical standing, time, etc.
- *Address counterarguments.* To prevent counterarguments or misunderstandings from undermining your case, take time in your speech to address and rebuke these counterarguments preemptively.

Speaking for Eloquence. A policy speech is more complex than an informative speech and more focused on a particular outcome than a public deliberation dialogue; therefore, a policy speaker needs to deploy language that is more complex in order to effect persuasion in their audience. As we discussed in Chapter 9, speaking for eloquence is the speaking style best equipped for most policy speeches. Speaking for eloquence enables the speaker to simplify complex ideas for an audience, draw on their emotions, emphasize their points with imagery, build the need for action with rhythm, and inspire action. Speaking for eloquence offers an array of tropes and figures the speaker can use; therefore, the speaker should be diligent in selecting only those stylistic devices that they deem most effective given their particular topic and primary speech goal.

Calling for Specific Action. In addition, a policy speech must feature a specific call to action. The call to action is typically the final aspect of any policy speech. In the call to action, the speaker makes a clear "ask" of the audience: vote this way, buy this product, volunteer for this group, etc. It comes at the end of the speech because we as speakers want there to be as little time as possible between our "ask" and the opportunity for the audience to act. Calls to action must be specific; vague or ambiguous calls leave the audience without direction and ultimately undermine the speaker's primary goal. For more of call to actions, see Chapter 7.

Anticipating Counterarguments. Finally, a successful policy speech is not just about arguing for a new policy but anticipating and addressing the counterargument to your speech by those who might disagree with you. **Counterarguments** are *claims raised in opposition to a proposed plan that identify its weaknesses and deficiencies.* Since problem-solving is a complex task, nearly every proposed solution has some sort of counterargument that can be raised against it. New government programs, for instance, might help address a problem, but might also become an unwieldy new expense that will be difficult to fund. Therefore, no speaker should expect that their proposed policy will be so good that it has no counterarguments. Instead, speakers should not wait for those who disagree with them to raise counterarguments but should do so themselves. If a speaker takes the time to raise the counterarguments against them, they may shrewdly show that they are an honest broker in a complex situation and that the counterarguments are not as problematic as the other side might suggest.

While these characteristics are essential for an effective policy speech, they alone may not drive the audience to the speaker's side. As such, policy speakers can also benefit from the use of organizational strategies that amplify the characteristics above.

Organizing for Persuasion

Earlier in this book, we devoted a chapter to general advice on organization that was effective for most kinds of speeches; however, that same chapter suggested that policy speaking in particular can sometimes demand more tested forms of organization to achieve the particular task of persuasion. In this section of the chapter, we will examine four (4) ordering patterns for policy speeches that policy speakers should highly consider to amplify their persuasive messages, all of which are illustrated in Table 15-1.

Problem-Solution. The first and simplest order pattern for policy speeches is the problem-solution ordering pattern. It offers the speaker a clear and distinct organization for an audience to follow that directly connects the need and the plan/practicality described previously. The problem-solution pattern maintains many of the most common features of our other ordering patterns: it starts with an introduction (including its five structural elements), ends with a conclusion, and has a body with points and transitions. What makes the problem-solution pattern distinct is its designation of the main points. In a problem-solution pattern, the speech has only two (2) main points. The first is the problem, which details the public problem identified by the speaker and a description of why it is a pressing need. The second is the solution main point. In the solution main point, the speaker details the plan to address the need and describes how the plan is practically implemented. The only other addition offered by the problem-solution pattern is the inclusion of a specific call to action somewhere in the concluding paragraph.

Problem-Cause-Solution. Closely related to the problem-solution ordering patterns is the problem-cause-solution ordering pattern. Like the problem-solution pattern, this pattern is a relatively clear and simple way of presenting the need, plan, and practicality for a policy speech. What distinguishes problem-cause-solution is the inclusion of another main point between the problem and the solution: the cause. In the cause point, the speaker moves beyond identifying and describing the problem in the first point to detailing what caused the problem in the first place. The speaker then moves on to offering the solution. The benefit of adding the cause point in this pattern is that it allows the speaker to advocate for a plan that is not simply a cosmetic or temporary fix; rather, in this pattern, the speaker can argue for eliminating the problem at its source and, thereby, stop it for good. Alternately, if the problem arises from many sources, this pattern allows the speaker to tailor their speech to specific dimensions of the problem (along with its solution). In other words, problem-cause-solution offers a speaker a more comprehensive approach to the problem.

Comparative Advantage. When the speaker aims to contrast two policies against each other, they should consider using the comparative advantage ordering pattern. As the name suggests, the pattern is focused on using comparison to illustrate a clear advantage in one policy over another. The patterns consist of an introduction, conclusion, and three main points: the first identifies the problem and describes the current approach to that problem, the second outlines the various way in which the current policy is inadequate (too expensive, counterproductive, inefficient, etc.), and the third point proposes an alternate policy and explains why it would be superior to the existing policy. This model works best when comparing two policies: an existing and a proposed policy. It does not work particularly well for proposing a new policy when no current policy is in effect.

Monroe's Motivated Sequence. The final policy ordering pattern for our consideration is called Monroe's Motivated Sequence. Derived from the study of the successful techniques of door-to-door salesmen in the early part of the 20th century, the motivated sequence is still used in sales, advertising, and marketing extensively today. It is radically different from the previous patterns we have examined, largely because it consists of five steps rather than a traditional I + 3 + C pattern.

In particular, Monroe's Motivated Sequence features a(n):

- **Attention step**. Replaces the introduction and serves as an extended attention getter.
- **Need step**. Details a current need in the audience, sometimes by raising a concern the audience did not even know they had.
- **Satisfaction step**. The speaker offers a solution to the audience to solve or mitigate their established need.
- **Visualization step**. The speaker helps the audience imagine how their life might look differently (in a large or small way) based upon their next choices. Visualizations can be positive or negative. Positive visualizations illustrate all the good that can come from following the speaker's plan; negative visualizations detail all that can go wrong if the audience ignores the speaker's plan.
- **Action step**. The speech ends with an extended call to action, with a particular focus on how the speaker can take immediate action along the lines the speaker suggests.

Table 15-1. Comparative Organizations of Policy Speech Patterns

PROBLEM-SOLUTION	PROBLEM-CAUSE-SOLUTION	COMPARATIVE ADVANTAGE	MONROE'S MOTIVATED SEQUENCE
Introduction	Introduction	Introduction	Attention
Main Point #1. Problem (Need)	Main Point #1. Problem (Need)	Main Point #1. Current Approach	Need (Need)
Main Point #2. Solution (Plan + Practicality)	Main Points #2. Cause	Main Point #2. Deficiencies in Current Approach (Need)	Satisfaction (Plan + Practicality)
	Main Point #3. Solution (Plan + Practicality)	Main Point #3. Alternative Approach (Plan) and Why It's Better (Practicality)	Visualization
Conclusion	Conclusion	Conclusion	Action

Fielding Questions After a Policy Speech

There are many situations that require the ability to field questions in a calm and convincing manner—job interviews, training sessions, professional presentations, and interpersonal debates. Policy speeches are chief among these occasions, but few of us are prepared to field questions in a Q&A session without practice. Therefore, we should spend a few minutes discussing how to think about Q&A and how to strategize doing it well.

Q&A Frame of Mind. Q&A sessions exist to achieve four primary objectives for a public speaker, namely to clarify information, expand or reinforce your arguments, bolster your credibility as a speaker, and assuage listener concerns. With these objectives in mind, it is vital that you anticipate and take questions in a Q&A session with the aim of emphasizing the following skills:

- **Competence**. A Q&A session should display your communication competence. Reinforce your claims for the audience and be prepared to explain and extend your arguments with new examples and additional evidence. There is usually information that you cannot include in your speech due to time constraints—this is your opportunity to share that information with the audience. Just as importantly: *Never fake it!* Audiences can spot a phony a mile away. Be willing to admit areas of ignorance by saying something like, "That's an aspect of the topic I haven't considered in depth," or "That's a good suggestion. I would like to pursue that in further research."

- **Collaboration**. A Q&A session is not a confrontation. You want to win over your audience, not beat them in an argument. Even though some audience members might bait you and try to engage you in confrontation, do not risk it. You will end up undermining your own credibility if you go "one-on-one" with a listener. Instead, emphasize areas of convergence between your arguments and the questioner's position. Listen carefully to the questions as audience members pose them. Be willing to admit areas of ignorance or weaknesses in your argument. Remember, the effectiveness of a speech is judged by how well it is adjusted to the audience.

- **Control**. When you are the speaker, you get to control the presentation. If you need a moment or two to think about a question before you respond, take it! Do not relinquish control of your topic by "buying into" someone else's premise. Do not allow one questioner to dominate the Q&A session—acknowledge others after you have given one audience member the opportunity for a question and follow-up question/response.

- **Common sense**. Do not feel that everyone is "out to get you" after you have given a speech. People have different motivations for asking questions—to seek clarification, to make themselves look smart, to help you support your claims, or to contradict you. Not all questions are hostile. That is why listening is an especially important skill during a Q&A session.

Q&A Strategies. While having the right mindset for a Q&A session is key to your success, you also want to be familiar with several particular strategies for answering questions effectively. These include:

- **Format**. After carefully listening to your audience's question and assessing the questioner's motivations, you will want to answer the question with a three-part response:

    1. Restate the question aloud if it needs clarification or if you want to make sure you are interpreting it correctly.

    2. State your answer succinctly.

    3. Support your answer. In other words, reiterate what you said in your speech or offer new information or evidence.

- **Nonverbal behavior**. When partaking in a Q&A session, do not forget that your audience is assessing your nonverbal behavior just as much as what you say in your answers. Therefore, as you answer a question, be sure to look at the questioner first before scanning the whole audience. Maintain a firm, authoritative stance. Try to minimize distracting gestures and movements. Finally, try to look and feel relaxed.

- **Watch for specific types of questions**. While we want many kinds of questions as a speaker in a Q&A session, it is important to recognize that not all questions are of equal caliber or made with the same intent. In fact, some questions can be either intentionally or unintentionally asked to raise problems for a speaker. As such, you'll want to be on the lookout for four types of questions and know how to answer them correctly.

- **Loaded questions**: *questions with assumptions or expectations already built into the questions.* An example of a loaded question is: "Don't you know that environmental regulation costs jobs?" To answer a loaded question, start by acknowledging the listener's position and/or emotions. Then, state your position without buying into the listener's premise. As a final step, try to emphasize areas of convergence between the two positions.

  Example answer: "It sounds like you're concerned about the economic implications of my proposal. That is understandable since previous regulations have had a negative effect on local economies. In fact, that was one of my main concerns as I was researching and developing this plan. However, by training businesses to use the environment more efficiently, I'm ensuring that the resources they need to keep their businesses going will be in plentiful supply for years to come. Without some sort of change in how businesses interact with the environment, local companies will have to shut down or move operations out of this region in just ten to twenty years."

- **Complex questions**: *questions with many parts, that go in many directions, or that may be too large for the time allotted in a Q&A*. For example: "I wonder which regulatory measures are best, most effective, and how much each costs?" To answer a complex question, start by stating that the question has several parts, and you will answer it piece by piece. Do not feel compelled to answer every issue. Feel free to focus on the most important/relevant question(s) in your response.

- **Vague questions**: *questions that do not clearly seek a particular kind of information or type of answer from the speaker*. For instance: "What do you think about NAFTA?" To answer a vague question, begin by trying to clarify with the questioner what she is trying to find out about before you attempt to answer. You might ask the questioner politely to pose their question again in a different way.

- **A non-question or statement of open disagreement/hostility**: *when a questioner offers a comment or critique to the speaker in the guise of a question*. An example would be: "I can't believe you cited something from PETA—they are the most radical animal rights group around. They care more about animals than people!" To answer a non-question is impossible because no question was actually asked; however, an effective speaker will note the non-question and respond appropriately. This response can productively start by telling the listener that you understand how he feels, answering the specific objection of the critique or statement, and finding areas of convergence if possible, and then move on to another question. Never allow hostility to escalate.

Of all the speeches we discuss in this book, the policy speech can be among the most multifaceted and therefore the most challenging; however, when done well, policy speaking offers speakers the opportunity to sway the minds of the audience on a vital issue the speaker cares about. In doing so, the speaker is actively participating in both public discourse and civic life.

Chapter 16

COMMEMORATIVE SPEAKING

Throughout history, communities have chosen to mark special events and occasions with speeches. The kind of speeches that are reserved for these special occasions are of a different tone and tenor than the others in this book. In particular, these speeches are what we call commemorative speeches. A **commemorative speech** is *a speech that praises a person or action as exemplary of a community value.* As this definition suggests, to speak on a special occasion—to mark a moment in time—is not just about celebrating, but about coming together as a community to affirm or reaffirm who we are and what matters to us. In this way, giving a commemorative speech is about putting life into perspective.

The need to put life in perspective tells us a lot about when and where commemorative speeches are given. It would be highly unusual, for instance, for someone to give a commemorative speech on a whim in the middle of the street or a city park, even if those places were common speechmaking venues. Instead, commemorative speeches cluster around moments of great transition: birth, death, victory, loss, achievement, failure, gatherings, and passings. It is in these moments that our sense of who we are—or who we were—can come into question. As such, it is also in these moments that we feel compelled to come together as a public, to reflect on the life that we share and, through the life and experiences of another person, rediscover ourselves.

The meaningfulness of commemorative speaking does not mean that these speeches are all serious; in fact, commemorative speaking is perhaps the best occasion for a speaker to be funny, entertaining, or clever. But we should never forget: no matter what the tone of a commemorative speech, it is always an act of doing something important and meaningful for ourselves and our communities.

Commemoration as Persuasion: A Speech of Values

While it may not be immediately apparent, a commemorative speech is a persuasive speech. More specifically, it is a particular kind of persuasive speech called a **speech of value**. A speech of value is *an address in which the speaker sets out a particular admirable belief as meriting adoption by the audience.* The speech has a persuasive aim because it asks the audience to adopt a value as important and impactful in their lives.

That a commemorative speech is persuasive in nature reveals a key part of how these kinds of speeches should be done, namely that they are only *partially* about the person, place, or event that is being commemorated. Certainly, a speech commemorating war heroes or praising a new scientific discovery is about these actual people and events: in our speeches, we will need to describe them, explain them, and go about praising them accordingly if we hope to make the speech commemorative.

But, in reality, a commemorative speech is just as much about the audience as it is the subject of commemoration. This is the inherent utility of a commemorative speech. Yes, commemorative speeches serve to honor someone or something, but their greater use is in *setting an example for others to follow*. In other words, commemorative speeches are about celebrating an individual only to the extent that that individual's achievement tells us something meaningful about who we are as an audience and how we might choose to live our own lives. Therefore, a speech commemorating war heroes is really about encouraging the audience to honor and practice bravery and service to country. Similarly, a speech marking a scientific discovery is about encouraging curiosity and the hard work it takes to make a breakthrough. In each case, marking the specific achievement is just part of broader purpose of the speaker.

Real-World Commemorative Speech Examples

Of all the speeches we will practice in this class, commemorative speeches are among the most likely that you will have to do, not just once but many times in the course of your life. Indeed, life is full of occasions that warrant commemorative speeches. For example, consider these extremely common commemorative speeches you will likely be asked to do some day outside of the classroom setting:

Toasts. A toast is *a very brief speech made with a raised beverage in which the speaker celebrates an accomplishment or gathering*. By its nature, a toast is often made at an event over dinner or another kind of meal. All toasts should be short, but the length can vary by occasion. A wedding toast by a member of a wedding party or parents should be short, but could reasonably last 2–3 minutes and end with the raising of glasses and the official "toast." By contrast a more casual toast over drinks must be incredibly brief; a toast over drinks that is too long is nearly unforgivable. What's too long? Consider the fact that your audience is holding something they want above their heads and they can't have it until you stop talking. Their arms will start to hurt after thirty seconds. Don't take that long.

Introductory Remarks. Another common type of commemorative speech is introductory remarks. Introductory remarks are *a short speech that introduces and celebrates the main speaker of an event*. As we now know, an effective public speaker needs to establish their credibility and expertise on a subject, something that can take up quite some time and, frankly, be embarrassing for some speakers to say about themselves. The role of an introductory speaker is to do this work for the main speaker. The introductory speaker should say warm things about the main speaker, describe their accomplishments and why they were asked to speak, and generally "pump up" the main speaker in the mind of the audience. You might think of introductory remarks as a warm-up act for the main event.

Acceptance Speech. Should you be so lucky to live an award-winning life (go you!), you'll want to know how to give an acceptance speech. An acceptance speech is an address by the winner of an award. We see these kinds of speeches all the time on televised award shows (the Oscars, Emmys, Grammys, etc.)—but they tend to be quite bad. However, televised award shows give speakers very little time whereas untelevised speakers are often given more generous time. The most important things to remember in an acceptance speech: know who is giving you the award, thank the award granters, thank those in your life who helped you, and briefly say something more general about what the award means to you. Also: not all awards come with the expectation of a speech, so only give one if asked!

Commencement Address. Graduations—whether from high school, college, or even kindergarten! —are among the most expected moments for the saying of celebratory words in U.S. culture. Commencement addresses—*longer speeches that celebrate the educational attainment of a group of students*—are thus something with which we are almost all familiar. Chances are we've heard both good and bad commencement addresses: the bad ones are all advice or all about the speaker whereas good ones are highly situated, usually funny, and primarily about the graduates.

Eulogy. It might seem odd to think of a eulogy—*a speech in celebration of the life of the deceased*—as a speech alongside other speeches for more happy occasions. But eulogies are certainly commemorative and, indeed, celebratory. They celebrate the life of someone who is no longer with us and they recognize that while that person may not be here anymore, their life can teach those of us who remain something about living life well. This is something eulogists can't forget: the speech is really for the living, not the dead.

Dedication. Closely related to introductory remarks or a eulogy is a speech of dedication—*an address that names a memorial, site, or space in honor of someone else.* Dedications can vary widely depending on what is being dedicated and when: if the person is still alive, it should be quite celebratory; if they are deceased, it may be more somber (although perhaps not). What is most important in a speech of dedication, though, is that the speaker detail how the life's work of the person honored will be continued through the memorial or space.

Throughout our lives, we are likely to have to give one or many of these kinds of speeches. However, while each speech is commemorative in its primary goal, be sure to pay attention to the significant differences between them. You cannot substitute a commencement address for a toast or introductory remarks for a eulogy without failing the speech situation.

Characteristics of a Commemorative Speech

In order to do a commemorative speech well, speakers will need to use the best practices for commemorative speaking. These best practices include:

Name a Value. All commemorative speakers will need to find a specific value to praise in the course of giving a commemorative speech. **Values** are *principles, standards, or beliefs that a person, people, or community hold as important and vital to the conduct of good personal and communal life.* While there are many values, common examples of values include principles like family, freedom, honesty, integrity, faith, persistence, responsibility, self-determination, flexibility, resilience, and service, just to name a small number. In the commemorative speech, you will need to reflect on what values matter to you and your community—and to be able to identify them in a clear and direct way. In your search for a value, a person, event, or act that inspires you might draw your attention first; however, if you think hard about it, you will find that there is a value embedded in your praise for that person that can be isolated and from which others can learn.

Root Your Speech in a Specific Person, Place, or Event. Once you have established your value, you will also want to identify the person, place, or event that exemplifies the value you want to praise. For some speakers, you might start with the person and move to the value; for others, you might begin with the value and move to the person. Either way, you do not want to give a commemorative speech about a value alone. A speech about "service," "friendship," or "perseverance" will always be vague and philosophical without rooting those values in the deeds or acts of a specific case. As we have already learned, using specific, concrete examples can help make our speeches relatable, relevant, and real to the audience.

Speak for Entertainment and/or Eloquence. A commemorative speech must also deploy language appropriate for the occasion in order to be successful. In general terms, a commemorative speech will usually qualify as either a speech for entertainment or a speech for eloquence (or a little of both). That means the speaker will be expected to avoid the simplistic and clear language of an informative address and will instead rely heavily on the stylistic tropes and figures more common to these other kinds of addresses. To review these various tropes and figures common to entertaining or eloquence, see those sections in Chapter 9.

But Can I Be Funny? While we might be most familiar as an audience with commemorative speeches that are serious and somber, we should recognize that it is entirely possible for a commemorative speech to be funny. Think about the "ideal" wedding toast as depicted in popular culture as an example. In almost all cases, it starts with some light and good-natured joking—even poking fun at the bride or groom—before eventually ending with some heartfelt praise and good wishes for the future. As such, wedding toasts are excellent examples of commemorative speeches that are both funny and touching. In contrast, there are some occasions that it is hard to see the humor in, particularly a tragic death or violent act. In those cases, staying away from humor is probably the best idea for a novice speaker.

Use a Manuscript. With the exception of a toast over drinks, which should be so short you can easily commit it to memory, commemorative speakers should consider using a manuscript to help them deliver their speech. There are several reasons why this makes sense. For one, some of these speeches are quite long; they also involve entertaining and eloquent language, which is difficult to deliver off the cuff. Introductory remarks and dedications often require great and specific details about a person you likely do not know well. Eulogies can be quite emotional; you'll want the full text there to go back to if you need it.

While these characteristics will give you a good sense of your expectations in a commemorative speech, there are other resources available to you in creating this very different kind of speech. In particular, students should check out the short essay on *Preparing Your Commemorative Speech* by Dr. Carl Burgchardt, which is available on Canvas.

Commemorative speeches often seem cute or even cookie-cutter at first glance, the stuff of silly toasts and entertaining occasions. But look again and you will see: every time we rise to commemorate a person, act, or event, we are rising to do the serious work of re-inscribing the moral and ethical compass of our family, community, and society.

Chapter 17

SPEAKING IN DIGITAL ENVIRONMENTS

Throughout the history of public speaking, technological advances have regularly altered the needs, opportunities, and challenges of public speakers. Advances in design, architecture, and acoustics enabled speakers to improve their projection and the size of their audience but also created distance from the audience. Inventions like microphones and visual aids provided speakers better ways to reach more people, but also altered the expectations and training of speakers. Recording and sharing public speeches, first on radio then television, radically upended our assumptions about how a public speaker should prepare, dress, perform and circulate their messages. In short, technology has always changed and with it, so has the training of the public speaker.

Today, our technological advances have again radically altered the training of the public speaker. In particular, while much of what we do as public speakers in topic selection, organization, research, and so on remains very much the same, a prepared public speaker in the 21st century must also be ready to speak effectively in digital environments. By **digital environments**, we mean *the sites where people gather to share ideas in new ways made possible by contemporary technological advances*. These digital environments are numerous with many distinctive features. For example, audiences may encounter a speech in a digital environment today when it is posted on social media, livestreamed through an online platform, uploaded to a site like YouTube, recorded in real time on their phones, or even delivered simultaneously through a business streaming interface.

Yet, while each of these digital environments is distinct, they also share significant dimensions that a speaker must consider to excel in all of these situations. Providing students with the opportunity to learn and consider these shared dimensions of speaking in a digital environment is the focus of this chapter.

Any Speech Can Be Digital (for Better or Worse)

Before we go any further in considering speaking in a digital environment, it is important to make one thing clear: any speech can be delivered in a digital environment. Indeed, unlike other types of speeches in this unit of the class, speaking in a digital environment is not distinctive because of its primary goals; rather, what makes speaking in a digital environment unique is *the venue in which it appears*. As a result, while all the speeches we will discuss in this chapter take place in a digital sphere of some sort, the goals, aims, or topics of those speeches can be of any sort. In other words, QuickStart, informative, public deliberation, policy, and commemorative speeches can all be done in digital environments.

Nonetheless, while it may be increasingly possible to deliver any type of speech in a digital environment, that does not mean that every speech *should* be given in that way. Indeed, in some instances, when a speaker chooses to give a speech in a digital environment, they may be undermining their speaking goals. Consider, for example, a eulogy—a well-established type of commemorative speech. Traditionally, a eulogy is delivered to honor the deceased, to soothe the mourners, and to praise the value of the deceased's life for the audience. When speaking at a funeral in person, the eulogist is well positioned to achieve these goals, particularly with their ability to interact face-to-face with the audience. By contrast, a digital eulogy would face some significant rhetorical challenges. A digital eulogy, for instance, might harm the speaker's credibility if the audience assumes that the speaker did not care enough about the deceased to come to the funeral in person. Similarly, a pre-recorded digital speech cannot be adjusted to the mood of the room—to tell if a joke landed well or to change the speaker's delivery—and thereby become less effective.

By contrast, other types of speeches with different speaking goals may not face the same challenges by speaking in a digital environment. For example, this same digital format may not be nearly as consequential in a witness's testimony (an informative type of speaking) in a courtroom or a businessperson's introduction via Skype.

In fact, some speakers might find their goals better achieved through speaking in a digital environment. A social media influencer, for instance, simply cannot be effective at influencing opinion on social media if they only speak to their followers in face-to-face settings. Given this speaker's audience and aims, choosing *not* to speak in a digital environment is a poor decision that will likely undermine their brand and their influence. Similarly, if a speaker is invited to give a lecture via Skype to a class at another institution, but the speaker insists that they will only deliver their lecture in person, the speaker is likely to be disinvited to speak at all. In other words, speaking in a digital environment when invited, asked, or assigned is typically an excellent reason to know how to speak in a digital environment comfortably.

The big takeaway here is this: Any kind of speech can be given in a digital environment; *however, as a speaker, you will always need to consider whether opting to speak in a digital format to your audience will enhance or harm your speaking goals.* In this way, the digital realm is just another factor in the public speaking situation that a speaker must always consider.

Real-World Examples of Speaking in a Digital Environment

On a daily basis, public speaking in a digital environment happens millions of times around the globe. Indeed, since the founding of the public-facing Internet in 1990, speaking in online and/or digital environments has become extremely common. Undoubtedly, speaking in digital environments will become more common and more complex over the decades to come with advancements in new technologies like holograms and virtual reality. However, at the moment, the most common ways in which public speakers address audiences in digital environments are:

Skype Presentations. Transmitted in real-time across the web, Skype presentations are an increasingly common form of public speaking, particularly after the 2008 Recession when companies, universities, and other institutions turned to technology to save money on the expense of flying speakers in for face-to-face presentations. Today, it is not unusual to have business meetings, job interviews, conference presentations, and the like conducted over Skype or similar live video streaming or teleconferencing services.

Online Lectures. If you've ever taken an online or hybrid course during your college career, you've likely seen public speaking in a digital environment through an online lecture. Increasingly popular with the rise of online learning, online lectures are typically video recordings of face-to-face lectures that are then uploaded to a Learning Management System (like Canvas) or some other interface. Sometimes, online lectures are augmented with graphics or videos to enhance the online experience.

Live Streaming Mobile Speeches. As we know, not all speeches are planned well in advance or given in friendly territory; however, these constraints can make the delivery of these speeches all the more important. In these situations, we sometimes see speeches livestreamed through mobile video recording technology like Periscope. In particular, apps like Periscope have offered audiences access to speakers in the midst of protests, house-arrest, and civil unrest.

TED Talks. This brand name format of public speaking in a digital environment is one commonly found on sites like YouTube. TED Talks show well the power of delivering highly planned, practiced, and packaged speech in an online setting. The high production value, short time, and well-rehearsed and tested topics make for entertaining and effective public speaking.

Podcasts. While most popular forms of public speaking in digital environments rely heavily on video, podcasts' exclusive focus on audio is the exception. Featuring single speakers or a group of speakers engaged in a lengthy dive into a single topic, podcasts are often well-researched and thoughtfully written speaking events focused on content, organization, entertainment, and audio delivery. Unlike these other formats, podcasts don't care what the speaker looks like or how they use their bodies to deliver their ideas—as long as they can be understood and speak in a compelling way.

Online Tutorials. Sites like YouTube are full of a very particular genre of public speaking in a digital environment: online tutorials. In essence, online tutorials are informative speeches delivered in a digital environment where the goal is to teach the audience how to do something. What that something is varies widely, though some of the most popular tutorials online focus on makeup, fashion, cooking, home repair and improvement, video games, and other lifestyle subjects.

Online Political Announcements. This relatively new genre of online public speaking has become quite popular in the last few years. Where it was once common and expected for a politician to announce their candidacy for office in a formal speech at a particular site, the last few election cycles have seen a mountain of candidates turn to short, highly-produced online announcement speeches delivered in a digital environment instead. Any why not? Candidates for office want a flawless, totally controlled, highly tailored message that can be widely circulated across all platforms to millions of people who likely do not know them. Speaking in a digital environment offers all of those options in one 2–3 minute video package posted online.

Considerations for Speaking in a Digital Environment

While we know now that any type of speech can be given in a digital environment, we also know that digital environments provide a significant set of concerns and opportunities a speaker must consider in order to do any of these speeches well. Regardless of platform or changes in digital speaking technology over the next few years, public speakers in a digital environment must consider the following:

Audio. Audio is an issue of concern for all communicators in a digital space, including public speakers. While in a face-to-face public speaking setting, we might worry about the projection of our voice or the quality of a microphone, in an online setting, speakers should be concerned that their voice is being recorded clearly, understandably, and at an appropriate level for everyone who will listen to your speech. You might consider the use of a voice capture aid in the recording of your speech (a digital microphone, headset, etc.). Also consider the implications for your audio if you select to deliver your speech on the move and farther away from your recording device when speaking in a digital environment.

Video Quality. Like audio, video quality is an essential concern for online public speakers. Without good-quality video of your speech, you are likely to have significant issues as it relates to understanding and clarity. However, video quality also has a large impact on credibility in a digital space. Videos with excellent video quality and high production value are likely to be watched, shared, and trusted by viewers more so than a poor-quality video recording of a speech. Luckily, technology has advanced so much that most recent cellphones offer stunning video quality standard. Speakers can enhance this technological quality by ensuring good lighting, simple backdrops, and steady filming or harm this quality with poor lighting, messy or distracting backdrops, or shaky or erratic filming. In addition, if you will be live streaming your speech, be sure to check for a strong and reliable Wi-Fi signal and streaming platform prior to starting the stream.

Framing. In a digital environment, public speakers have the benefit of controlling their **framing**: *the proximity and background of their speech as perceived by the audience*. In real life, public speakers often obsess about the position from which they are seen or the setting of their speech to little benefit; frankly, most of us have little control over the setting of our speeches or our appearance offline. By contrast, in digital settings, a lot of speakers have complete control of these factors; however, this control is a double-edged sword. Because speakers have almost complete control in crafting how they are framed on-screen, flaws in framing can be catastrophic and met with little forgiveness. For most speeches, speakers will be rewarded for backgrounds that are clean, appropriate, and not distracting; many more professional online speakers will use a green screen to neutralize and control their background. Cardinal sins of framing in a digital environment include embarrassing backgrounds, messy rooms, distracting noises, poor lighting, and unexpected visitors.

Unexpected Visitors: Crashing the BBC Interview

Robert Kelly, a professor and expert in East Asian affairs, was by all accounts excited and prepared to be interviewed live on the BBC about the resignation of the leader of South Korea in early 2017. However, viewers at home could not take him seriously when, behind Kelly on his live Skype stream, two adorable children burst into his room and started playing around behind his back. Kelly tried to recover—his wife even ran into the room to try and usher the kids out—but it was too late. Kelly's credibility was gone and the two cute kids stole the show. Luckily, things worked out in the end. "I made this minor mistake that turned my family into YouTube stars," Kelly told the *Wall Street Journal*. "It's pretty ridiculous." Check Canvas to watch the video of Kelly and his run-in with framing mistakes during his BBC interview over Skype.

Length. The length of a speech in a digital environment is not a minor factor to consider as a public speaker. In our attention-starved world *offline*, we already know that the old expectations for how long a speaker can hold their audience's focus have changed. Online, these changed expectations are even more remarkable. Today, while speakers might be able to hold an audience's attention for 10 to 15 undistracted minutes offline, in a digital environment, that limit is probably closer to 5 to 7 minutes max. Many great public speeches in digital settings can even achieve their primary goal in an effective 2–3 minutes speech. Alternately, if a speaker knows they will need to speak for longer than 5 minutes in a digital space, the speaker must add multiple, meaningful, and effective ways to reengage the audience as they move through their address. Otherwise, their audience is likely to be shopping for shoes or watching cat videos before they even get to their first main point.

Permanence. One of the conventional weaknesses of public speaking offline is ephemerality, the fact that speeches don't last and are easily forgotten with time and inattention. In digital environments, speeches do not suffer from this ephemerality; rather, a speech shared online can live on indefinitely, particularly if it goes viral. However, while this may seem like a benefit compared to more traditional public speaking, the permanence of speeches in a digital environment can also be problematic. Because these speeches stick around, your words are never really forgotten. And sometimes speeches you deeply believe in at the time do not age well. Don't forget: old speeches online can easily be brought back up to be used against you in your professional, personal, and civic pursuits. Therefore, whenever you speak in a digital environment, choose your words carefully, consider before you consent to be filmed, and be mindful of how your topic may change in the future.

Circulation. Like permanence, circulation is also an issue unique to speaking in a digital environment. While we may have very targeted ways in which we intend our digital speeches to be seen and shared, once we click "send" much of that perceived control goes out the window. This can often work to our advantage: if more people see and share our speeches, our chance of affecting our speech goals likely rise. Yet, at the same time, if our speeches do not go well, our bad speaking experience will probably not be immune from the same forces that make other videos go viral. As speakers, we can make reasonable decisions about circulation to help limit the downside and increase the upside: maintain strict control over our videos, make them harder to copy or capture, or share them only within safer, more trusted institutional venues like your class's Canvas site. We should also be mindful to never submit a speech digitally without reviewing it for mistakes, errors, misstatements, or other embarrassing problems—a good practice for speaking IRL, too!

Audience. By now we know that audience is always a central concern for the public speaker; however, in digital environments, our audiences are often much harder to analyze or anticipate. We cannot control exactly who will see our live stream or how video of our speech might circulate online. As such, speakers in a digital environment should always assume they are speaking to a broader audience than might seem obvious at first. To put it another way: it is always best to assume you are speaking to a general audience when you speak in a digital environment. That might mean your speech loses some of it specificity: you will want to avoid inside jokes, nicknames, or humor that might not be appreciated by people who you do not know, for instance. But better safe than sorry. In reality, your digital speech may only be seen by people you know well and have a stated relationship with; but if your speech does circulate more widely, you want to know that you can stand by what you said in front of any audience that might see it. To put it in a way that most people can relate to: don't say or do anything in your digital speech that you wouldn't feel comfortable having a perfect stranger see!

Unexpected Audience: Mitt Romney and the 47%

As the Republican candidate for President of the United States in 2012, now-Senator Mitt Romney made a fatal flaw in his campaign by forgetting that any speech can circulate to audiences beyond those immediately in front of you. In particular, at a private donor dinner, Romney made the mistake of saying that:

> "There are 47 percent of the people who will vote for [Obama] no matter what...there are 47 percent who are with him, who are dependent upon government, who believe that they are victims, who believe the government has a responsibility to care for them, who believe that they are entitled to health care, to food, to housing, to you-name-it. That that's an entitlement. And the government should give it to them. And they will vote for this president no matter what..."

While this argument appealed to Romney's core supporters in the room, a server working for minimum wage at the event recorded Romney's remarks and shared them with the press.

When those remarks circulated on national television before the entire country, Romney lost significant support. Evidence suggests that Romney's comments swayed undecided voters who were open to voting against the president, but who took offense to Romney's characterization of them. Ultimately, political historians largely agree that Romney's run-in with an unexpected audience played a large part in his electoral loss that November.

Format and Advances in Technology. As the technology that makes digital public speaking possible continues to grow and expand, it is prudent for a speaker to be mindful about the platform they use to make their speech, how it does or does not interface with other communication technologies, and how your speech can be formatted and/or saved. For example, do you want your speech saved on a personal hard drive, posted on an institutional platform like Canvas, posted on a commercial platform like YouTube or Vimeo, or in the cloud? How will this choice shape how you share, promote, control, or limit access to your speech? Also, is your file made using proprietary technology, so it can only be viewed by those with access to that same technology? How will this shape the diversity of your audience and who it reaches? Questions like these are important to consider to ensure an effective and ethical speech in the digital environment.

Speaking in Digital Style. Finally, as a public speaker in a digital environment, you'll want to make sure that you speak in a digital style. As we discussed elsewhere in this book, there are two primary ways in which most people use style to deliver their ideas: written style and oral style (see Chapter 3). The former is used in writing, which by its very nature allows for complex words and organization, good length, and regular reconsideration by the reader; the latter is used in public speaking with an emphasis on clear, easy-to-understand words, easy-to-follow organization, and an emphasis on listenable speech that can be absorbed in one sitting by an audience. However, in digital environments, we can speak differently, in what we might think of as a **digital style**. This is because digital speechmaking offers ways for us to combine and add to both written and oral style. Like written style, digital style is permanent and can be replayed at will, so digital speakers need not emphasize repetition, rely as much on signposts, or avoid complex words, terms, or organization. Like oral style, digital speeches tend to favor a conversational tone, less grammatically strict language, and an immediacy of speaking in real time with your audience. In addition, because of its digital nature, a digital style allows a speaker to add things they could not do in either other style like:

- Embed live links to research and sources within the video file
- Use graphics to title your speech, move between sections, and gain your audience's attention
- Spilt screens between the speaker and their visual aid
- Introduce background music at key points
- Use voiceovers to augment or emphasize points

To be sure, not all public speakers in a digital environment will have the technical knowledge or resources to incorporate all of these added features into their digital speeches; however, if you do have this access or training, feel free to try them out. Regardless, all speakers in a digital environment should recognize: speaking effectively online is not writing for video or speaking on camera—it has the potential to be a radically different style of speech all its own.

As a practice, speaking in a digital environment is still a new and unfolding form of public speaking. Nonetheless, by trying your hand at speaking in this context sooner than later, you better prepare yourself for what are sure to be important changes in the nature of public speaking in the digital world to come.

Appendices

Appendix A

STUDENT INFORMATION SHEET

Semester:________________________ SPCM 200 Section #:______________

Full Name:____

Nickname or Preferred Name: ______________________________

Phone #: ____

E-mail:____

What, if any, public speaking experience have you had?

What are your initial thoughts, questions, or concerns about this class?

Final exam notice: SPCM 200 has a **common final exam**. You are required to take the final exam at the time designated in the official university final exam schedule. You will not be permitted to take the exam early due to travel or other plans, and you will not be able to make it up if you miss it. If you have multiple exams scheduled on the day of the SPCM 200 final and are hoping to rearrange your testing schedule, **plan to rearrange your other exams**. Since there are only a few common finals scheduled by the university, they must take precedence.

Please sign below to verify that you understand the SPCM 200 final exam policy, as well as the other policies and requirements outlined in this *Coursebook*.

Student's Signature ____

Appendix B

SPEECH ASSIGNMENT: QUICKSTART SPEECH

Prepare and present a 2–3 minute speech on a topic specified by your instructor. This speech is designed to "diagnose" your speaking strengths and areas that need improvement. It will be graded on a pass/fail basis. If you attempt to complete the assignment in good faith, ***you will pass***.

The QuickStart Speech Assignment Emphasizes the Following Skills:

☑ *Organization*: Make sure your speech has an identifiable introduction, body, and conclusion.

☑ *Extemporaneous Delivery*: Engage your audience with a dynamic speaking style and sustained eye contact. Deliver the speech from a "bare bones" outline on index cards.

☑ *Time Management*: Practice your speech so that you conform to the time limit. This is probably the most important rule. If several students take more than 3 minutes, there will not be enough class time for everyone to speak.

Speaker ______________________________

Topic ______________________________

QuickStart Speech

+ Excellent **✓ Satisfactory** **-- Needs improvement** **0 Failed to complete**

INTRODUCTION
Captured audience attention ______
Previewed main points ______

BODY
Main points clear ______
Main points developed ______

CONCLUSION
Signaled start of conclusion ______
Reviewed main points ______
Decisive/artistic last line ______

DELIVERY
Maintained eye contact ______
Used vocal variety ______
Projected adequately ______
Pronunciation correct ______
Articulation clear ______
Rate appropriate ______
Paused effectively ______
Gestures purposeful ______
Mannerisms appropriate ______
Facial expression ______
Spoke fluently ______
Extemporaneous style ______
Effective use of speaking notes ______

ADDITIONAL ITEMS
Completed in time limit ______
Topic appropriate ______
Fulfilled assignment requirements ______

Specific strengths and areas for improvement:

Instructor comments and suggestions:

Time: ________

Grade: Pass/Fail

Speaker ______________________________

Topic ______________________________

QuickStart Speech

+ Excellent **✓ Satisfactory** **-- Needs improvement** **0 Failed to complete**

INTRODUCTION
Captured audience attention ______
Previewed main points ______

BODY
Main points clear ______
Main points developed ______

CONCLUSION
Signaled start of conclusion ______
Reviewed main points ______
Decisive/artistic last line ______

DELIVERY
Maintained eye contact ______
Used vocal variety ______
Projected adequately ______
Pronunciation correct ______
Articulation clear ______
Rate appropriate ______
Paused effectively ______
Gestures purposeful ______
Mannerisms appropriate ______
Facial expression ______
Spoke fluently ______
Extemporaneous style ______
Effective use of speaking notes ______

ADDITIONAL ITEMS
Completed in time limit ______
Topic appropriate ______
Fulfilled assignment requirements ______

Specific strengths and areas for improvement:

Instructor comments and suggestions:

Time: ________

Grade: Pass/Fail

Appendix C

SPEECH ASSIGNMENT: INFORMATIVE SPEECH

Prepare and present a 4–6 minute speech that conveys useful or interesting information to an audience. Cite at least 4–6 *different sources* for your audience during the speech (put the names of your sources in parentheses when you cite them within the body of your outline, as well as additional and appropriate citation information), and include *a minimum of one speaking aid* prepared specifically for this assignment. Prior to the delivery of the speech, submit one copy of a typed preparation outline, including a Works Cited page, to your instructor. Upload that identical file (with your name removed) to VeriCite. *Students who do not submit to VeriCite may receive a zero on their speech.* Avoid spelling, typographical, or grammatical errors.

The Informative Speech Assignment Emphasizes the Following Skills:

☑ *Organization*: Focus on clarity in this speech. Your speech should have a well-developed introduction, distinct and logical main points, transitions between points, and a concise, compelling conclusion.

☑ *Research*: This will be your first research-based speech of the semester. You should not only find a variety of credible sources and interesting supporting material, but you also must cite your sources clearly for the audience.

☑ *Outlining*: A well-prepared complete-sentence outline will enable you to fulfill the organizational and research requirements of this assignment. Make sure you follow the outlining models on Canvas carefully.

☑ *Speaking Support*: This assignment allows you to practice two skills related to speaking aids: 1) preparing professional-quality speaking aids, and 2) using them in a way that enhances (rather than detracts from) your credibility.

- ☑ *Speaker Credibility*: Every aspect of your performance, from topic selection to research to delivery, should evidence your personal credibility as a speaker.
- ☑ *Audience Adaptation*: Prepare your speech with your specific audience in mind. Devise strategies to give them useful information, keep them interested, and adapt to their knowledge of your topic.

Name____

Date________________________

Informative Speech

Propose two potential topics for your Informative Speech. List them below, in order of preference, and explain what strategies you would use to adapt each topic to your class audience.

Topic 1:

Specific purpose:

Thesis statement:

Proposed speech main points (2–4 main points—remember you will only have about 1 minute to discuss each main point):

1.

2.

3.

4.

What will you use for your speaking aid(s)?

Topic 2:

Specific purpose:

Thesis statement:

Proposed speech main points:

1.

2.

3.

4.

What will you use for your speaking aid(s)?

Instructor Comments:

Topic 1 __ Approved __ Not Approved

Topic 2 __ Approved __ Not Approved

Speaker ______________________________

Topic ______________________________

Informative Speech

+ Excellent **✓ Satisfactory** **-- Needs improvement** **0 Failed to complete**

Specific strengths and areas for improvement:

INTRODUCTION

Gained audience attention ______
Established credibility ______
Introduced topic clearly ______
Related topic to audience ______
Had concise thesis/preview ______

BODY: ORGANIZATION

Main points were clear ______
Ordered main points logically ______
Effective transitions ______

BODY: RESEARCH

Main points fully supported ______
Adequate variety of sources ______
Used credible sources ______
Cited sources orally ______

CONCLUSION

Signaled end of speech ______
Summarized main points ______
Ended with artistic last line ______

DELIVERY

Maintained eye contact ______
Used vocal variety ______
Projected adequately ______
Pronunciation correct ______
Articulation clear ______
Rate appropriate ______
Paused effectively ______
Gestures purposeful ______
Proxemics effective ______
Mannerisms appropriate ______
Facial expression ______
Spoke fluently ______
Extemporaneous style ______
Effective use of speaking notes ______

SPEAKING AID

Clear and easy to engage ______
Professionally designed ______
Incorporated well into speech ______
Used technology appropriately ______
Added clarity to content ______

OUTLINE

Complete sentence format ______
Logical subordination ______
Labels included ______
Works Cited page ______
Accurate spelling ______
Correct grammar ______
Free of typos/errors ______

ADDITIONAL ITEMS

Topic challenging ______
Topic interesting ______
Topic unique ______
Adapted to audience ______
Completed in time limit ______
Fulfilled assignment requirements ______

Instructor comments and suggestions:

VeriCite? Y / N

Time: ________

Score: ________ /100

Speaker ______________________________

Topic ______________________________

Informative Speech

+ Excellent **✓ Satisfactory** **-- Needs improvement** **0 Failed to complete**

INTRODUCTION

Specific strengths and areas for improvement:

Gained audience attention ______
Established credibility ______
Introduced topic clearly ______
Related topic to audience ______
Had concise thesis/preview ______

BODY: ORGANIZATION
Main points were clear ______
Ordered main points logically ______
Effective transitions ______

BODY: RESEARCH
Main points fully supported ______
Adequate variety of sources ______
Used credible sources ______
Cited sources orally ______

CONCLUSION
Signaled end of speech ______
Summarized main points ______
Ended with artistic last line ______

DELIVERY
Maintained eye contact ______
Used vocal variety ______
Projected adequately ______
Pronunciation correct ______
Articulation clear ______
Rate appropriate ______
Paused effectively ______
Gestures purposeful ______
Proxemics effective ______
Mannerisms appropriate ______
Facial expression ______
Spoke fluently ______
Extemporaneous style ______
Effective use of speaking notes ______

SPEAKING AID

Clear and easy to engage	______
Professionally designed	______
Incorporated well into speech	______
Used technology appropriately	______
Added clarity to content	______

OUTLINE

Complete sentence format	______
Logical subordination	______
Labels included	______
Works Cited page	______
Accurate spelling	______
Correct grammar	______
Free of typos/errors	______

ADDITIONAL ITEMS

Topic challenging	______
Topic interesting	______
Topic unique	______
Adapted to audience	______
Completed in time limit	______
Fulfilled assignment requirements	______

Instructor comments and suggestions:

VeriCite? Y / N

Time: ________

Score: ________ **/100**

Appendix D

SPEECH ASSIGNMENT: PUBLIC DELIBERATION SPEECH

You will prepare a 5–7 minute speech to explore an issue and then moderate a 3–4 minute dialogue with your class colleagues (maximum of *12 minutes total* for the speech and dialogue). Then you will present a brief conclusion (no more than one minute) summarizing your speech content and dialogue. Your topic should be potentially suitable for the policy speech assignment, and you should use the dialogue as an opportunity to 1) potentially find a topic for your policy speech, and/or 2) gain a greater understanding of and appreciation for your audience's diverse perspectives before you design your policy speech. Cite at least ***5–7 different sources*** for your audience during the speech (put the names of your sources in parentheses when you cite them within the body of your outline). On the day of your dialogues, turn in one copy of a *typed outline* of your public deliberation speech with *dialogue question prompts* listed at the end and a Works Cited page. Upload that identical file (with your name removed) to VeriCite. *Students who do not submit to VeriCite may receive a zero on their speech.* Avoid spelling, typographical, or grammatical errors.

The Public Deliberation Speech Assignment Emphasizes the Following Skills:

☑ *Organization*: A dialogue can be organized to facilitate clear and comprehensive exploration of an issue.

☑ *Dialogue*: Before you can ethically and effectively urge your audience to adopt a particular policy, you must appreciate the multiple sides to every issue and value your audience members' unique perspectives.

☑ *Speaker Credibility*: In order for audience members to value your opinion, they must feel that you respect them. You can demonstrate this respect in this speech.

☑ *Language*: Your specific word choices matter greatly in demonstrating care and concern for your audience and their viewpoints.

☑ *Audience Adaptation*: When audience members feel that you respect them as equals, you value their views, and you will allow them to determine their own courses of action, they are more likely to participate in communicative exchanges in an authentic and meaningful way.

Name____

Date____________________

Public Deliberation Speech

Propose two potential topics for your Public Deliberation Dialogue. List them below, in order of preference.

Topic 1:

Thesis statement:

What other perspectives on this topic are necessary to consider as you organize your speech?

If this topic is approved, what kind of questions might you ask as part of your facilitation? Be sure to include examples of open-ended questions.

Topic 2:

Thesis statement:

What other perspectives on this topic are necessary to consider as you organize your speech?

If this topic is approved, what kind of questions might you ask as part of your facilitation? Be sure to include examples of open-ended questions.

Instructor Comments:

Topic 1 __ Approved __ Not Approved

Topic 2 __ Approved __ Not Approved

Speaker ______________________________

Topic ______________________________

Public Deliberation Speech

+ Excellent **✓ Satisfactory** **-- Needs improvement** **0 Failed to complete**

Specific strengths and areas for improvement:

INTRODUCTION

Gained audience attention ______
Established credibility ______
Introduced topic in an open-minded way ______
Related topic to audience ______
Clear thesis/preview ______

BODY: ORGANIZATION

Main points were clear ______
Presented topic fairly ______
Effective transitions ______
Incorporated deliberative language ______

BODY: RESEARCH

Main points fully supported ______
Adequate variety of sources ______
Used credible sources ______
Cited sources orally ______

DIALOGUE

Smooth transition to dialogue ______
Appropriate question prompts ______
Facilitated effectively ______
Deliberative environment ______
Allowed multiple people to participate ______

CONCLUSION

Summarized main points ______
Ended with artistic last line ______

OUTLINE

Complete sentence format ______
Logical subordination ______
Labels included ______
Works Cited page ______
Accurate spelling ______
Correct grammar ______
Free of typos/errors ______
Include appropriate discussion questions ______

DELIVERY

Maintained eye contact ______
Used vocal variety ______
Projected adequately ______
Pronunciation correct ______
Articulation clear ______
Rate appropriate ______
Paused effectively ______
Gestures purposeful ______
Proxemics effective ______
Mannerisms appropriate ______
Facial expression ______
Spoke fluently ______
Extemporaneous style ______
Effective use of speaking notes ______

ADDITIONAL ITEMS

Topic appropriate ______
Completed in time limit ______
Fulfilled assignment requirements ______

Instructor comments and suggestions:

VeriCite? Y / N

Speech Time: ________ **Dialogue Time:** ________ **Total Time:** ________

Score: ________ **/200**

Speaker ______________________________

Topic ______________________________

Public Deliberation Speech

+ Excellent **✓ Satisfactory** **-- Needs improvement** **0 Failed to complete**

Specific strengths and areas for improvement:

INTRODUCTION

Gained audience attention ______
Established credibility ______
Introduced topic in an open-minded way ______
Related topic to audience ______
Clear thesis/preview ______

BODY: ORGANIZATION

Main points were clear ______
Presented topic fairly ______
Effective transitions ______
Incorporated deliberative language ______

BODY: RESEARCH

Main points fully supported ______
Adequate variety of sources ______
Used credible sources ______
Cited sources orally ______

DIALOGUE

Smooth transition to dialogue ______
Appropriate question prompts ______
Facilitated effectively ______
Deliberative environment ______
Allowed multiple people to participate ______

CONCLUSION

Summarized main points ______
Ended with artistic last line ______

OUTLINE

Complete sentence format	______
Logical subordination	______
Labels included	______
Works Cited page	______
Accurate spelling	______
Correct grammar	______
Free of typos/errors	______
Include appropriate discussion questions	______

DELIVERY

Maintained eye contact	______
Used vocal variety	______
Projected adequately	______
Pronunciation correct	______
Articulation clear	______
Rate appropriate	______
Paused effectively	______
Gestures purposeful	______
Proxemics effective	______
Mannerisms appropriate	______
Facial expression	______
Spoke fluently	______
Extemporaneous style	______
Effective use of speaking notes	______

ADDITIONAL ITEMS

Topic appropriate	______
Completed in time limit	______
Fulfilled assignment requirements	______

Instructor comments and suggestions:

VeriCite? Y / N

Speech Time: ________ **Dialogue Time:** ________ **Total Time:** ________

Score: ________ **/200**

Appendix E

SPEECH ASSIGNMENT: POLICY SPEECH

Prepare and present a 6–8 minute speech that proposes a plan to solve a current public problem. After your 6–8 minute speech, field 2–3 minutes' worth of questions from the audience. You may arrange your policy speech into the problem-solution organizational pattern, the problem-cause-solution pattern, the comparative advantages organizational pattern, or Monroe's motivated sequence. Make sure to relate your discussion of the problem and proposed solution specifically to your class audience. **It is highly recommended that you do not come up with your own policy, but *find* a policy to advocate or adopt for a new context**. Cite at least *6–8 different sources* for your audience during the speech (put the names of your sources in parentheses when you cite them within the body of your outline). Prior to the delivery of the speech, submit one copy of a typed preparation outline, including a Works Cited page, to your instructor. Upload that identical file (with your name removed) to VeriCite. *Students who do not submit to VeriCite may receive a zero on their speech.* Avoid spelling, typographical, or grammatical errors.

The Policy Speech Assignment Emphasizes the Following Skills:

- ☑ *Organization*: Choose an organizational pattern that suits your topic and persuasive goals.
- ☑ *Argument*: Well-developed arguments should support your persuasive claims. Include clear logical appeals, appropriate emotional appeals, and thorough research.
- ☑ *Speaker Credibility*: Every aspect of your performance, from topic selection to research to delivery, should evidence your personal credibility as a speaker.
- ☑ *Audience Adaptation*: Your speech should show evidence of careful audience analysis and specific audience adaptation. Anticipate and respond to potential counterarguments against your proposed plan.
- ☑ *Speech Support*: Speaking aids are optional this time, but strongly suggested. Speaking aids can help illustrate and support your persuasive claims.

Name ____________________

Date ____________________

Policy Speech

TOPIC PROPOSAL

Review the policy model requirements for the assignment. Then, identify two potential topics for your policy speech and do preliminary research on both. Make sure that your topics are unique, narrow enough to cover in the time allotted, and adapted to your class audience. List them below in order of preference.

Problem 1:

A. State succinctly the nature of the public problem:

B. List the ways in which this problem causes serious harms to people, property, institutions, nature, etc.

C. What proposal(s) for change do you plan to offer to solve this problem?

List at least three articles you have found on this topic **FROM THIS YEAR AND LAST YEAR ONLY**:

1. Author ____________________ Title ____________________
   Publication ____________________ Pages__________ Date__________
2. Author ____________________ Title ____________________
   Publication ____________________ Pages__________ Date__________
3. Author ____________________ Title ____________________
   Publication ____________________ Pages__________ Date__________

Problem 2:

A. State succinctly the nature of the public problem:

B. List the ways in which this problem causes serious harms to people, property, institutions, nature, etc.

C. What proposal(s) for change do you plan to offer to solve this problem?

List at least three articles you have found on this topic **FROM THIS YEAR AND LAST YEAR ONLY**:

1. Author ______________________________ Title ________________________________

   Publication ___________________________ Pages__________ Date____________

2. Author ______________________________ Title ________________________________

   Publication ___________________________ Pages__________ Date____________

3. Author ______________________________ Title ________________________________

   Publication ___________________________ Pages__________ Date____________

Instructor Comments:

Topic 1 __ Approved __ Not Approved

Topic 2 __ Approved __ Not Approved

Speaker ______________________________

Topic ______________________________

Policy Speech

+ Excellent **✓ Satisfactory** **-- Needs improvement** **0 Failed to complete**

INTRODUCTION
Gained audience attention ______
Established credibility ______
Introduced topic early ______
Related topic to audience ______
Clear thesis/preview ______

BODY: ORGANIZATION
Main points were clear ______
Effective organizational pattern ______
Effective transitions ______

BODY: RESEARCH
Main points fully supported ______
Adequate variety of sources ______
Used credible sources ______
Cited sources orally ______

BODY: ARGUMENT
Sound and clear reasoning ______
Clear problem (Need) ______
Clear solution (Plan) ______
Plan workable (Practicality) ______
Advantages outweigh disadvantages ______
Addresses counterarguments ______

BODY: AUDIENCE ADAPTATION
Adapted to audience ______
Effective use of pathos ______
Effective use of ethos ______

CONCLUSION
Signaled end of speech ______
Summarized main points ______
Ended with artistic last line ______

Specific strengths and areas for improvement:

CRITIQUE SHEET

Q&A

Listened carefully to questions ______
Managed session well ______
Answered questions clearly and effectively ______

DELIVERY

Maintained eye contact ______
Used vocal variety ______
Projected adequately ______
Pronunciation correct ______
Articulation clear ______
Rate appropriate ______
Paused effectively ______
Gestures purposeful ______
Proxemics effective ______
Mannerisms appropriate ______
Facial expression ______
Spoke fluently ______
Extemporaneous style ______
Effective use of speaking notes ______

SPEAKING AIDS (optional)

Clear and easy to see ______
Professionally designed ______
Incorporated into speech ______
Used technology appropriately ______
Added clarity to speech ______
Content ______

OUTLINE

Complete sentence format ______
Logical subordination ______
Labels included ______
Works Cited page ______
Accurate spelling ______
Correct grammar ______
Free of typos/errors ______

ADDITIONAL ITEMS

Topic challenging/appropriate ______
Completed in time limit ______
Fulfilled assignment requirements ______

Instructor comments and suggestions:

VeriCite? Y / N

Time: ________

Score: ________ **/250**

Speaker ______________________________

Topic ______________________________

Policy Speech

+ Excellent **✓ Satisfactory** **-- Needs improvement** **0 Failed to complete**

Specific strengths and areas for improvement:

INTRODUCTION

Gained audience attention ______
Established credibility ______
Introduced topic early ______
Related topic to audience ______
Clear thesis/preview ______

BODY: ORGANIZATION

Main points were clear ______
Effective organizational pattern ______
Effective transitions ______

BODY: RESEARCH

Main points fully supported ______
Adequate variety of sources ______
Used credible sources ______
Cited sources orally ______

BODY: ARGUMENT

Sound and clear reasoning ______
Clear problem (Need) ______
Clear solution (Plan) ______
Plan workable (Practicality) ______
Advantages outweigh disadvantages ______
Addresses counterarguments ______

BODY: AUDIENCE ADAPTATION

Adapted to audience ______
Effective use of pathos ______
Effective use of ethos ______

CONCLUSION

Signaled end of speech ______
Summarized main points ______
Ended with artistic last line ______

CRITIQUE SHEET

Q&A
Listened carefully to questions ______
Managed session well ______
Answered questions clearly and effectively ______

DELIVERY
Maintained eye contact ______
Used vocal variety ______
Projected adequately ______
Pronunciation correct ______
Articulation clear ______
Rate appropriate ______
Paused effectively ______
Gestures purposeful ______
Proxemics effective ______
Mannerisms appropriate ______
Facial expression ______
Spoke fluently ______
Extemporaneous style ______
Effective use of speaking notes ______

SPEAKING AIDS (optional)
Clear and easy to see ______
Professionally designed ______
Incorporated into speech ______
Used technology appropriately ______
Added clarity to speech ______
Content ______

OUTLINE
Complete sentence format ______
Logical subordination ______
Labels included ______
Works Cited page ______
Accurate spelling ______
Correct grammar ______
Free of typos/errors ______

ADDITIONAL ITEMS
Topic challenging/appropriate ______
Completed in time limit ______
Fulfilled assignment requirements ______

Instructor comments and suggestions:

VeriCite? Y / N

Time: ________

Score: ________ **/250**

Appendix F

SPEECH ASSIGNMENT: COMMEMORATIVE SPEECH

Prepare and present a 4–5 minute speech that pays tribute to a person, concept, organization, or institution. This speech will be delivered from manuscript. Organize your speech's main points according to the virtue(s) exhibited by the subject you have chosen to amplify. Incorporate stylistic devices into your speech, and label them on your manuscript. **Be sure to select a topic that is praiseworthy for general audiences** (praising excessive alcohol/marijuana use or violence are bad topics for general audience, for instance). Making sure your topic is approved by your instructor will ensure you pick an appropriately praiseworthy topic. Prior to the delivery, submit a typed, double-spaced copy of your manuscript to your instructor. Upload that identical file (with your name removed) to VeriCite. *Students who do not submit to VeriCite may receive a zero on their speech.* Avoid spelling, typographical, or grammatical errors.

The Commemorative Speech Assignment Emphasizes the Following Skills:

☑ *Commemoration and Community Values*: Identify and illustrate the virtues possessed by your subject.

☑ *Decorum*: Make speaking decisions that show appropriate attention to your audience, topic, and occasion.

☑ *Language Use*: Choose each word carefully and employ colorful, concrete, and evocative language.

☑ *Delivery*: Have a carefully polished delivery that employs dramatic pauses, vocal variations, and artistic phrasing. Because there is no research required for this speech, you are expected to put extra time into practicing your delivery.

Name____

Date____________________________

Commemorative Speech

Propose two potential topics for your Commemorative Speech. List them below, in order of preference, and explain why you think your subjects are praiseworthy.

Topic 1:

List 2–3 virtues exemplified by your subject, and briefly note the anecdotes or examples you will use to illustrate each virtue.

Topic 2:

List 2–3 virtues exemplified by your subject, and briefly note the anecdotes or examples you will use to illustrate each virtue.

Instructor Comments:

Topic 1 __ Approved __ Not Approved

Topic 2 __ Approved __ Not Approved

Speaker ______________________________

Topic ______________________________

Commemorative Speech

+ Excellent **✓ Satisfactory** **-- Needs improvement** **0 Failed to complete**

INTRODUCTION
Gained audience attention ______
Set proper mood ______
Clear/artistic preview ______

BODY
Main points were clear ______
Virtues clearly identified ______
Virtues well illustrated ______
Concrete language/vivid descriptions ______
Use of imagery ______
Use of rhythm ______
Pathos ______
Quality transitions ______

CONCLUSION
Reinforced mood ______
Virtues restated ______
Meaningful/artistic last line ______

DELIVERY
Maintained eye contact ______
Used vocal variety ______
Projected adequately ______
Pronunciation correct ______
Articulation clear ______
Rate appropriate ______
Paused effectively ______
Gestures purposeful ______
Proxemics effective ______
Mannerisms appropriate ______
Facial expression ______
Spoke fluently ______
Effective use of manuscript ______

Specific strengths and areas for improvement:

MANUSCRIPT

Labeled stylistic devices	______
Accurate spelling	______
Correct grammar	______
Corresponds to presentation	______
Free of typos/errors	______

ADDITIONAL ITEMS

Subject praiseworthy	______
Completed in time limit	______
Fulfilled assignment requirements	______

Instructor comments and suggestions:

VeriCite? Y / N

Time: ________

Score: ________ **/100**

Speaker ______________________________

Topic ______________________________

Commemorative Speech

+ Excellent **✓ Satisfactory** **-- Needs improvement** **0 Failed to complete**

Specific strengths and areas for improvement:

INTRODUCTION
Gained audience attention ______
Set proper mood ______
Clear/artistic preview ______

BODY
Main points were clear ______
Virtues clearly identified ______
Virtues well illustrated ______
Concrete language/vivid descriptions ______
Use of imagery ______
Use of rhythm ______
Pathos ______
Quality transitions ______

CONCLUSION
Reinforced mood ______
Virtues restated ______
Meaningful/artistic last line ______

DELIVERY
Maintained eye contact ______
Used vocal variety ______
Projected adequately ______
Pronunciation correct ______
Articulation clear ______
Rate appropriate ______
Paused effectively ______
Gestures purposeful ______
Proxemics effective ______
Mannerisms appropriate ______
Facial expression ______
Spoke fluently ______
Effective use of manuscript ______

CRITIQUE SHEET

MANUSCRIPT

Labeled stylistic devices ______
Accurate spelling ______
Correct grammar ______
Corresponds to presentation ______
Free of typos/errors ______

ADDITIONAL ITEMS

Subject praiseworthy ______
Completed in time limit ______
Fulfilled assignment requirements ______

Instructor comments and suggestions:

VeriCite? Y / N

Time: ________

Score: ________ /100

NOTES

1 Claude E. Shannon and Warren Weaver, *The Mathematical Theory of Communication* (Urbana: University of Illinois Press, 1949).

2 David K. Berlo, *The Process of Communication* (New York: Rinehart and Winston, 1960).

3 Francesca Levy and Christopher Cannon, *The Bloomberg Job Skills Report* 2016, February 9, 2016, https://www.bloomberg.com/graphics/2016-job-skills-report/.

4 Incitement has been defined by the U.S. Supreme Court to mean "advocacy of the use of force… directed to inciting or producing imminent lawless action" that is "likely to incite or produce such action." See *Brandenburg v. Ohio*, 395 U.S. 444 (1969).

5 See Tom Head, "6 Major U.S. Supreme Court Hate Speech Cases," *ThoughtCo*, January 6, 2019, https://www.thoughtco.com/hate-speech-cases-721215.

6 Audre Lorde, "Age, Race, Class, and Sex: Women Redefining Difference," in *Sister Outsider* (Berkeley: The Crossing Press, 1984), 123

7 Jennifer Van Hook and Barrett Lee, "Diversity is on the Rise in Urban and Rural Communities, and it's Here to Stay," *The Conversation*, February 20, 2017, http://theconversation.com/diversity-is-on-the-rise-in-urban-and-rural-communities-and-its-here-to-stay-69095

8 John Inglod, "Colorado's Population Substantially More Diverse," *Denver Post*, May 4, 2016, https://www.denverpost.com/2011/02/23/census-colorados-population-substantially-more-diverse/

9 Kevin Simpson, "Rural Colorado's White Population is Declining, and Minorities are Transforming the Region's Culture and Economy," *Denver Post*, November 12, 2017, https://www.denverpost.com/2017/11/09/colorado-rural-demographic-minority-increase/

10 Phillip Bump, "What America Will Look Like in 2050, in 4 Charts," *Washington Post*, April 3, 2015, https://www.washingtonpost.com/news/the-fix/wp/2015/04/03/what-america-will-look-like-in-2050-less-christian-less-white-more-gray/?utm_term=.fe60f15e6bed

11 Bump, "What America Will Look Like."

12 National Academies of Sciences, Engineering, and Medicine, "The Economic and Fiscal Consequences of Immigration," (Washington, DC: The National Academies Press, 2017), https://doi.org/10.17226/23550.

13 Kenneth Burke, "Definition of Man," in *Language as Symbolic Action* (Berkeley: University of California Press, 1966).

14 Brian Arao and Kristi Clemens, "From Safe Spaces to Brave Spaces: A New Way to Frame Dialogue Around Diversity and Social Justice." In *The Art of Effective Facilitation.* Stylus Publishing, 2013: 135–150.

15 "Here are Jerry Seinfeld's 10 funniest jokes," *New York Post*, April 17, 2014, https://nypost.com/2014/04/17/here-are-jerry-seinfelds-10-funniest-jokes/

16 Karen Kangas Dwyer and Marlina M. Davidson, "Is Public Speaking Really More Feared Than Death?" *Communication Research Reports* 29, no. 2 (2012): 99–107, http://dx.doi.org/10.1080/08824096.2012.667772.

17 "America's Top Fears 2016," Chapman University, October 11, 2016, https://blogs.chapman.edu/wilkinson/2016/10/11/americas-top-fears-2016/

18 Graham D. Bodie, "A Racing Heart, Rattling Knees, and Ruminative Thoughts: Defining, Explaining, and Treating Public Speaking Anxiety," *Communication Education* 59, no. 1 (2010), 72–73, http://dx.doi.org/10.1080/03634520903443849.

19 Levy and Cannon.

20 J.A. Daly, A.L. Vangelisti, H.L. Neel, and P.D. Cavanaugh, P. D, "Pre-performance concerns associated with public speaking anxiety." *Communication Quarterly* 37 (1989): 39–53.

21 Behnke, R. R., & Sawyer, C. R. (1999). "Milestones of anticipatory public speaking anxiety," *Communication Education*, 48, 165–172; Behnke, R. R., & Sawyer, C. R. (2000). "Anticipatory anxiety patterns for male and female public speakers," *Communication Education*, 49, 187–195.

22 Stuart Brody, "Blood pressure reactivity to stress is better for people who recently had penile-vaginal intercourse than for people who had other or no sexual activity," *Biological Psychology* 71 (2006): 214–222.

23 Megan Meads, "The Effects of Internal and External Expressions of Felt Luck On Performance," *Yale Review of Undergraduate Research in Psychology* 5 (2015): 46–54, http://www.psychology.pitt.edu/sites/default/files/u58/YRURP%20Spring%202015%20Issue.pdf#page=46; Gretchen Rubin, "Who Knew? Lucky Charms Actually Work," *Psychology Today*, September 10, 2013, https://www.psychologytoday.com/blog/the-happiness-project/201309/who-knew-lucky-charms-actually-work; Carl Bialik, "The Power of Lucky Charms," *Wall Street Journal*, April 28, 2010, https://www.wsj.com/articles/SB10001424052748703648304575212361800043460.

24 Walter R. Fisher, "Narration as a human communication paradigm: The case of public moral argument," *Quarterly Journal of Speech* 51, no. 1 (1984): 1–22, https://doi.org/10.1080/03637758409390180.

25 Richard Weaver, "Language is Sermonic," in *Dimensions of Rhetorical Scholarship*, ed. Roger E. Nebergall (1963).

26 Richard Lanham, *The Economics of Attention: Style and Substance in the Age of Information* (Chicago: University of Chicago Press, 2006), 6.

27 C.K. Ogden and I.A. Richards, *The Meaning of Meaning: A Study of the Influence of Language upon Thought and of the Science of Symbolism* (New York: Harvest, 1923), 7.

28 Burke, "Definition of Man," in *Language as Symbolic Action*, 13–15.

29 J.L. Austin, *How to Do Things With Words* (Cambridge: Harvard University Press, 1992), 12–13.

30 Michel Foucault, *History of Sexuality: An Introduction* (New York: Pantheon, 1978), 43.

31 Richard A. Lanham, *A Handlist of Rhetorical Terms* (Los Angeles: University of California Press, 1991), 92.

32 Amanda White, "Smells Ring Bells: How Smell Triggers Memories and Emotions," *Psychology Today*, January 12, 2015, https://www.psychologytoday.com/us/blog/brain-babble/201501/smells-ring-bells-how-smell-triggers-memories-and-emotions.

33 Allison Prasch, "Reagan at Pointe du Hoc: Deictic Epideictic and the Persuasive Power of 'Bringing Before the Eyes,'" *Rhetoric & Public Affairs* 18, no. 2 (2015): 247–276.

34 "Our Work," Center for Public Deliberation, 2017, https://cpd.colostate.edu/about-us/.

35 Martín Carcasson, "Tackling Wicked Problems through Problems of Engagement," October 2013, https://www.adams12.org/sites/default/files/uploads/documents/Carcassion_Article.pdf.

36 Maria Konnikova, "The Psychological Research That Helps Explain the Election," *New Yorker*, December 25, 2016, https://www.newyorker.com/science/maria-konnikova/the-psychological-research-that-helps-explain-the-election.

37 Charles G. Lord, Lee Ross, and Mark R. Lepper, "Biased Assimilation and Attitude Polarization: The Effects of Prior Theories on Subsequently Considered Evidence," *Journal of Personality and Social Psychology* 37, no. 1 (1979): 2098–2109, https://nuovoeutile.it/wp-content/uploads/2014/10/BIASED-ASSIMILATION-AND-ATTITUDE-POLARIZATION.pdf.

38 Dan Kahan, "The Cultural Cognition Project at Yale Law School," *Yale Law School*, http://www.culturalcognition.net/dan-kahans-publications/.

39 Karen Stenner, *The Authoritarian Dynamic* (New York: Cambridge University Press, 2005).

40 Brendan Nyhan and Jason Reifler, "When Corrections Fail: The Persistence of Political Misperceptions," *Political Behavior* (forthcoming), http://www.dartmouth.edu/~nyhan/nyhan-reifler.pdf.

41 Richard E. Petty and John T. Cacioppo, "The Elaboration Likelihood Model of Persuasion," *Advances in Experimental Social Psychology* 19 (1986), 123–205, https://ac.els-cdn.com/S0065260108602142/1-s2.0-S0065260108602142-main.pdf?_tid=252e2e9c-0a41-4ce1-888e-0d1b60db6088&acdnat=1529513896_ebe97f1e5a5bf2236ca1dec0d0a31494.

42 For example, Robert Frank Weiss, "Repetition of Persuasion," *Psychological Reports* 25 (1969): 669–670.

43 David Broockman and Joshua Kalla, "Durably reducing transphobia: A field experiment on door-to-door canvassing," *Science* 352, Issue 6282 (2016): 220–224, DOI: 10.1126/science.aad9713. NOTE: This is not the original debunked essay on this approach, but a new test of validity conducted by the scholars who debunked the original essay.

44 Matthew Feinberg and Robb Willer, "From Gulf to Bridge: When Do Moral Arguments Facilitate Political Influence?" *Personality and Social Psychology Bulletin* 41, no. 12 (2015): doi: 10.1177/0146167215607842; See also, Olga Khazan, "The Simple Psychological Trick to Political Persuasion," *The Atlantic*, February 1, 2017, https://www.theatlantic.com/science/archive/2017/02/the-simple-psychological-trick-to-political-persuasion/515181/.